The Dream And Its Amplification

The Dream And Its Amplification

Edited by

Erel Shalit and Nancy Swift Furlotti

The Dream And Its Amplification

The Fisher King Review Volume 2

Fisher King Press
5485 W 170th St N
Skiatook, OK 74070
www.fisherkingpress.com
info@fisherkingpress.com
+1-831-238-7799

Front Cover Image: A Giant Dream©
from an original painting by Howard Fox
www.howardfox.com

Acknowledgments

We would like to express our gratitude to the eminent Jungian analysts who generously contributed chapters to this book. Each enlightening tale was spun by the personality, life, and experience of these wonderful authors. Yet, the book itself belongs to the reader, who is invited to commence a journey of curiosity to pick up the yarn and follow the threads of the stories into the depths and expanses, through the twists and the turns of the dreaming mind.

We are grateful to Mel Mathews, editor and publisher of Fisher King Press, for his steadfast support and insightful guidance in bringing this venture to fruition. With expertise and sensitivity, patience and devotion, he has led the way over the inevitable hurdles to bring this book to publication.

Beyond our eyes, we were fortunate to have two seasoned editors to smooth out the manuscripts. We thank Margaret Ryan for her exceptional language editing and Karen Farley for her superb proofing, formatting, and editing of the chapters into their finished print-ready form. Karen, with her precise artistic eye, designed the cover of the book to be an invitation to the reader, to step into the rich world of dreams.

We want to thank Howard Fox for granting permission to reproduce his painting "A Giant Dream" on the cover of this book.

Howard Fox's paintings are in the genre of magical realism, depicting a realm of fantasy with precise details, creating an illusion of reality so often found in dreams.

In this painting, we see the more personal side of the psyche being drawn deeper into the unconscious, as reflected by the different figures whose attention turns to the sleeping giant. The policeman, who halts a couple from approaching the sleeping giant on the bridge, might represent that aspect of consciousness which, out of fear, prevents access to the archetypal realm, to the underworld of dreams.

We may wonder, who is he, the dreaming giant? Is he, perhaps, a giant image of the dream's central focus, "the royal road," the grand bridge between consciousness and the unconscious mind? He is seen, and on the verge of being approached by consciousness. Lying on the bridge, the giant delineates the boundary, and represents the connecting intersection, between the more personal narratives in the foreground of the psyche (and the painting) and the psyche's roots in nature, which in the distance becomes increasingly whole and unified.

The giant uses a red fire engine for a pillow. While asleep, a fiery libido is subdued. What will happen when the giant wakes up, waking up our consciousness? Or, similarly, when we approach the images in our dreams?

The painting is an image with a story to be looked at, read, explored, contemplated, and partly understood.

We invite the readers to circumambulate the image of the dreaming giant, and to trace the embedded stories in this giant dream, just as we hope the chapters in this book will inspire the reader to explore the amplifications of their dreams and images.

Erel Shalit and Nancy Swift Furlotti

Contents

The Amplified World of Dreams

by Erel Shalit and Nancy Swift Furlotti

The dream is a little hidden door in the innermost and most secret recesses of the soul, opening into that cosmic night which was psyche long before there was any ego-consciousness, and which will remain psyche no matter how far out ego-consciousness extends.

—C. G. Jung[1]

Humans have always expressed themselves in images of their outer and inner worlds—seemingly a characteristic of our genetic structure. The dream is a communication from the psyche in the form of images arising from the realms of the unconscious, beyond conscious ego control. The deeper layers within us speak to us nightly through dreams, mostly appearing during the stage of REM (rapid eye movement) sleep, usually at the end of each of the four to six sleep cycles a night. Whether we remember our dreams or not, they affect us.

Constantly at work, the psyche brings forth that which is positive and creative, as well as all that is negative and destructive in the depth of our soul. The psyche may guide us or lead us astray; it behooves us to consciously take part in determining which direction we are led. We participate by attempting to understand the meaning of our dreams and by discerning the inner voices that speak to us, to distinguish between the inner figures of wisdom and the ghosts behind our complexes.

In this book we focus on the amplification method that Jung developed to uncover the meaning of the dream, a procedure that reflects his approach to the psyche and the understanding of dreams. In contrast to free association, which reflects a causal view of neurosis, amplification indicates the movement from etiology toward understanding the *meaning* and symbolic *value* of the image. Rather than reductive causal explanations of the individual's symptoms, amplification aims at enhancing consciousness by focusing on the image. As the term implies, we attempt to enlarge the dream image by amplifying it—by relating it to its roots in the objective psyche and its appearance in culture, history, mythology, and religion. The psyche speaks in images; thus, in order to gain from its wisdom, we need to understand the language of images, to be aware of their depth and meaning, and to study them in their personal as well as collective contexts.

Dream and Culture

From the beginning of humanity, a wide tradition of dream work has existed in count-less cultures. In the oldest preserved myth, the four-thousand-year-old Gilgamesh epic, we are told one of humanity's oldest reported dreams, dreamed by the king and inter-preted by his mother Ninsun, queen of the wild cow, the wise and all-knowing god-dess.[2] She explains to Gilgamesh that the star that in his dream has fallen down to him, which he is unable to remove, is his companion. We might say that the star pertains to that aspect of fate that cannot be evaded.

Jung gave examples of dreams and how they were interpreted in other cultures, as well as in antiquity. Referring to a series of dreams, Jung, relying on Josephus Flavius,[3] concluded that Simon the Essene,[4] who was a skillful dream interpreter, understood dreams not only sensibly, but in a way similar to his own.[5] Analyzing Nebuchadnezzar's second dream in the Bible,[6] in which he dreams of a tree growing up to heaven that is cut down and the king turned into a beast, Jung followed Daniel's interpretation of the dream. Jung wrote that it was "easy to see that the great tree is the dreaming king himself. Daniel interprets the dream in this sense. Its meaning is obviously an attempt to compensate the king's megalomania, which, according to the story, developed into a real psychosis."[7] Jung considered this historical dream, "like all dreams," to have a *"compensatory function"*[8] of counterbalancing the king's disproportionate sense of power. For him to achieve a semblance of wholeness, Nebuchadnezzar's psyche deemed that the tree must be cut down to size. Jung aptly summarized Nebuchadnezzar's con-dition as "a complete regressive degeneration of a man who has overreached himself."[9]

Daniel similarly understood the meaning of the dream as referring to the king's inflation and warned him "to repent of his avarice and injustice."[10] Since the king did not repent, he was cast out to live as a beast.

In Africa, Jung understood that "magic is the science of the jungle."[11] He visited the Elgonyi in East Africa, from whom he learned the distinction between the ordi-nary and the "big" dreams—dreams that affect the entire group and are dreamed by the medicine man, who would know "where the herds strayed, where the cows took their calves, and when there was going to be war or a pestilence."[12] Now, however, the medicine man wept and told Jung that even he had no dreams anymore, "since the British came into the country." Because the colonizers knew "when there shall be war; … when there are diseases," there was seemingly no need for dreams as "guidance of man in the great darkness."[13] Jung traced the tribally significant "big dreams" in different cultures, including "in the Greek and Roman civilizations, where such dreams were reported to the Areopagus or to the Senate."[14]

"Big" dreams seem to emerge at important periods in one's life and may reflect a transition from one stage of development to another, during which the individual is particularly open to collective, archetypal imagery that is believed to be pertinent for the group. "These dreams in particular make us understand why the ancients attributed a pronounced prognostic meaning to their dreams. Throughout the whole of antiquity, and to a large extent still in the Middle Ages, it was believed that dreams foretell the future."[15]

Many ethnic groups developed specific ways of sharing dreams and cultural codes for their interpretation. Jung reported that in some parts of Africa, the indigenous people were shy about sharing their dreams, perhaps out of fear that "harm may come to them from anyone who has knowledge of their dreams." The Somali and Swahilis, on the other hand, says Jung, consulted an Arab dream book and turned to Jung for advice on their dreams.[16]

In Ancient Greece there was a widespread practice of using dreams for healing. The word *incubation* comes from the Latin *incubare*, to sleep in a sacred precinct, which was a practice in ancient Greece of seeking healing dreams in a sacred place.

In her initial dream in analysis, a woman dreams that she walks to a house "further away, a bit on the side; no one has been here for quite some time. It is like a hide-out, set apart from the rest of the city. I lie down to sleep." In the dream, she is guided to the place of incubation, a condition of openness to dreaming and symbolization, which here takes place in the dream itself.

Around the third century B.C.E. there were more than four hundred sanctuaries creating a network of what we would regard today as general and mental health clinics. These sanctuaries were termed *Asclepieia*, after *Asclepius*, the god of medicine and healing. Hippocrates, for example, was director of the Asclepeion at the island of Cos.

Henry Miller explained how he had not known the meaning of peace until he visited the principal sanctuary of Asclepius at Epidaurus, where dream incubation began around 600 B.C.E. "There was a stillness so intense that.... I heard the great heart of the world beat," he writes, and he makes it clear the sanctuary is really an internal space "in the heart."[17]

In the procedure of dream incubation at the Asclepeion, the person seeking healing first underwent a ritual cleansing bath. Then, the "patient" visited the temples of Aphrodite (of love and nature) and of Apollo (of understanding and clarity). Finally, the person would be called into the *abaton* of the Asclepeion.

The *abaton* was the innermost sanctuary, the sleeping chamber, where the person slept on a couch, called *kline* (from which we have the word "clinic"), until a healing dream would appear. (*Abaton* means "an impassable place," or metaphorically, "pure or chaste.")[18] The person was to await patiently for the arrival of an initial dream in which Asclepius would appear—that is, until a transference dream occurred in which the image of the healer would evoke and be attached to the internal healing function. Asclepius could appear, for instance, in the shape of a bearded man or a boy, as god or as dog. In particularly powerful treatment, Asclepius might appear as a snake: What can kill and poison can also heal, a reality of which the physicians' snake-coiled staff, the *caduceus*, reminds us. In fact, it was with this staff that Hermes, the mediator god, put people to sleep and sent them dreams.

According to Barbara Tedlock,[19] cultures frequently have rules concerning the sharing and interpreting of dreams. For instance, dreams involving the ancestors or the earth deities are shared with the shamans, who are dream interpreters.[20] However, there may be forbidden dreams that are not told to anyone. For the Zuni, telling a good dream would diminish its positive effect on the dreamer; therefore, more bad dreams are shared than good ones. In the Momostenango culture, all dreams, whether good or bad, even small fragments, are shared. Initially they are told in private but later shared at length in public groups with initiated "daykeepers," who are the official dream interpreters. Chronic bad dreams are thought to cause illness. The Zuni and Quiché believe that all dreams provide information about future events.[21]

A dream sequence, especially if told to others, moves from its original state of mere sensory imagery in one's mind to a verbal form. This form is then filtered through language-centered, secondary-process thinking and shaped into a cohesive narrative.

Quite naturally, different languages can impart a completely different meaning to the dream. Each dream can be interpreted in various ways, depending on the interpreter.

Additionally, the underlying implied purpose of the dream can be different in different cultures. For example, the word for *dream* in Zuni is a verb, indicating that the dreamer acts upon something, whereas in Quiché it refers simply to a state of being. The English word *dream* refers to the imaginal sensations that pass through a person's mind when sleeping. The Germanic origin of the word refers to deception, illusion, ghost, apparition, merriment, and noise. On the other hand, the old English word for *dream* referred to joy, mirth, music, and vision.

The Hebrew word for dream, *chalom*, has the same root as *hachlama*, meaning *recovery*. In Arabic, it means both *dream* and *to mature*, as well as *seminal fluid*. In Hebrew, the word originally meant *soft*, *moist*, and *viscous*. This is the state of "healthy humors," when one's body liquids, or humors, are free and flowing. In this condition imagination can spring forth, and growth can take place. This life-enhancing moisture can be compared with the nurturing part of the egg, the yolk (in Hebrew, *chelmon*!), in which the fetus develops.

"Emission of seminal fluid" and "to attain puberty"[22] are noted as the key meanings of the root for *chalom*, dream. Furthermore, a development has been suggested from the Tigre language, wherein the root means "coming of age," to the Arabic and Hebrew "sexual dreams," on to the generalized meaning of "dream."[23]

So what we have is a conglomerate of moisture, sex, and maturity, all combined in the dream, *chalom*. Maturity of soul is achieved by raising instinct into imagery—and what is more powerful than sexual imagery! In the dream, instinct is expressed by imagery, which then powerfully activates the instinct. The moisture of imagination may then drive the person to nightly emissions during a sexual dream.

Jung's View on Dreams and the Unconscious

Although Jung credited Freud with the "boldest attempt ever made to master the enigma of the unconscious psyche on the apparently firm ground of empiricism,"[24] his view of the unconscious was strikingly different from Freud's. For Jung, the unconscious is limitless and cannot be fully known, even by consciousness. It is not merely a repository of repressed thoughts and emotions, which, when these are made conscious by interpretation, will be emptied out. Rather, the unconscious is a vast ocean from which consciousness emerges as an island. "It is from these all-uniting depths that the dream arises," said Jung. "No wonder that in all the ancient civilizations an impressive dream was accounted a message from the gods!"[25]

Explicating his view of the unconscious, Jung stated,

> It remained for the rationalism of our age to explain the dream as the remnants left over from the day, as the crumbs that fell into the twilit world from the richly laden table of our consciousness. These dark depths are then nothing but an empty sack, containing no more than what falls into it from above.... It would be far truer to say that our consciousness is that sack, which has nothing in it except what chances to fall into it.[26]

Jung's writings speak the language of images, rather than the more ego-centered language of mechanisms, such as in the term *defense mechanisms*. The dream's real meaning does not lay hidden, latent, lurking behind the overt text. Rather, for Jung, the dream is "part of nature, which harbors no intention to deceive, but expresses something as best it can, … but we may deceive ourselves, because our eyes are shortsighted."[27] According to Freud, the instinctual truth of the unconscious hides behind the manifest dream text. Jung, on the other hand, viewed the individual's consciousness as small and shortsighted, whereas the unconscious is honest and healing.

Furthermore, Jung differentiated between the personal and the collective unconscious. The personal unconscious, said Jung, "contains lost memories, painful ideas that are repressed, subliminal perceptions, … and finally, contents that are not yet ripe for consciousness."[28] Complexes reign over the personal unconscious whether in their purposeful task of bringing archetypal energy and images into personal experience, or when autonomous, detracting energy that would otherwise be accessible to the ego.[29]

In sweeping contrast, the collective unconscious, according to Jung, "contains the whole spiritual heritage of mankind's evolution, born anew in the brain structure of every individual."[30] It is in this universal layer of the unconscious that mythological motifs reside, sometimes rising into consciousness. We deduce the existence of archetypes in the collective unconscious from the appearance of archetypal images in, for instance, mythology and culture. In Freud's view, the mythical structure of the psyche needed to be *resolved* (e.g., the Oedipus complex), whereas for Jung, the modern mind would be *ensouled* by an encounter with the mythical layer.

The dream is a picture from the unconscious that reflects the soul's capacity to produce images and symbols. We might say that the dream is a prism and a mirror of the soul. Through this prism, elements from the archetypal layer of the unconscious emerge and crystallize as images, persons, events, and symbols. The dream serves as the Self's mirroring of the psyche, which enables us to reflect on our behavior and the one-sidedness of our consciousness.

The individuation process, when taking place in analysis, for instance, means making the unconscious, conscious—but Jung also said,

> Consciousness must confront the unconscious and the balance between the opposites must be found. As this is not possible through logic, one is dependent upon symbols which make the irrational union of opposites possible. They are produced spontaneously by the unconscious and are amplified by the conscious mind.[31]

That is, more important than tracking the rational mind's logic and interpretation is to allow the spontaneous symbol-forming activity of the unconscious to come into sight. Jung came to see the dream as a manifestation of the Self's image-creating and symbol-forming capacity, not as the result of "non-creative dream-work." The dream is, said Jung, a "*spontaneous self-portrayal, in symbolic form, of the actual situation in the unconscious.*"[32]

The fundamental element of the dream is the symbol. Symbols are the powerhouses of the psyche, equivalent to the mitochondria of the cell. They are representations of wholeness and the union of opposites, thus carrying the potent and current connection between humanity and the greater Self.

Symbols act as transformers of psychic energy, libido.[33] Jung pointed out that the symbol "has an eminently 'healing' character, that it helps to restore wholeness as well as health … by removing and transforming the blockages and obstructions of psychic energy."[34] One experiences a charge, a sense of *numinosity*, when presented with a symbol, like having come into contact with something truly other. Unlike *signs*, symbols contain more than the mere fact of what they represent. When a symbol no longer carries its potency because of a change in the culture or religious beliefs, new, living symbols emerge from the psyche to maintain the human-spirit connection and to reconcile the opposites on both individual and cultural levels. The psyche offers up symbols as a way to help us reconcile these opposites within ourselves, ultimately leading us to develop a working relationship with the greater Self, the archetype of wholeness and meaning. The Self both guides the process and is its goal. Through its guidance, the Self offers us symbols and images in our dreams to direct our way.

Symbols are archetypal representations. The word *archetype* is derived from *arche* or "first principle," which points to the creative source that cannot be represented or seen, and from *typos*, "impression" or "imprint," which refers to a manifestation of the first principle. Archetypes are universal patterns or motifs appearing in the form of symbolic images in religions, mythology, fairy tales, legends, and psychological symptoms. They are the primordial, structural elements of the human psyche seen in images and symbols that manifest through universal patterns of human behavior. Like crystals with many facets, we cannot see or understand an archetype in its totality. We may discern one or more facets at any one time, but never the whole crystal.

Archetypal images express patterns of human existence, and complexes represent the actual embodiment of these patterns. Complexes contain a set of archetypal motifs or images at their core, with a web of related behavior patterns around that core. It is through the body and our emotions that the archetypes touch ground in material reality, manifesting these common human patterns. Archetypal images mostly appear in our dreams in the shape of personalized complexes; that is, the complexes in our dreams give personalized shape to the archetypal images, so that these can be assimilated into the ego and consciousness.[35]

The ego is the center of consciousness and contains all that the person is aware of, including thoughts, feelings, sensations, and intuitions. Through the process of individuation we increasingly assimilate unconscious elements and integrate complexes as aspects of our personalities. This is a continuing process of enlarging the ego complex by bringing the darkness of the unconscious into the light of consciousness. Jung believed that this process was the meaning and purpose of life itself and that it is facilitated by the Self's offering up dreams for us to unveil. Clarifying the themes in Jung's *Answer to Job*,[36] Edinger considered the process of making conscious what is unconscious to be the ultimate task of transforming the dark, unconscious side of the god image.[37]

Jung pointed out that he differentiated "the dream process according to how the reactions of the unconscious stand in relation to the conscious situation."[38] From his study of dreams in different cultures and in his work with patients, he distinguished four ways in which dreams offer us meaning and comment on our lives:

1. Dreams can be the unconscious reaction to the conscious situation, resulting in content that compensates or is complementary to what transpired during the day.

2. Dreams can show us a conflict that exists between the unconscious and consciousness; the unconscious offers us another viewpoint that is in conflict with our current attitude.

3. Very significant dreams try to actively change the conscious attitude.

4. Dreams may give us archetypal material from the unconscious that has no connection to our daily lives; these are the "big dreams" that are experienced as illumination.

Jung emphasized that this last category of dreams can occur before the outbreak of mental illness, when contents from the unconscious may break through into consciousness. Jung also clarified that,

> Dreams prepare, announce, or warn about certain situations, often long before they actually happen. This is not necessarily a miracle or a recognition. Most crises or dangerous situations have a long incubation, only the conscious mind is not aware of it. Dreams can betray the secret.[39]

Freud warned against an excessive respect for "a mysterious unconscious."[40] Rather, "*[w]hen the work of interpretation has been completed,*" wrote Freud, in italics, after having completed the first psychoanalytic dream interpretation, *the dream can be recognized as a wish-fulfilment.*"[41] An apparent example of wish-fulfilment (and sleep protection) is a dream in which the dreamer, who has been asked by her employer to arrive one hour earlier for work, dreams: "I wake up, get dressed, take my pajamas to work, and there I go back to sleep." The important aspect of Freud's hypothesis is perhaps that the "dream takes the place of action,"[42] which has wider implications than mere wish-fulfilment.

Jung believed that dreams result from five main causes and conditions:

1. Somatic stimuli, body positions, illness, and physical perceptions. (How many times have you dreamed you had to go to the bathroom, to finally wake up to that pressing physical need?)

2. Other environmental stimuli such as light and temperature, or an alarm clock going off;

3. External psychical stimuli that affect the unconscious (e.g., distress of a family member, moods, or secrets); family members can be so attuned to each other that they dream each other's dreams;

4. Past events, whether forgotten personal ones or historical events that contain archetypal contents;

5. Anticipation of the future, both what may transpire in actual life, as well as psychical and emotional changes in the dreamer, even if not yet recognizable to him or her.

Furthermore, Jung claimed that, except in posttraumatic dreaming, dreams do not repeat a previous experience exactly.[43]

Personal dreams are limited to the affairs of everyday life and one's personal process, offering information and guidance pertaining to what is going on in our current lives. These are the everyday dreams, the "bread and butter" of the dream world. It is frequently the small, seemingly insignificant dreams, easily forgotten, that offer us important information about our inadequate conscious standpoint.

The big dream, as mentioned, stretches beyond the boundaries of the current affairs in one's life. Jung's experience prior to World War I is interesting in light of his category of prospective dreams. He had a horrific series of nine visions and three dreams, showing scenes of blood flowing in the streets of Europe, frozen landscapes, and dead bodies. Some of these images erupted into his waking state as visions. At first he wondered if he were having a psychotic break, but with the commencement of World War I, he realized that the images were portraying a collective reality, revealing what would happen during this war. A number of other people across Europe at this time experienced the same phenomenon. It was a powerful reaction from the unconscious, commenting on what was "in the air" but not yet a reality. The dreams spoke to the collective situation as well as to Jung's own impending descent into the unconscious to explore the nature of the psyche.[44]

Jung viewed dreams as stages in the classical drama and believed a great many dreams have a definite structure to them. "The whole dream-work is essentially subjective," said Jung, "and a dream is a theatre in which the dreamer is himself the scene, the player, the prompter, the producer, the author, the public, and the critic."[45]

Jung followed the Aristotelian outline of the structure of drama:[46]

1. The *introduction* or *exposition* states the setting, time, and place, what is said and not said, the people, and the statement of the problem to be

addressed, the theme of the dream. For example, "I was in an old house and it was dark outside."

2. The *development* is the movement of the plot through which things become complicated, and we do not know what will happen next: "Suddenly, someone knocked on the front door and when I went to answer, there was no one there, so I left the room. Just then, my grandmother saw someone's face in the window and was terrified. She screamed out for me."

3. The *peripeteia* is the twist of the story, crisis, or the turning point: "I ran back into the room and opened the window. I saw my brother walking across the lawn and called after him."

4. The final stage is the *lysis*, the solution or conclusion, whether the way out or catastrophe: "This had been the first time we had seen my brother in years. We were happy to see him, and I sat talking with him into the morning after our grandmother went to bed."

Furthermore, we can observe the progression of images by studying entire dream series. In the natural rhythm of the psyche, images emerge into consciousness, replacing others that return to the waters of the unconscious, in a constant progression, cycling through the vegetative, the animal, and the spirit realms.

Dreams are not moral. Nature does not necessarily take a side between good and evil or between other opposites. It is up to our ego consciousness to filter the dream through our cultural sensibility to determine the value of the message.

By actively interacting with dreams, we realize the centrality of the Self as a guiding force in our life. Through dreams we are able to see where libido, or life energy, is blocked and where it wants to go. Although dreams can be viewed from different perspectives and understood in more than one way, they always move us toward a more conscious life by helping to locate the source of creativity, the water of life within. By attending to our dreams, we can gain clues to help us balance the opposing aspects of our personalities, such as our instincts, with our spiritual needs.

Amplification

The psyche speaks to us in metaphors, a language we must learn as we embark on our journey to reveal the meaning of dreams. Jung wrote,

The "manifest" dream-picture is the dream itself and contains the whole meaning of the dream.... What Freud calls the "dream-façade" is the dream's obscurity, and this is really only a projection of our own lack of understanding. We say the dream has a false front only because we fail to see into it.... We do not have to get behind such a text, but must first learn to read it.[47]

The means that Jung devised to "read" the text of the dream was the process of amplification, which deciphers meaning through comparison. Metaphors and analogies depict scenes of life, and the dream images show that of which we are unconscious. In contrast to the view that dreams "were not designed by nature to serve any function—not rehearsal of instincts, not release of otherwise unreleasable impulses. Nothing, *nada*, just noise, like the gurgling of the stomach,"[48] we recognize that images emerge in our psyche to send us messages. These messages are offered for our understanding, although the interpretation can vary depending on the interpreter, as we filter these metaphors through our own unique psychology.

Jung's method of amplification reflects his distinction between the personal and the collective layers of the psyche. Parallel to the ego as center of consciousness, and as one's conscious sense of identity, the Self encompasses both consciousness and the unconscious. The (capital *S*)[49] Self stands as a guardian at the crossroads between the personal and the objective layers of the psyche. In its capacity as archetype of *meaning*, the Self provides the archetypal foundation on which the ego and consciousness develop, the blueprint on which the house of conscious identity is erected. As the psyche's *symbol-forming faculty*, the Self brings archetypal images into the personal level of awareness, dressed in the garb of complexes, appearing as images in our dreams.

The technique of free association enabled Freud to abandon hypnosis as a means of going beyond the limits of ego consciousness. By means of free associations, a dream image will find its place in the context of personal complexes and repressed memories. By amplification, on the other hand, the conscious ego reaches out toward the meaning and symbolic value of the image. The image and its roots in the objective psyche become the focal issues.

With amplification, the focus turns from the dream leading the ego into the personal unconscious, to providing the objective psyche a way to manifest in the world of consciousness.

Even though not explicitly using the term, Jung introduced the idea of amplification in a 1914 lecture "On Psychological Understanding." He contrasted a causal-reductive standpoint with a synthetic (or "constructive") approach, whereby the question is asked how "out of this present, a bridge can be built into its own future"?[50] Jung then differentiated between a reductive approach, leading a male patient to his father-complex, and amplifying the image of a sword in the patient's dream, enabling him "to face the dangers of life through firm and brave decision," as illustrated by "the words 'I will' [as] mankind's oldest heritage [which] have helped it through innumerable dangers."[51] Jung mentions how, from a comparative analysis, "typical formations can be discovered."[52]

Amplification is not merely an intellectual expansion of personal dream images, but a way of tapping into the treasures of humankind's spiritual heritage, so that the fountain can bring the living waters to nourish the individual psyche by means of the image. The images, in fact, serve in the role of angels, which, "are personified transmitters of unconscious contents that are seeking expression."[53]

Jung clearly explained his thinking behind the process of amplification:

> It is simply that of seeking the parallels. For instance, in the case of a very rare word which you have never come across before, you try to find parallel text passages, parallel applications perhaps, where that word also occurs, and then you try to put the formula you have established from the knowledge of other texts into the new text. If you make the new text a readable whole, you say, "Now we can read it." That is how we learned to read hieroglyphics and cuneiform inscriptions and that is how we can read dreams.[54]

The dreamer's personal associations are always a starting point in working with dreams, whether predominantly personal or of a more archetypal nature. Jung emphasized this point by "making sure that every shade of meaning which each salient feature of the dream has for the dreamer is determined by the associations of the dreamer himself."[55] Unlike free association, which leads to a person's core complexes, it is crucial to remain within the context of the specific dream image. Thus, the dreamer's associations are bound to the specific image, exploring it by circumambulation, that is, by staying close to the image, circulating around it.

With the personal associations flushed out, there may remain obscure images that would benefit from archetypal amplification. We enter fairy tales and legends, explore the mythical dramas, and turn to comparative religion. We go back to the language that has been formed over the course of human history and that draws from the emerging creative imagination of humanity. We find the archetypal associations in the deep well of human, divine, and nature's wisdom. These supplement and support our personal associations, which together allow us to decipher the meaning of the dream, which has arisen to us from the Self. Particularly, it is the big, archetypal dream that we remember all throughout life. But the archetypal kernel is present even in the simplest of dress; often it may be the simpleton, the common clerk, barely noticeable, the unsophisticated neighbor, who serves as psychopomp, as guide along the road of our soul's travels.

The task, then, is to find similarities or associations between the dream image and mythic stories and fairy tales, in culture and religious thinking. The story will open up the gates to a world of experience for the dreamer to see and ponder. The psyche beyond our consciousness may often help us find the stories and the archetypal representations that expand the information transmitted through the dream.

Active Imagination

Amplification means more than seeking cultural and other parallels. In *active imagination*, the ego reaches out to grasp the archetypal essence and meaning of the drama and the images in the dream.

Jung considered his method of active imagination to be a "spontaneous amplification" of archetypal material. In active imagination, the person assumes an attitude of passive consciousness, enabling openness to "unconscious influences."[56] "On this natural amplification process," Jung continued, "I also base my method of eliciting the meaning of dreams, for dreams behave exactly in the same way as active imagination; only the support of conscious contents is lacking."[57] Amplification by means of active imagination can take place in a variety of ways, such as writing down dialogues with dream figures or circumambulating the images of a dream.

For example, after a year in analysis, a fifty-year-old highly successful male CEO dreamed the following:

> It is nighttime. I am milking a cow, but there is no milk coming. I am then told [by what amounts to an inner voice] to bring the cow to the entrance of Jerusalem, to bury it there in a pit and let it cook for several hours or days, and then bring it to Mount Scopus, where we have to run to change the buckets because it gives so much milk.

The dreamer amplified the dream by active imagination, going through the events of the dream in a state of reverie, writing down his experience. The following is abbreviated from his active imagination:

It is night, very dark. I am not the one who decides here about this. I am being led, not leading. Wouldn't imagine myself milking a cow! But ok, that's my task, and I accept.

This cow is huge, much bigger than real cows. She is majestic. I approach hesitantly, but she doesn't move. I start milking, but no milk comes. I don't know what to do—to try harder? I ask her, but she doesn't answer, just stares back at me, as if reproaching me.

Then I hear this voice, don't know from where. It's a very strong voice—strong but soft, not loud at all, almost a whisper, yet very clear, penetrating. It's clear to me that this voice knows something that I don't, and I do as I am told—I start walking toward Jerusalem, a long and uphill road, pulling the big cow by a rope. It follows silently. I almost feel like I am riding an elephant, though I am pulling the cow behind me. It's simultaneously easy, I feel elevated, and heavy and burdensome.

We get to the gates of the city, and even though it's at night, I can see the people who have gathered there: beggars and thieves, all kinds of outcasts. And here I come with my cow! Looks kind of funny! Don't know if I am inside or outside the gate, but I am in that area, on a hilly slope, where I dig a pit. It feels terrible to bury the cow, but she doesn't seem to mind. I am quite horrified, in fact. The big cow lies there, melting in the boiling water, bubbles of water.

I sit and wait. I just wait. Very strange mood. It's so quiet. No life around. Really nighttime. I am all alone. Nothing happens. Very long time. Nothing I can do. I hardly move as I watch those bubbles in the boiling water as the cow is cooking. It's as if nothing is ever going to happen.

Then the sun rises, the cow climbs out of the pit, and I know I have to take it to Mount Scopus. I am not surprised at all that she is well and alive—it's all very natural, I think.

There, on top of the mountain, the view of Jerusalem and its surroundings is breathtaking. A bird's-eye view, seeing it all, but without really being there—nearby, but not fully inside the city. Yet, getting the full map of it.

It's incredible to feel how the milk flows! Don't know who all the people there are—I think it might be all those that I met at the entrance to the city, at the city gates. But it's too much milk, we can't handle it all. Somehow I need to back down, or find a solution.

In the absence of personal associations, this dream is not a personal, but predominantly an archetypal dream, as the magical cow that is cooked, brought back to life, and then found to be overflowing with milk clearly indicates.

The meaning of the dream's message is unveiled by associations bound to each image in the dream. Jung suggested that one think of a circle with rays emanating from its circumference. Each ray represents one image in the dream.

In order to make sense of the nonlinear time of the unconscious, as we wake up from a dream we place the images in linear sequence, even though actually any image can come first. The images are arranged around the circle of the diagram or the central meaning of the dream.

In this dream, the cow that accompanies the dream ego all through the dream is undoubtedly the main image to explore. We go through this process for each image, and then look at the bigger picture we have created, to find the thread that leads to an understanding or a statement of meaning. The images we would then explore by amplification are the cow, the absence and then the abundance of milk, the inner voice, the entrance to Jerusalem, cooking the cow in a pit, Mount Scopus, running to get buckets, and the others in the dream, described as beggars, thieves, and outcasts.

A cow represents a domesticated animal associated with milk and nurturing; in archetypal terms the cow is associated with the Great Mother. We find her as the cow goddess Isis from Egyptian mythology, and in Ninsun, the wise dream interpreter and queen of the wild cow, as well as in Hindu mythology, where Kamadhenu is the mother goddess of all cows. The sacred red cow can be found in both Jewish and Christian tradition, as well as in Greek mythology.

This cow, however, gives no milk. She is not a nurturing cow and is unable to properly support the dreamer. This man's cow instinct has dried up. The cow reproaches him, because he has ignored her for too long.

His relationship with and attitude toward the unconscious, represented by the Great Mother, do not nurture him and need to be reestablished. He has lost the ability to extract the warm, sweet milk in life—a metaphor for joy, nurturing, care, and relationship. Now, however, this successful man, clearly with a strong ego, agrees to do the humble work.

Compensation from the unconscious comes in the form of the voice of the Self, guiding the dreamer to bring the cow back into its fructifying state, and thereby to bring himself into relationship with it. He needs to bring the cow to the entrance of Jerusalem and let it cook in a pit for several hours or days.

The gates of the city signify an entrance to a center, pregnant with archetypal meaning and symbolic significance. Here Jerusalem is a city in a dream—Heavenly Jerusalem, as a representation of the Self—rather than Earthly Jerusalem, which might have emerged through personal associations. The shadow, represented by the beggars and the thieves, stands at the gateway to the Self.

The big cow now needs to boil in water for hours or days. Although the dreamer feels terrible about this apparent brutality, he needs to remain in a state of being rather than doing, succumbing to forces and processes beyond his ego's control. The scene is quite ritualistic and similar to what we see in fairy tales about animals that must die and be reborn in a new form in order to help the protagonist. This cow represents an instinctual part of the dreamer that has become a huge burden and lost its creative juices, the nurturing milk. It needs to be transformed at the threshold of the city, at the point of transition.

The ritual takes place during the night. There is a need "to sit in the dark," to patiently remain in a state of depression, or in the alchemical *nigredo*, waiting for the sun to rise and the light of consciousness to emerge, as the dreamer contemplates the transformation of the cow energy.

This is the time of thoughtful introversion as the cow boils and then emerges transformed as the sun rises. The light of consciousness has awakened the new cow image in the dreamer. Now the cow has to be taken to Mount Scopus, where the dreamer is then confronted with the problem of the transformed cow's providing *too much* milk. The dream ego does not know what to do with all this libido, flowing in such abundance. The dreamer is put to work with the group of shadow figures to collect the milk. He needs to relate both to those shadow figures and to the nurturing cow to keep the flow of the milk in balance—without the participation of the shadow elements, he would be too one-sided. This hard work might be necessary as a way for the dreamer to reengage with a feeling aspect of his life that is connected with feminine instinct and feminine spirit.

From Mount Scopus the dreamer has a "bird's-eye view" of Jerusalem and its environs. He is not in the center, at the heart of the city, but can see it from above. The stage has moved from the *nigredo*, or sitting in depression, to *albedo*, or whitening, where there is an influx of conscious awareness, the clear view of the bird flying overhead, seeing the map of the city. The map or the layout of the terrain is clear, but it is overwhelming; too much view, too high, too much white milk.

Figure 1.1 Sculpture of Kamadhenu,
Mother Goddess of Cows,
At the Batu Caves, Malaysia
Photograph by Christian Haugen

The next stage in alchemy is the reddening or *rubedo*, which involves the embodiment of the transformation whereby one makes it one's own. This dreamer is not there yet, but instead is quite overwhelmed by the experience of change. The inner voice, Jerusalem, Mount Scopus, the magical cow all point to a spiritual attitude that perhaps needs to be mediated by reality before it can be realized.

The image in the dream of more milk than the dreamer can contain points to an important psychological issue. The flood gates of the psyche have been opened and the dreamer is inundated with creative energy, more than he can handle. At such times it is crucial that the ego step in and object by taking a stance against the psyche, asking that it curtail the flood, reducing its offering to just enough energy for the person to manage. The dream image of the cow's milk swings from its absence, the lack of psychic energy, to too much. A balance between the extremes needs to be found, and it is the ego's job to find it by taking a strong stance at the doorway between consciousness and the unconscious.

The dreamer allowed himself to follow the inner voice and was willing to be changed by the process, but he must then, as well, find a balance between his ego and his deeper resources.

Amplification of images from the objective layer of the psyche is important if one is to achieve a more complete picture and meaning of a dream, in conjunction with the personal experience and associations. The chapters that follow, written by prominent Jungian analysts, illustrate the many ways in which the meaning of dreams can be deepened by a variety of approaches to amplification. Each of the contributors to this volume has chosen a particular direction, whether art and poetry, myth and fairytale, culture and religion, or initiation to the stages of our life, to paint a kaleidoscopic gestalt of the dream and its amplification.

Notes

1.   C. G. Jung, *CW* 10, par. 304.

2.   Stephen Mitchell, *Gilgamesh*, 83.

3.   Josephus Flavius, *The Jewish War*, 2.111–115.

4.   The Essenes, a Second Temple Jewish sect, lived mainly near the Dead Sea. The Dead Sea Scrolls are often considered to have been part of their library.

5.   *CW* 18, par. 240–244.

6.   Daniel 4.

7.   *CW* 8, par. 485.

8.   *CW* 18, par. 247 (italics in original).

9.   *CW* 18, par. 246.

10.   *CW* 18, par. 246.

11.   *CW* 10, par. 128.

12.   *CW* 10, par. 128.

13.   *CW* 18, par. 674.

14.   *CW* 3, par. 525; the Areopagus functioned in classical times as a High Court of Appeal.

15.   Jung, *Children's Dreams*, p. 380.

16.   C. G. Jung, *Memories, Dreams, Reflections*, 265.

17.   Henry Miller, *The Colossus of Maroussi*, 70f.

18.   Edward Tick, *The Practice of Dream Healing*, 4.

19.   Barbara Tedlock, *Dreaming: Anthropological Interpretations*, 22.

20.   Barbara Tedlock, *The Role of Dreams and Visionary Narratives in Mayan Cultural Survival*, 459.

21.   *Dreaming: Anthropological Interpretations*, 105–131.

22.   Francis Brown, S. R. Driver, and Charles A. Briggs, *Hebrew and English Lexicon of the Old Testament*, 321.

23.   Ludwig Koehler, Walter Baumgartner, and Johann Jakob Stamm, *Hebrew and Aramaic Lexicon of the Old Testament*.

24.   "In Memory of Sigmund Freud," *CW* 15, par. 64.

25.   *CW* 10, par. 305.

26.   *CW* 10, par. 305.

27.   Jung, *Memories, Dreams, Reflections*, 161f.

28 CW 7, par. 103.

29 See Erel Shalit, *The Complex: Path of Transformation from Archetype to Ego.*

30 CW 8, par. 342.

31 CW 11, par. 755.

32 CW 8, par. 505 (italics in original).

33 CW 5, par. 344.

34 Jolande Jacoby, *Complex / Archetype / Symbol*, 100, 103.

35 Cf. Erel Shalit, *The Complex: Path of Transformation from Archetype to Ego.*

36 CW 11, par. 745–747.

37 Edward Edinger, *Transformation of the God-Image*, 122.

38 Jung, *Children's Dreams*, 7.

39 CW 18, par. 473.

40 Sigmund Freud, Remarks on the Theory and Practice of Dream-Interpretation, *S.E. XIX*, 112.

41 *The Interpretation of Dreams, S.E. IV*, 121.

42 *The Interpretation of Dreams, S.E. IV*, 123.

43 Jung, *Children's Dreams*, 8–18.

44 Sonu Shamdasani, Introduction, in Carl Gustav Jung, *The Red Book*, 202.

45 CW 8, par. 509.

46 CW 8, par. 561–564.

47 CW 16, par. 319.

48 Owen Flanagan, *Dreaming Souls*, 24.

49 Although Jung himself did not capitalize the *Self*, it is a convenient distinction from the more common uses of the term, including its application in other psychoanalytic thinking.

50 CW 3, par. 399.

51 CW 3, par. 400–403.

52 CW 3, par. 413.

53 CW 13, par. 108.

54 CW 18, par. 173.

55 Jung, *Dream Analysis*, 72.

56 CW 8, par. 403.

57 CW 8, par. 404.

References

Brown, F., Driver, S. and Briggs, C. *Hebrew and English Lexicon of the Old Testament.* London: Oxford University Press, 1906.

Edinger, E. *Transformation of the God Image.* Toronto, Canada: Inner City Books, 1992.

Flanagan, O. *Dreaming Souls: Sleep, Dreams, and the Evolution of the Conscious Mind.* Oxford: Oxford University Press, 2000.

Freud, S. *Standard Edition of the Complete Psychological Works,* 24 vols., London: Hogarth Press, 1953-1973.

Jacobi, J. *Complex/Archetype/Symbol in the Psychology of C. G. Jung.* New York: Bollingen, 1971.

Jung, C. *Children's Dreams: Notes from the Seminar Given in 1936–1940.* Princeton, NJ: Princeton University Press, 2008.

_____. *Dream Analysis: Notes of the Seminar Given in 1928–1930.* Princeton, NJ: Princeton University Press, 1994.

_____. *The Collected Works.* Princeton: Princeton University Press, 1953-1979.

_____. *Memories, Dreams, Reflections.* Edited by Aniela Jaffé. New York: Random House, 1989.

_____. *The Red Book: Liber Novus.* S. Shamdasani (Ed.). M. Kyburz, J. Peck & S. Shamdasani (Trans.). New York: W. W. Norton, 2009.

Koehler, L., Baumgartner, W. and Stamm, J. *Hebrew and Aramaic Lexicon of the Old Testament.* Leiden: Brill Academic Publishers, 2000.

Miller, H. *The Colossus of Maroussi.* New York: New Directions Books, 2010.

Mitchell, S. *Gilgamesh.* New York: Free Press, 2004.

Shalit, E. *The Complex: Path of Transformation from Archetype to Ego.* Toronto: Inner City Books, 2002.

Tedlock, B. *Dreaming: Anthropological Interpretations.* Santa Fe, NM: School of American Research Press, 1992a.

_____. The Role of Dreams and Visionary Narratives in Mayan Cultural Survival. *Ethos, 20*(4), 1992b, 453–476.

Tick, E. *The Practice of Dream Healing: Bringing Ancient Greek Mysteries into Modern Medicine.* Wheaton, Il: Quest Books, 2001.

Pane e' Vino
Learning to Discern the Objective, Archetypal Nature of Dreams

by Michael Conforti

Life is driven by the presence and workings of universal principles. These archetypal regularities are observable in virtually every facet of life, including our engagement in rituals which insure that food will be on our table, that our children are safe, and that our spiritual needs are attended to. And each and every day we strive to maintain the primacy and sanctity of these practices in our lives.

And then there is pane e' vino, bread and wine. Bread insures that our stomachs will be full, and wine, the elixir of life, melts away the veil of manifest reality, bringing us into the domain of the transcendent.

When we enter the world of pane e' vino, we enter a domain of time which transcends the secular world and allows us to sense the eternal. This is the realm of sacred time referred to by Rabbi Heschel in *The Sabbath*. For Heschel, the beginning of the Sabbath represents entry into an eternal moment. He writes that "the highest goal of spiritual life is … to face sacred moments … a religious experience … a spiritual presence."[1] Susannah Heschel adds that, once within the temenos of the Shabbat, we "enter not simply a day, but an atmosphere."[2]

Citing from the Zohar, Heschel adds, "We are within the Sabbath rather than the Sabbath being within us."[3]

So too in the Catholic tradition there are these moments which transcend temporality. During the Transubstantiation phase of the Mass, where the bread and wine are transformed into the body and blood of Christ, and also at the Benediction, we experience yet another sacred moment in time termed by the Catholic theologians as the *anamnesis*. These moments are not rituals or a reenactments, but an actual experience of eternal time—of transcendence, where we are allowed to share in the living mystery of the numinous.

In "Transformation Symbolism in the Mass," Jung speaks of a reality strikingly similar to Heschel's experience of the Sabbath:

> The *mysterium* … The manifestation of an order outside time involves the idea of a *miracle* which takes place "vere, realiter, substantialiter" at the moment of transubstantiation, for the substances offered are no different from natural objects … whose nature is known to everybody, namely … bread and wine.[4]

Jung proceeds in saying that the mass allows for a "… revelation of something existing in eternity, a rending of the veil of temporal and spatial limitations which separates the human spirit from the sight of the eternal."[5]

From the Mass to the Sabbath to pane e' vino, we enter the domain of the ineffable. Here we listen to the whispers of the wise ones who came before us, the sages and dreamers who brought us to the sea to listen—to see, and to feel the reality of the psyche, and the voice of the ancient wisdom traditions.

Footprints of the divine, these are the imprints left by all those who came before us seeking meaning in life and a way to commune with something greater than oneself. Theirs was an animistic world where the Gods, if pleased, brought the needed rains and the migration of the buffalo, but if displeased, brought calamity. Early cultures knew their lives depended on a relationship to these divine influences, which required learning how to appropriate these Gods in a manner fitting their divinity. At times there was a meal, a jug of wine, and moments of being brought to their knees in devotion, or fear of the unseen forces which shaped their lives. Helpless to shift the tides of these divine winds, they quickly learned the language of the Gods and spirits. Theirs was a domain, a language, and way of life far removed from that of everyday life.

Jung was a "mediatore," a bridge-builder between these worlds. His approach to psyche represents a confluence of two worlds, referred to in *The Red Book* as the "Spirit of the Times" and the "Spirit of the Depths." It is through the dream that we learn of the "Spirit of the Depths," this natural order of life and the ways of psyche and Self.

Jung and the sages and dreamers before him understood that the ways of psyche, Self, and the divine were best approached through a reverence for the wisdom traditions. While Jung's formative years were influenced by the birth of the psychoanalytic movement and its focus on pathology, the creative daemon which burned inside his soul could never accept this reductive, mechanistic view of human nature. Instead, Jung writes that,

The main interest of my work is not concerned with the treatment of neuroses but rather with the approach to the numinous. But the fact is that the approach to the numinous is the real therapy, and inasmuch as you attain to the numinous experiences you are released from the curse of pathology. Even the very disease takes on a numinous character.[6]

As Jung looked to the dream as an expression of the numinous, he realized that psyche represents itself through iconic images, carrying with them a richly textured world of meaning. It was the "antique soul" that was revealed through these archetypal images. For more than sixty years, he studied the ancient texts on symbolism, spirituality, alchemy, and other expressions of Self in art, religion, and literature to learn about the workings of psyche and its unique iconographic language. As Jung came to realize the specificity and rich meaning inherent in these images, he chided his students who felt the need to create their own context and meanings for these archetypal images.

It is our human propensity towards hubris, coupled with a deep fear of the unknown, which drives our subjectivist approach to dream images. Instead, Jung taught that the dream never concealed its meaning, but revealed it through the presentation of universal images.

The image is embedded within its own archetypal field and is expressed through a series of highly specific images which Neumann terms the "symbol canon" to connote the inexorable relationship between archetype and image. Jung often spoke of the native meaning of an image and encouraged us to allow the dream to reveal its own nature. In *The Way of the Image*, Kaufmann continues to build on this theme of the inherent, objective meaning of images when discussing the experience of listening to a concert performance of classical music:

It is a mark of artistry that each of them (the performers) imbued the music with their own individuality, which was very distinctive. I used to be able to tell, by listening to a record, who the performer was. However, they all played the same score! The objective reality was the written score, the notes in a particular key, in a specific sequence. The subjectivity was the particular shading, the individual nuances … Thus it is possible for a musical critic … to write that a particular performer took considerable liberties with the music, but it was all within the spirit of the composer, whereas another artist infused the music with so much of his individual personality that it was no longer the piece written by the composer. Subjectivity was no longer within the well-defined boundaries, it was no longer bowing to the dictates of the objective reality.[7]

Through years of poring over ancient alchemical texts and images, Jung came to learn a great deal about the language of the archetypes and their associated images. From the symbols of sulfur, the Virgin Mary, the different stages in the alchemical process, to a rich ethological understanding of the nature of each animal, Jung sought to enter the unique and specific field of these images. Here we can speak to an inherent symmetry between field and form and between image and archetype.

For instance, we find a number of different species of bears, including the black, brown, grizzly, and polar bears. And when working with the image of a particular bear, we realize that each is distinct and goes about the business of life and survival in a manner specific to its species. So with the eye of an ethologist, we come to appreciate the specificity of the animal, in much the same way as we approach the specificity of a dream image. Through a careful reading of the inherent properties of a particular animal or image, we begin to understand something essential about the intrinsic nature of the constellated issue represented by the dream symbols. This archetypal, ethological approach allows us to understand some fundamental properties of nature's and psyche's habits. As each animal lives within the confines of its native instincts, tendencies, and habitat, we are given an important lens from which to understand some essential aspects of the animal as a carrier of psychic energy. Brown bears will rarely prosper where black bears live, nor will the black bear make a life where polar bears roam. Each image, each symbol, each aspect of life represents an unfolding of an ontological essence, an archetypal regularity inherent within the natural world, and so too, within the life of the psyche.

Consider a contemporary dream of a polar bear in the wild. In order to understand the meaning of this dream we need an in-depth understanding about the essential aspects of the polar bear's nature. Our ancestors spent years learning about the nature and spirit of their totem animal. To worship this aspect of the Self, it was imperative to know as much as possible about the animal's nature, including its mating habits, its relationship to parenting, and the specific nuances of its movements. Theirs was a mimetic, ritualistic experience, an entry into the archetypal field and domain of the animal-image.

While the continuance of life is a primary task of every living being, it is this very issue of survival which is most prominent when addressing the world of contemporary polar bears. Modern scientists and naturalists have come to the painful realization that polar bears may be at the brink of extinction. Once the masters of adaptation in the polar north, they learned to survive and prosper under some of the harshest conditions found in the world. One central feature of survival depended on their ability to swim from one section of land to another and to rest during these long and grueling journeys, where they had to swim from ten to twelve miles before finding the next piece of solid ground. As ice floes were abundant in the far north for centuries, the bears came to depend on these needed resting places during their sojourns. However, one of the most damaging aspects of global warming is the sudden melting and disappearance of the landmass and ice floes, which since the beginning of time have offered survival and life for these bears. With the disturbing discovery of a large number of polar bears found dead in the sea, naturalists now predict that this catastrophic change in their habitat will cause their extinction within our lifetime. Their time-honored instinctive practices of survival no longer suffice amidst these dramatic changes in their habitat.

In learning the seriousness of the polar bear's plight, we are struck by the magnitude and danger now facing this animal. So why would psyche present such an image and psychological situation to a dreamer? The reason may well be that the dreamer is now facing an unprecedented challenge to their survival. So we begin to fear that our dreamer's early and successful modes of adaptation may no longer suffice in the face of dramatic changes in their psychological and perhaps even physiological landscape. The question is, will the dreamer be able to create a novel and adaptive response to these life-threatening changes? It is significant that while an outcome is not overtly indicated in the dream itself, the outer world plight of the polar bear may unfortunately suggest the unspoken *lysis* for this dreamer. However, we do well to hope that a creative solution and approach to this situation will emerge.

A Subjective, Relativistic Perspective on Dreams— Or How We Go on Making the World What We Want It to Be

Jung was a naturalist and understood that the archetypes are an expression of the natural order of life. In sharing this archetypal, collective history, we see that our life is influenced by the same eternal ways that have spoken to humanity since the beginning of time. Every expression of life, from the biological and economic to the psychological and spiritual, is governed by a set of universal, autonomous processes, operating across domains. Janstch makes this point when stating that,

Science is about to recognize these principles as general laws of the dynamics of nature. Applied to humans and their systems of life, they appear therefore as principles of a profoundly natural way of life.[8]

We see how it is that trees grow, learn something about the relationship between the acorn and the mighty oak, the eternal migratory routes of animals, and the branching patterns of tree roots to learn about the parallels occurring within the natural world, the human body, and the individual and collective psyche. It was M. L. von Franz who spoke of archetypes as "nature's constants," which poignantly captures this underlying order between individual and world. These shapers of individual and collective experience represent the archetypal and morphological constants within the psyche. It was Jung's original discoveries of the presence of innate, *a priori* ordering processes within the psyche which provides each of us access to the repository of the world's wisdom traditions and prepares the way for us to remain in relationship to these eternal life principles.

While psychology focuses on individual dynamics, Jung's archetypal perspective looks at the individual in relationship to the ontological. It is this form-generating field which is the focal point for many of the early Jungians and which remains as the frontier for understanding the source for much that is good and bad in the world. All actions, be they benevolence or the atrocities of genocide, spring from an *a priori*, transpersonal, psychoidal domain. It is here, in this matrix of experience, that Jungian psychology may perhaps make its greatest contributions in learning about these motive forces existing within the individual and collective psyche.

Dream

The dream in this next section speaks to this psychoidal domain and demonstrates the need to learn about the objective nature of an image. This dream comes from a man named Peter, who has just crossed the threshold into the retirement phase of his life. After many years of a rich and satisfying career as a clinician and academician, he now looks to the world of carpentry as a way to live out this next part of his life. Approximately six months into the analysis, he had the following dream:

> I had discovered a large amount of wood under the water that had been there for at
> least fifty years. It was all log-length, some trees more than 30–40 feet in length, which

had been de-limbed, and bound with rope on both the front and rear. While I knew that wood exposed to water for a sustained period generally turns to pulp, I still wondered if there could be enough salvageable wood to use for heat in my wood stove.

The dream ends with these questions, so we never do learn of the condition of the wood or what in fact he would do with it. However, the dream's message is a powerful one, and tells of a profound discovery.

I asked Peter his reactions to this dream, and especially his thoughts about the image of the wood under water. He replied that he had never heard anything about this, nor did the image evoke any feelings or memories. However, I strongly felt that the specificity of this image was compelling and suggested its archetypal origins.

I experienced a meaningful synchronicity a few days before the appearance of this dream which directly related to this symbolism of the wood. National Public Radio (NPR) covered a story of the owner of a lumber mill who had found log-length wood under water. Similar to Peter's dream imagery, these de-limbed logs had been intentionally bound by rope in the front and rear and had clearly been lying on the bottom of the water for many years. Also, like Peter, the man decided to bring this wood to his mill and began the milling process to see the effects this storage under water had on the wood. He was shocked to discover that this wood had the most exquisite grains, textures, and details he had ever seen in his many years of working with lumber. Through his own research, he learned that this was indeed some of the most precious and valuable wood ever found, and this method of storing it under water had been practiced for thousands of years by ancient boat builders and others as a means of curing. In fact, it was the Viking ship builders who understood that the water had the effect of curing and strengthening the wood, and this process, while maintaining the integrity of the wood, allowed the craftsman to bend the wood to fit the contours of the boat. So too was such wood used for the creation of many of the world's finest instruments.

While we could have engaged in a lot of imaginative and clever footwork regarding this dream, including looking at the image of "getting the wood up," the dream itself suggested that we attend to the objective, universal meaning of the image. In beginning this process, I discussed the contents of this radio interview and the additional details I had learned about this art of curing wood as a way of translating and grounding the archetypal nature of this dream, in the hope we could find a way to bring the depth of this message into Peter's life.

I explained that the dream revealed that something of immense value had been curing, gestating for many years, and was now ready to be brought to consciousness. I then added that the alarming message in the dream suggested the potential to misuse something of tremendous value, represented in his plan to use the wood for heat in his stove. I went on to say that while it is important to heat his internal alchemical stove, the inherent value, exquisite grains, and uniqueness of this wood really should be reserved for a much more valuable purpose. In realizing the beauty and importance of this wood, we have to ask why he would put something of this value into a wood stove, especially when he can buy wood of a much lesser value and at a fraction of the cost to heat his home. To bring home this point, I asked if he would really want to use a beautiful diamond for a building task when a stone from his garden could accomplish the same results.

The Archimedean point from which to understand this dream rests in the objective meaning of this image. Images represent worlds and domains unto themselves and are energetic epicenters of psychic activity and energy. As their meaning is innate and intrinsic to the archetypes they seek to describe, they are not to be placed upon some Procrustean Bed, to be stretched, or shortened, to fit either the dreamer's or the therapist's ideas about them. It was Saul Lieberman, the Talmudic Master, whose approach to these sacred texts closely resembled Jung's work on the objective meaning of dreams. Lieberman's way to the sacred suggests that,

> … the scholar's understanding of a given version [of a text; the word version is writ-
> ten in Hebrew, "*girsah*"] depends on what he brings to it: the more he knows, the less
> likely he is to engage in conjectures not justified by the facts; the less likely he is to
> "doctor" a text that should be left alone; the less likely he is to offer a labored, intricate
> explanation …[9]

For Lieberman, Jung, von Franz, and the ancients who knew of the wisdom traditions, it was the Self, God, the objective psyche, and not the conjectures and machinations of the conscious mind which revealed the greatest meaning in life and psyche. Elie Wiesel acknowledged the connection between development of a conscious mind and the ability to rationalize our actions, certainly a note about the shadow aspects of conjecture and subjectivity.[10] Instead, our task in working with dreams is to create conditions which allow for the emergence and understanding of their innate, archetypal meaning, and in this way, we can learn of the dream's specific mandates for the individual.

It is the emergence and discovery of this precious gift, and the need to use this in a meaningful way, that represents the central issue in this dream. However, the dreamer's intention to use this wood for fuel provides a chilling revelation about his conscious attitude toward these gifts.

So what is it that he has suddenly discovered? While we may never fully understand the scope and depth of this treasure or how it may be expressed in his life, we do, however, know that it has been curing for many years and is now ready for inclusion in the dreamer's life. What is paramount in this dream work is to articulate the meaning and orientation of the image and to bring this psychic potentiality into his daily life.

What do we do with the gifts we've been given? It is a refrain we often hear in life. There are times when we are able to create a rich and meaningful life from these resources, and then again, there are times when we cannot. It's all too easy to squander one's gifts. So once again, let's turn to the dream for guidance about Peter's gifts and ability to use what the Self has provided for him.

Especially as we approach midlife and the later stages of life, there is an even greater urgency to bring our inherent gifts to fruition. It is a difficult truth to admit that we have misused a precious gift given to us from the Self. Here, when we approach that much-needed and often-dreaded reflection on our lives, we gaze in the mirror and find an older version of what we ever imagined to see, and we ask if we are living the life we were destined to live.

As the dream spoke of a potential to misuse something of great value, I had to question if his intention to take all his years of education, working with clients and students, and his love of this work, and now turn to the world of carpentry, was an expression of this tendency.

There are certainly carpenters who are true artisans, and I have a particularly high regard for this group of craftsmen. A number of years ago, I hired a senior artisan carpenter to rebuild my kitchen. At seventy-two, both age and the signs of a quickly advancing arthritic condition slowed his movements. However, after just two days of work, I realized that, not only was his work truly outstanding, but he accomplished more than a team of four men working together. So too was my paternal grandfather, Eugenio Conforti, who learned his carpentry skills in his native Italy. Coming to America as an immigrant, he quickly rose to the ranks of a finish-carpenter. His particular gift was to hand-build those complex double and triple ceiling moldings found in older homes. Then too, there are the archetypal roots of carpentry extending back to

Jesus and Joseph. Perhaps it was this field of carpentry that Peter needed to access, but instead he chose to concretize the movement into this archetypal field.

And why fifty years? Again, a question we can never fully answer, but we can say that for Peter, now sixty-two years old, this curing process began when he was twelve years old, which is when he developed a deep interest in the natural world. Since childhood he'd had a sense of wonder, which later evolved and matured in his career as an educator. As a professor, friend, and father, he touched the lives of so many people from around the world. He was loved by so many, and to all he brought this sense of wonder.

In response to the dream, I suggested that he consider giving up working as a carpenter and instead keep it as a personal avocation while dipping his foot back into the world of education. He could teach a course at the community college to see how it would feel to again be teaching. He agreed and arranged to teach a course for the local college. While a far cry from the hallowed halls of his prior academic institution, it was his love of teaching and inspiring students that carried him on in this process. On the wings of angels he soared, and so too did his students. From the first class with only seven enrolled students, to the third week where the numbers suddenly swelled to over twenty-five, word had already spread that a truly gifted teacher had entered their ranks, and, almost overnight, he was the most highly regarded instructor at the college.

In this return to teaching, he once again found meaning and greater peace in his life. He was within a temenos that was right for him, and his gifts as an educator, honed over many years, were now once again part of his life. Clearly there will be other manifestations of this precious wood in his life, and this re-entry represented an essential aspect of learning how to value his gifts and allowed him to once again walk hand in hand with his destiny.

It was this dream which illuminated the path for the next portion of his life, especially by showing him the magnitude of this gift. It also spoke to his propensity to take a gift and use it inappropriately. In many ways this dream is as meaningful for the collective as it is for Peter, reminding humanity of the responsibility we each have to our creative daemons. This is especially true in today's world, as the demands of modern life often eclipse our relationship to soul and psyche.

In conclusion, I am reminded of an event which occurred a number of years ago while I was lecturing about a dream image which neither the dreamer nor the analyst was familiar with. It had to do with turtles hatching at a time of year that was out of sequence with the natural order of their life cycle.[11] If in fact they were to be born at the time indicated in the dream, they would have surely perished. An older analyst in the audience responded by stating that "the psyche would never present an image that neither he nor his patient was familiar with." This was a moment when I was glad to have had that second cup of espresso after lunch! I responded to him by speaking Italian, saying that after this lecture, I was looking forward to returning home, to be with my family. I asked if he understood what I had said, to which he said no, because he did not speak Italian! The central point here is that his inability to understand my comments in no way invalided the objective reality of what was being said to him. Archetypes as "nature's constants" are invariants within the psyche and will not be silenced by our individual relationship to it.

The objective psyche speaks to the inherent reality of Self and nature and is not predicated on one's frame of reference or personal understanding of what has occurred. So, like the dream, which presents images and material which the dreamer or analyst is also unfamiliar with, the tendency is to either dismiss any meaning that is not part of their own frame of reference or to import what is foreign into a world shaped by humanity's experiences. Our speculations and fantasies about an image are just that—speculative and filled with subjective renderings, which often veer from the inherent meaning. Here one seeks to import experiences outside of their awareness into a pre-conceived, personal framework, where conjecture replaces objective meaning.

One of Jung's greatest contributions was his discovery and ongoing research into the reality of the psyche. A reliance on subjectivity will only occlude the mysteries and forward-moving dimensions of the Self. Spirituality and transcendence are not to be bounded by the lens of conventional thought. There is a rising above, a seeking to know more, a hunger to be touched by what is new, that are the hallmarks of spirituality. Heschel speaks to this very point in his piece entitled "Ineffable," when he writes,

> The search for reason ends at the shore of the known; on the immense expanse beyond it only the sense of the ineffable can glide. It alone knows the route to that which is remote from experience and understanding.... reason cannot go beyond the shore, and the sense of the ineffable is out of place where we measure.... We do not leave the shore of the known in search of adventure or suspense ... We sail because our mind is like a fantastic seashell, and when applying our ear to its lips we hear a perpetual murmur from the waves beyond the shore.[12]

The point to my refrain in Italian was grasped by many in the audience, and, shortly afterwards, I was at the airport for my return trip home, knowing that it was again time for some *pane e' vino con la mia famiglia*—for some bread and wine with my family.

Notes

1 Abraham Heschel, *The Sabbath*, 6.
2 Susannah Heschel in Abraham Heschel, *The Sabbath*, XV.
3 Susannah Heschel in Abraham Heschel, *The Sabbath*, XV.
4 CW 11, par. 307.
5 CW 11, par. 307.
6 C. G. Jung, *C. G. Jung Letters*. vol. 1, 377.
7 Yoram Kaufmann, *The Way of the Image*, 3.
8 Erich Janstch, *The Self-Organizing Universe: Scientific and Human Implications of the Emerging Paradigm of Evolution*, 8.
9 Meir Lubetski (ed.), *Saul Lieberman: Talmudic Scholar and Classicist*, 4.
10 Elie Wiesel, *And the Sea is Never Full*.
11 I am grateful to Dr. Jane Carr for presenting me with this image.
12 Abraham Heschel, *I Asked for Wonder*, 1.

References

Conforti, M. *Field, Form and Fate: Patterns in Mind, Nature and Psyche*. Louisiana: Spring Journal, 1999.

Heschel, A. J. *The Sabbath*. New York: Farrar, Straus and Giroux, 1951.

_____. *I Asked for Wonder*. New York: Crossroads, 2001.

Janstch, E. *The Self-Organizing Universe: Scientific and Human Implications of the Emerging Paradigm of Evolution*. New York: Pergamon, 1980.

Jung, C. Transformation Symbolism in the Mass. *Psychology and Religion, CW 11*. New Jersey: Princeton University Press, 1969.

_____. *C. G. Jung Letters*. Selected and edited by Gerhard Adler in collaboration with Aniela Jaffé, 2 vols., New Jersey: Princeton University Press, 1973.

_____. *The Red Book*. New York: W. W. Norton, 2009.

Kaufmann, Y. *The Way of the Image*. New York: Zahav Books, 2009.

Lubetski, M. (ed.). *Saul Lieberman: Talmudic Scholar and Classicist*. New York: Edwin Mellon Press, 2002.

Neumann, E. *Origins and History of Consciousness.* New Jersey: Princeton University Press, 1954.

Von Franz, M. *Archetypal Patterns in Fairy Tales.* Toronto: Inner City Books, 1997.

Wiesel, E. *And the Sea is Never Full.* New York: Alfred A. Knoff, 1999.

Amplification
A Personal Narrative

by Thomas Singer

Introduction

Amplification as an idea or a technique is relatively easy to understand. As a living reality, it is far more elusive to evoke than to explain. The lived reality of weaving an amplification can take on a richness and texture that is as elegant as any of the finest fabrics in the world. And amplification, when lived, is a fabric that is woven by time, memory, image, feeling, sensation, idea, and perhaps even a glimpse, at times, of divinity.

The goal of amplification is to catalyze a transformative process in the relationship between the personal, cultural, and archetypal levels of the psyche. The study and use of amplification should begin with the specificity and uniqueness of an individual's life that expands into the life of specific cultures and ultimately finds its roots in the archetypal or universal dimensions of human experience. The quest to find meaning in symbolic imagery by tapping into archetypal sources can transform an individual's life trajectory and release unexpected creative energies.

Personal Story and Original Dream Image

This chapter offers a personal narrative of my experience of amplification. The initial context and setting for this story occurred more than forty years ago and remains alive inside me to this day, because the wondrous thing about an amplification living in the psyche is that it continues to weave its magic and meaning over time, as long as one pays attention to it. In the fall of 1965, I enrolled as a first-year student at Yale Medical School, having just returned from a year of teaching in Greece following graduation from college. The year in Greece had been one of glorious discovery and the awakening of a thirst for life. I imagined myself following in the footsteps of Nikos Kazantzakis and his *Zorba the Greek*. I explored modern Greece, its magnificent landscapes and people, always accompanied by the haunting memories of earlier eras that murmur to one in the stones, the trees, the sky, the sea.

You might imagine how I felt when I returned to the United States and moved into the medical school dorm. New Haven was quite a long way from Greece and quite a brutal way to sober up from the intoxication of Greek adventures. My newly acquired taste for life vanished almost instantaneously. I felt a dread settle over me. Most of my classmates came charging into medical school, armed with anatomy, physiology, microbiology, and the other basic medical sciences already under their belt from undergraduate studies. I had taken my basic premedical course early in college and hadn't taken a science course in three years. Yale was enormously forgiving and, unlike any other medical school in the country, had almost no exams for the first two years, which afforded me some time to get my feet on the ground. Yale had the strange idea that the students they admitted would find their way and didn't need to be sadistically tortured into becoming good doctors. So, I found myself desperately struggling to catch up in the first two years but not flunking out because we had no tests or grades.

The third year is when we began our clinical rotations, and all of my efforts to stay afloat failed when I was tested for the first time. Until then, I had been able to sneak by. I felt like I had landed in New Haven from another planet, had no sense of belonging, and whatever identity I had consolidated to date began to crumble almost immediately when I began my internal medicine rotation. On the first day of my clerkship I was assigned to examine a man who had been admitted to the ward with a stroke. When I entered the room, he was surrounded by a family in great distress. Whatever primitive medical and human skills I had begun to develop deserted me. I fumbled through taking a history from the family and performing a physical exam on an elderly man who was comatose. For me, it was an agony of incompetence and being overwhelmed with fear and doubt.

Shortly after that, I was called to join our "rounds" of all the patients on the ward. Rounds included the resident, interns, medical students, and an attending physician— a virtual sea of white coats swooping into hospital rooms and often the most difficult moments in people's lives. The attending physician asked us how one could tell the difference between a midbrain stroke and one that had occurred higher up in the brain. I froze—I only knew that the man I had tried to examine couldn't talk and didn't respond to any stimuli. I did learn in those rounds that someone with a midbrain stroke is staying alive with only the so-called "vegetative functions" intact—respiration and heart beat. But, after the rounds, I simply walked off the wards, went back to my dormitory room, closed the door, and didn't come out for two days. Eventually, the resident phoned and asked what had happened to me. I said that I couldn't come back. I went to the Student Health Department, began to talk to a resident psychiatrist, and, within about six weeks, found myself meeting a Jungian analyst for the first time.

Talking with someone who took my pain seriously got my own psychic midbrain going. I was able to tell the analyst about my childhood, Greece, and the choice to become a doctor. One childhood memory kept recurring with a surprising poignancy. I remembered throwing a rock at a friend and drawing blood from his forehead when I was eight years old. I was competitive but not combative. At the time, his father was my mother's doctor and my mother was suffering severe ulcerative colitis that required major abdominal surgery and the removal of a large portion of her small intestine. As a result of the disease and surgery, my mother lost twins with whom she was pregnant. I didn't understand any of this as an eight-year-old; I only knew that I had drawn blood from the son of my mother's doctor. And now, I was training to be a doctor.

Often in driving to those first sessions with my analyst, I would experience excruciating headaches. It is in this context that I remember my first experience of "amplification." My analyst was trying to help me connect my experience in Greece with my childhood memories of my mother's illness and my being in medical school. She left the room and brought back a book of photographs of classical Greek sculptures. She showed me an image of a boy being carried on the shoulders of an older, strong Greek man. I think she was trying to help me connect my deep feelings of being a very vulnerable boy with potential feelings of manly strength. I think she was showing me what she imagined would be helpful.

I could sense that my analyst was attempting to broaden my story, to give it a deeper context, to connect it with an eternally recurring human situation so that I wouldn't feel so alone in my suffering. That didn't happen. What did have meaning to me was the thought that one day I might be initiated into the Jungian mysteries and the sacred rite of amplification. I also learned that our techniques carry no guarantee of their working. I was an "amplificatee manqué."

However, other Jungian approaches, directly related to amplification, began to become real for me in those early analytic encounters and eventually offered a gateway into an authentic experience of amplification that has been deeply important in my development. I learned to remember my dreams; I began to draw dreams; and I learned to think symbolically about my life experiences. It was the remembering and drawing of a dream that led in time to a real experience of amplification. For me, the difference between the first, failed attempt at amplification and the later, more compelling experience was that the content of the material that led to a rich amplification arose in a dream. It came from an unknown but potent place within, and the innerness of its origin made connecting it to a source from another time and place real and powerful. The gateway to my initiation into the value of amplification as the royal road to the unconscious came via a "big dream" in 1969:

> I stand face to face with a large "circus" snake. I don't know how I know it is a "circus" snake or even what a "circus" snake is. The name simply announces itself to me in the dream. I know that I want to flee from the snake. My mother stands behind me and insists that I stand my ground. The snake stands as tall or even taller than I and is glowing and radiating energy. We look one another straight in the eye, and I sense that its intentions towards me are not malevolent. They might even be good.

Figure 3.1. Dream of Snake, Boy, Mother
Source: Author's drawing

Snake as phallus, snake as healer, snake as *kundalini*, snake as the mystery of death, rebirth, and immortality—the living symbol came alive in me, although I knew nothing of the multiple symbolic meanings of the serpent at the time of the dream. The word "circus" came over time to suggest magic, illusion, play, fantasy, mystery, and the hint of other realms of being that I later came to recognize as belonging to "psyche" as elaborated in such films as *Pan's Labyrinth* or Fellini's *Amarcord*. All of these possibilities accrued to the dream in the process of amplification over many decades.

In my first reactions to the dream, I only knew that I was facing something terrifying which my mother insisted that I take on directly. Two associations presented themselves to me at the time of the dream:

1. I had run from the medical wards in the horror of seeing a dying man and his grieving family, propelled by my own feelings of utter inadequacy. My analyst as mother helped me begin to face more squarely the mysteries of life and death that were terrifying me.

2. My own mother had done much the same thing on another occasion that actually came the summer before my meltdown on the medical wards. I had finished my first two years of medical school and had the summer off. I arranged to travel to Bolivia with a close friend whose father was stationed in La Paz as part of a U.S. Aid program. We were going to work with a medical missionary and Indians who were being relocated from the 11,000 foot Altiplano to the sparsely populated sea-level jungle territories.

Before traveling to Bolivia, I went back to St. Louis, Missouri, to visit my mother and father. My father was scheduled for a neurosurgical procedure related to osteoarthritis of the spine. I wanted to see him before going to South America. I was scheduled to leave a few days before his surgery. On the appointed day I said my goodbyes, went to the airport, boarded the plane, and, before we had begun to taxi away from the gate, the man sitting next to me died instantaneously of a heart attack. He was laid out in the aisle, and I remember looking at his short, black socks and the white, hairless skin above them. The flight was delayed for the body to be removed from the plane. The thought of my father about to undergo neurosurgery and the corpse lying next to me made me insist on exiting the plane. The airline officials were reluctant to let me disembark, but I didn't take "no" for an answer and left the plane with the body. When I arrived home by taxi, my mother was surprised. I told her what happened. Her response astounded me. She said that I could only stay home for twenty-four hours and then I would have to leave. I later came to realize that she did not want me to stop my life just as it was beginning in the fear of death. She was fearful that I would be trapped in the guilt and mutual dependency of caring for ill parents which had been a significant part of my father's fate in having to look after his own father, who lived to the age of 99. My mother wanted me to face the realities of illness and death head-on and to embrace their painful truths by affirming life. It was a brutal lesson. These were among my personal associations to the dream of the "glowing and radiating" serpent.

Cultural and Archetypal Amplification of a Dream Image

The amplification of the dream came later, when I managed to graduate from medical school and begin my psychiatric residency in San Francisco. I resumed my analysis with a second Jungian, and, as he became familiar with my personal history, he suggested that I read Jane Harrison's *Themis*, an exploration of the mythology of matriarchal, pre-classical, pre-Olympian Greeks. I took his suggestion to heart in the belief that my analyst knew something of undiscovered value that would bring meaning to my life. The process of amplification can originate in a positive transference to the wise old analyst, who is seen as having wisdom about mysterious things that hold the key to understanding one's past, present, and future.

It was the introduction to *Themis* that began the amplification of the serpent dream in which the archetypal dimensions of the snake began to come into focus. I read and reread *Themis* over many years. Eventually, perhaps thirty years after my dream of the serpent, I "saw" for the first time that my own drawing of 1969 had a parallel image in Harrison's book.

Figure 3.2. Mother, Snake, Child, and the Wealth of Harvest Fruits
Jane E. Harrison, *Themis: A Study of the Social Origins of Greek Religion*, p. 286

I came to understand that the two images—one from my psyche and one from the psyche of the pre-classical Greeks—are grounded in the same archetypal reality. Sometimes, explorations of the psyche are like a detective story with surprising twists and turns in unraveling a mystery.

Amplification, in its goal of connecting personal material to the cultural and archetypal foundations of human experience, often opens up a whole new world view to an individual. In the amplification of my snake dream, I began to appreciate the magnificent world view of the earliest Greek society to which the serpent will be our focus and guide.

1. *Mana* and the Snake

Looking more closely at my drawing (Figure 3.1), one notices the simple, radiating lines that surround the serpent, suggesting the huge energies that emanate from its being.

I came to see the energetic vibrations in my primitive drawing as representations of *mana*. *Mana* is a mysterious power that resides in all things. It connects the seen and the unseen, the living and the dead, the organic and the inorganic. *Mana* is the indwelling, vitalizing force inherent in all created matter. In the yogic traditions, the *mana* of the snake has been fully elaborated into a way of understanding *shakti*, the serpentine libidinal energy that is coiled at the base of the spine. One can easily imagine the snake in my drawing as an image of *kundalini* as well as of *mana*.

I stumbled on a moving example of *mana* in the mid-1970s while wandering through the Plaka, the old section of Athens beneath the Acropolis. I came across a store window full of stones with human faces and animal forms. Inside sat a haggard, middle-aged woman who told me the story of her son's murder during the student uprising against the Greek Colonels' regime in November, 1973, when the Colonels sent a tank through the university gates. She described falling into a prolonged depression in the grief over her lost son. One day she noticed a stone on the ground and saw a face in it. She picked it up and started collecting stones in which she saw figures that she would highlight. She slowly came back to life by seeing life in the stones and opened the store to memorialize her son. The store, the stones, and the woman herself were all filled with the *mana* of how a grieving mother came back to life in rediscovering the *mana* of life itself in seemingly inanimate matter.

2. Totemism, The Tribe, and the Snake

In the evolution of the human psyche, totemism is a central station along the way in the development of consciousness. Totemism links the psyche of the group to the natural and supernatural realms. Totemism is a world view in which interpenetrating *mana*, or life force, shares in common being. Totemism is built on the intimate relationship between a group of kindred people on one side and a species of natural or artificial objects on the other side. What happens to one member of the totem group happens to all. In the totemistic stage of belief, people rarely see themselves as separate from their tribal identity or the nonhuman world around them.

One does not need to scratch very far beneath the surface of contemporary life to see that the belief in *mana*—the belief in the shared identity of belonging to a particular totem group and the belief that what happens to that totem group is essential to the ongoing vitality of the tribe and all its members—is alive and well today. For instance, those in countless cities around the United States united in the love of baseball and its totem bird or animal share in their city's common being and fate. The depth of feeling and reverent attitude to the baseball season, in which many experience year in and year out rebirth in the spring and, for most, death in the fall, mirrors the ancient cycle of totem life as experienced by the ancient Greeks. Everybody in the community of fans participates in the course of the season, and what happens to one happens to all as part of the tribe. And, perhaps closer to home for the readers of this book, many believe that belonging to the Jungian totem group is essential to the ongoing vitality of our own tribe and the world.

3. Life Daimon, Rebirth, and the Snake

For the earliest Greeks, the snake was believed to be the source of regeneration and immortality. As a *life daimon*, the serpent was closely associated with the Great Mother and her mysteries of renewal. The souls of the dead, as well as the seeds of the plants, were returned to the underworld, where they participated in the preparations for rebirth. The shadow of the dead, the *keres*, took the form of small, winged creatures, whereas the strength and vitality of the dead, the *thumos*, passed into the serpent. The reincarnation of the tribe as a whole, not a specific individual, occurs through the *thumos* of the snake.

In this regard, the snake bears a striking resemblance to the phallus; each has remarkable regenerative capacities and each has a mind of its own. It is an occasional achievement of mankind to regulate the spermatic contribution of snake as phallus to the ongoing life of the tribe.

The snake was viewed not only as the source of the tribe and the city, but as the source of life itself. This accounts for the importance of the snake in the pre-patriarchal world view of the Greeks, which was most clearly visible in *Python's* central role at Delphi, the religious center of Greece in both its pre-patriarchal and Olympian eras.[1] Python, the serpent, was later replaced at Delphi by Apollo, who became the symbolic representative of the patriarchal era.

4. The Snake in Transformation and Healing

As a natural extension of the ancient Greeks' understanding of the cycle of life, death, and rebirth, a cult of healing and transformation grew up around the figure of Asclepius who, like the Great Mother, also had as his companion or non-human representation the snake. The Asclepian cult emphasized a therapeutic ritual in which suffering human beings would dream their way to a cure by a journey to the underworld where, if they had good fortune, the serpent would initiate their healing. In our modern formulation, we would say that the psyche was encouraged to go into the unconscious to find the healing bite of the snake that would lead to regeneration, renewal, and healing.

5. Evil, Death, Distrust, Paranoia, and the Snake

Harrison focuses almost exclusively on the buried, matriarchal strata of the human psyche in which the snake as a positive attribute of the Great Mother is all but forgotten in contemporary consciousness. Just as the matriarchy fell under the power of the patriarchy at Delphi, the snake was banished to the darker realms of human experience. Harrison bypasses these later, negative aspects of the snake that are more familiar to us and which are essential to any complete amplification of its symbolic meaning. We all know that the snake is not exclusively about renewal, regeneration, vitality, and energy. It has a potently dark side as well.

The snake is not just about healing (φάρμακο) and rebirth. It can also be about death, poison, evil, distrust, and paranoia. In fact, most of us know about the serpent as a seducer who introduces the knowledge of good and evil into the Garden of Eden. The more sinister sides of snake symbolism appear in the poisonous distrust and paranoia that enter intrapsychic processes, interpersonal relationships, group dynamics, and international relationships.

In our contemporary world, one can easily imagine two snakes paired off against one another as being at the archetypal heart of the deep suspicions that bring death and destruction to opposing international forces—such as those between the Western and Islamic worlds. To connect personally with the archetypal power of the serpent requires that one locate the living serpent in oneself—in its creative and destructive potential, in its healing and poisonous potential, in its capacity for death and rebirth, and in the terrifying potential for distrust, suspicion, paranoia, and evil in one's own being.

Bringing the Cultural and Archetypal Amplification of a Dream Image Back Home

In providing this quick tour of the amplification of the snake image, my goal has been to bring the reader into an ancient world view that is quite different from 21st century consciousness. It is a view of man, nature, and spirit that saw its flowering around 1500 B.C. or some 3,500 years ago. Imagining the world from that point of view, I feel quite upside down. It is such an alternative view to that of our modern psyche that there is no way I can or should take it on entirely, as if I could totally replace one world view with another. But, I do find myself taking in pieces of that radically different way of seeing the world which opens up, broadens, and complements how I look at experience both in the inner and outer world.

In digesting Harrison's *Themis* over many decades, I find myself inhabiting the world just a bit differently—in a way that is more receptive to and animated by the serpentine energies of life. The Earth Mother and her consort, the snake, have initiated me into a more natural embrace of instinctual life and its blessings. Living with the snake as a partner/guide results in a heightened sensitivity to the vibrations of both inner and outer reality. The snake's sway can be slow and rhythmic when in tune with the flow of life or sudden and violent in striking out when threatened.

I think of the realm of the snake as offering a bottom-up, non-rational center of consciousness rather than a top-down, rational view in which the mind orders everything. Trying to integrate the ancient snake psyche of Harrison's Greeks and the contemporary rational mind is akin to what the Jungian tradition speaks of as bringing the unconscious and conscious mind into dialogue. It is absurd, although tempting, to think that I could relocate into the archaic, magnificent world view of Harrison's

Themis. Rather, the challenge is to develop the capacity to move back and forth between these two world views on certain occasions, with the hope that they might at times be complementary rather than antagonistic.

Amplification of a symbolic dream image challenges us to look at our familiar point of view through new eyes and with new understanding—and to bring that alternative psyche into dialogue with our contemporary consciousness. With that in mind, I want to circle back to the beginning of the chapter and bring this amplification of the snake back into relationship with my personal life. I consider this exercise essential because it is only in the meeting of the uniquely personal and the archetypally universal that amplification of a dream symbol takes on the depth of its potential meaning. "Healing" as an abstract principle is relatively meaningless without connection to the specific and unique suffering of the individual. Personal and archetypal, unique and universal need one another for the living reality of the amplification of a dream image/symbol to weave its magic. For archetypal "healing" to be real, it requires the specificity of a unique human situation to come alive.

Some forty years after my original snake dream, the healing reality of Asclepius came alive in my psyche. It occurred in the context of a serious health problem I developed as I approached my 70th year, just as my original snake dream occurred as a youthful medical student facing serious illness and death decades before. The snake itself is not present in the two dreams I am going to relate, but the serpent energy as Asclepian healing wisdom emerges from the unconscious, making its point of view available to consciousness. The upside-down wisdom of the unconscious speaks to the top-down knowledge of the rational mind in this anecdotal story.

A few years ago I developed such severe back pain that I could hardly walk and at times had to use a cane and then a walker. I wondered if I was now walking in my father's footsteps when he faced a deteriorating spine as I was heading off to Bolivia as a young man. Workups of my spine, including x-rays and MRIs, revealed severe stenosis at several levels of the lumbar spine. I trusted my spine doctor, who worked very closely with the orthopedic surgeon. After months of conservative physical therapy failed and my pain was only getting worse, we all agreed that I needed surgical intervention, and a spinal fusion at two levels was recommended and scheduled. A few weeks before the surgery, I woke up with a short dream:

> I am lying on the operating table as the surgery is about to begin. I realize that I have
> not signed the consent form for the operation.

The anticipation of major surgery makes all of us anxious, but this dream suggested I was not prepared. I told the dream to my spine doctor, a sensitive and thoughtful man. A day or so later he called back and said that, at a routine review of upcoming surgical cases, it was decided that they would do a fusion at one level rather than two. A few weeks later, I awoke with a second dream:

> I am on the operating table. The procedure is going well and is nearly finished. At the last minute, the surgeon takes out a hammer and chisel—which doesn't look too good to the "me" as hovering observer over the "me" on the operating table.

Again, I communicated the content of the dream to my physician. And again, he took my case to the weekly surgical review board and they decided to do a simpler laminectomy rather than a fusion. This time, I actually did go forward with the less radical surgery and it went well. I experienced a dramatic reduction in pain and improvement in mobility. I had some subsequent complications which responded well to injections and currently—"Δόξα τω Θεώ," "Thanks be to God"—I am doing well. There are several doctors and many gods to thank for my positive outcome to date, and at least one of them has to be Asclepius and his healing snake, because dream incubation figured prominently in my therapeutic healing. An active dialogue between conscious and unconscious, a sensitive doctor who responded to the dream communication, and a fine surgeon all contributed to my improvement. The serpent has its own wisdom, which is different from the wisdom of the rational mind. We can think of "the wisdom of the serpent" as a non-rational "tool" which provides a different attitude towards illness, healing, and the psyche. It does not have to be seen as oppositional to conventional, modern healing techniques, but as complementary. For example, I did proceed with surgery, which was beneficial, but the "wisdom of the serpent" helped guide the decision about which surgery was best for me.

Conclusion

I have come to believe that amplification is most valuable when one is attentive to the personal, cultural, and archetypal levels of psychic reality. A purely archetypal approach is a great "trip" but often has little connection to one's actual life. And focusing only on the personal level cuts off the potential for depth that comes through connecting with the archetypal dimension. And both personal and archetypal experiences are most often filtered through a cultural level that mediates between the two. Equal attention to all three gives the greatest possibility for the "royal road" of amplification to become a living tapestry of great riches.

Notes

[1] Joseph Fontenrose, *Python: A Study of Delphic Myth and Its Origins*

References

Fontenrose, J. *Python: A Study of Delphic Myth and Its Origins.* Berkeley and Los Angeles: University of California Press, 1980.

Harrison, J. *Themis: A Study of the Social Origins of Greek Religion.* Cambridge: Cambridge University Press, 1912.

Kazantzakis, N. *Zorba the Greek.* London: Faber and Faber, 1965.

Redeeming the Feminine
Eros and the World Soul

by Nancy Qualls-Corbett

"The dream is a little hidden door in the innermost and most secret recesses of the soul, opening into that cosmic night which was psyche long before there was any ego-consciousness, and which will remain psyche no matter how far our ego-consciousness extends," Dr. C. G. Jung explains. He continues,

> In dreams we put on the likeness of that universal, truer, more eternal man dwelling in the darkness of primordial night. There he is still the whole, and the whole is in him, indistinguishable from nature and bare of all egohood. It is from these all-uniting depths that the dream arises …"[1]

Jung explores not only the mysteries of the personal unconscious but also that of the collective unconscious. His theory was of the "all uniting" archetypal world and how one's psychic life extends into a far greater sphere than that of an individual's ego con-sciousness. It is as if each individual soul was like a colorful silken thread comprising a miniscule yet very necessary part of a magnificent tapestry. It is the interweaving of the personal psyches with the "cosmic night," creating a far greater design, the world's psyche, the World Soul.

The concept of *Anima Mundi*, the World Soul,[2] has been with us for ages, albeit hidden in the practices or imaginings of ancient shamans, alchemists, and other gifted ones who dared to reach beyond the collective mindset of their times. "The cosmos is a single Living Creature which contains all living creatures within it,"[3] was Plato's de-scription of the world's soul. Renaissance artists and philosophers realized there was no split between spirit and matter; they understood *Anima Mundi* as the spiritual essence within all creation. Their creative designs were formed according to divine proportions found in nature. The shaman, a designated spiritual leader of the tribe, underwent rigorous rites of passage involving visions of dismemberment and re-memberment, symbolic death and rebirth. The shaman had the capacity to envision moving into the lowest depths as well as heavenly heights. He was one with the world of both spirit and matter. The alchemists realized that within the *prima materia*, the heavy, leaden aspect of humankind, there also was the gold, symbolic of the untarnished, indestructible element of one's psychic life. They identified Mercurius as a "life-giving power like a glue, holding the world together, and standing in the middle between body and spirit."[4]

Jung's work also tells of the *Anima Mundi*. He writes, "The soul of the world therefore is a certain only thing, filling all things, bestowing all things, binding and knitting together all things that it might make one frame of the world."[5] The source of wisdom and knowledge of the all-pervading essence of the *anima mundi* was "the inner-most and most secret numinosum of man."[6]

"As above, so below," an axiom attributed to the early alchemist, Hermes Trismegistus; the macrocosm is mirrored within the microcosm. Just as our dreams relate the complexities of one's internal soulful life, they seemingly may mirror the condition of the World Soul. Looking through this glass darkly, what do we see? What is this image we receive when viewing our collective consciousness? And perhaps more importantly, where does our blindness lie, what do we close our collective conscious mind's-eye to and fail to understand or simply ignore?

When viewing the condition of our contemporary world, we find in both women and men a dominant patriarchal attitude and demeanor governing politics and organized religion, resulting in materialism, endless warring to gain power over another, and hate crimes based on a false sense of superiority. Modern day bards sing of this critical issue: "People killin', people dyin'. People … got me questionin'. Where is the love?"[7] We value rational thinking and repress instinctual feeling. Logos dominates Eros. All of these factors contribute to the loss of balance or negation of the true manifestation of Eros. The name, Eros, the mythological god of love, was the name Jung enlisted to describe the feminine principle of the psyche. As a psychic aspect in both men and women, the feminine principle makes it possible for one to know and understand the emotional disposition of another. Eros facilitates one's ability to mediate, to reach out, to enable another, and to love. The repression or degrading of the feminine principle results in massive physical and psychic destruction and growing widespread need. The rape and abuse of Mother Earth and her environment is no less destructive than the rape and physical abuse and psychic trauma of human women of all ages and young boys that we find occurring throughout history and in many parts of our world today. Rape is an ultimate symbol of the misuse of power, the ultimate symbol of the loss of Eros.

Dr. Jung wrote, "Where love reigns, there is no will to power; and where the will to power is paramount, love is lacking."[8] These crucial words, "love is lacking," seemingly describe the condition of our contemporary world. Eros, the feminine principle, is underdeveloped and undervalued. Our dreams inform us of this critical issue.

An individual's dreams relate not only conditions of one's personal psychological framework, that is, the soulful interior life, but they may reflect a much greater view of our world's soul also. For instance, immediately after the terrorists' attack on the World Trade Center, many people's dreams depicted the horror far beyond their personal situation. A woman's dream, I recall, began with, "The world has shifted on its axis." Another's dream imaged the earth opening up and swallowing the people. These horrific events that occurred September 11th had cataclysmic effects not only in our personal psyches, but also in the *Anima Mundi*.

In the following dreams of a woman, Delores, we view not only her personal psychological condition, but also how her traumatized psychic life, "where power was paramount and love was lacking," resonates in the world's soul, that which reflects the similar condition of our universe from ancient to modern times. The absence of the feminine principle, Eros, is pervasive.

Delores is an attractive middle-aged woman, married and mother of two adult children. She is intelligent, well-educated, competent, and creative; nonetheless, her life was ruled by darkness. In the beginning of her analysis, she did not or could not experience much joy and happiness. She stated that she lacked a sense of deep feelings and doubted if she was capable of love. Her haunting memories of early childhood released one traumatic experience after another. As an adult Delores learned that an attempt had been made to abort her birth a few months after conception. Her mother was emotionally absent while her father abused her both physically and emotionally. She was sexually molested at an early age. Despite her many achievements and involvements with others, her continuous sense of self was that of being unwanted, unworthy, unloved, and unlovable.

Delores survived throughout her life by becoming very adaptive—role-playing as it were—that of a well-defended yet approval-seeking young girl, the popular teen-ager, an *ingénue* in young adult years. She wore a well-carved mask of the feminine persona. In such cases of abuse as Delores's, the feminine component of psyche, in order to protect itself from the onslaught of traumatic, debilitating emotions, becomes split off or hardened, as it were, and thus inaccessible to conscious development. This archetypal theme is seen frequently in fairy tales: the princess is imprisoned in a tower by her father, the ruling king, as in the Grimm's tale *Maid Maleen*. In the tale of *The Handless Maiden*, the father unknowingly sells his daughter to a demonic being and then must cut off her hands. Regardless of how well-adapted the outer shell of the feminine persona—that which one acquires and with which one's ego identifies—becomes, it is quite the opposite from the true essence of the feminine principle, Eros, that which is inborn. This results in a hollow feeling of incompleteness deep within, as if living a life of a false self.

This initial dream of Delores's conveys the governing situation of her psychic life:

> I am observing a scene by a river. There are woods all around and many trees have been cut forming a clearing in the middle. I see myself as an infant of eighteen months. I'm lifted skyward by a large pair of men's hands. I am wearing a white cotton dress embroidered with rosebuds. I hear a masculine voice from on high call my name. There is a look of devastation to the land where the trees have been cut. I feel frightened because with the trees gone, I am unprotected. I know that the Indians in the woods are watching and that they will harm me.

The dream takes place by the river and in the woods, deep within that primordial unconscious place where the water of life is flowing. The setting appears to be a ceremonial place where the infant girl child is being offered up by the superior masculine factor. Delores associated the white dress as her christening dress when eighteen months of age. Her name being called by a disembodied voice identifies her as a victim to be ritualistically sacrificed. She has no protection and feels in danger of being harmed by the unconscious savage life of the native men.

In the dream, the dreamer's ego was standing aside as if on an Archimedean point, objectively observing the events taking place. Delores in her formative years had experienced the little girl child at the mercy of parental authority and retained this feeling of persecution and subjugation throughout life. The feeling of warm, loving care or delight in her mother's eyes was absent. The nascent seed of the feminine nature was not nourished, nor was there fertile soil in which it could grow. In similar fashion we, both men and women, are also consciously observing the sacrifice of our infant feminine nature, of love and relatedness, as it is sacrificed to gods of power and materialism. We see the destruction of Earth and human nature; we feel in harm's way, being aware of the archetypal savageness that surrounds us.

This archetypal theme, as seen in Delores's personal history and in her dream, may be amplified when recalling the myth, *The Rape of Persephone.*

Briefly related here is the story of a young girl, Persephone. (In some versions of the myth she is called Kore, a name meaning "young maiden.") She was the daughter of Demeter, an Earth goddess, the goddess of harvest, of Spring, and of fertility of the earth. Hades, the god of the Underworld, was captivated by Persephone's beauty and wished to have her as his own. In some versions of the myth Hades enlisted help from his brother Zeus to devise this plan to kidnap her. One day, when Persephone was merrily walking in the green fields, she came upon a beautiful flower. The moment she plucked this rare blossom, the earth opened up and she tumbled into the underworld, the realm of darkness and death. Mother Demeter grieved so for her daughter that soon all the fertile lands became barren. The people and animal life were starving, and Zeus realized that, if this continued, there would be no living thing left on earth to worship him. He then ruled that Hades had to return Persephone to the upper world. Hades had to comply with Zeus's edicts, but first he devised a plan. He would lure Persephone into eating something and thus keep her connected to him and the underworld. But as Persephone only ate six pomegranate seeds, Zeus ruled that she would remain six months on earth and six months in the Underworld.

This myth is often recounted to explain the change of seasonal growth: the six months Persephone was connected to the divine feminine, Demeter, the earth was fertile and people flourished. The other six months was a time of darkness and dormancy, the wintertime of the earth. The myth, however, speaks to a much more profound issue than accounting for seasonal changes. It tells in symbolic form the abduction (or the sacrifice as in Delores's dream) of beautiful feminine nature and the resulting sterility in life, the wintertime of the soul. It also tells of the promising results when the young feminine nature is restored to its rightful place.

This theme of the rightful place of feminine nature continues throughout the following months:

> I am attending a fundamentalist church with several girl friends. None of us seem very engaged in the service. A family with about five children comes before the congregation to make their testimonial. The father is the dominant member. The mother is off to one side. The father introduces the children, and it is evident that he is especially proud of his sons. The youngest child, a girl, is wheeled inside in a grocery cart. The father says her name and then adds, "Sorry, baby girl, but you don't get to be a whole

person. I'm sorry, but you just don't." Although he focused his attention on the baby girl, it was evident that this was his attitude toward his wife and other daughters, too. The congregation moves toward meeting the family. My friends and I move quickly toward the door.

Delores had been raised in a Christian church, although one that was more liberal than one with fundamentalist beliefs. Her early experience was one of acceptance within the church community. Here her long-felt basic need of belonging was provided for. However, in her adult years she began to question some of the Christian tenets she had been carefully taught. Given her early history with her personal father, God, the father, took on the same wrathful disposition. And as in the dream, she had to find the nearest exit to escape the patriarchal symbolism of the Holy Trinity. At this time there were no female priests or women who were leaders in the church. The dream image of the girl child, the nascent feminine principle simply "carted around," not embraced by loving arms, was symbolic of the attitude Delores experienced in organized religion. Wholeness must also include the integration and acceptance of her feminine nature.

Although the basic concept of all world religions is based on a form of Eros, that is, loving one another, it is difficult to imagine that tenet being the prevailing belief in the hearts of humankind. Throughout the world we find various religious sects ignoring the spiritual essence of the feminine principle. As in the dream, the girl, the feminine principle, is not considered a whole person; the consideration of Eros is relegated to something inferior.

Throughout the course of analysis new dream images were brought to consciousness by which Delores could follow the transformative effect in her inner and outer life. There were a series of dreams that had the similar theme of adopting a daughter, or of rescuing a girl child from an institutional type of place or providing a safe haven for children. Delores was becoming more aware of her instinctual and emotional life that had long lain dormant, and was integrating this into consciousness. There often ensued dreams of the opposite effect, as well. In one dream Delores was assisting a child to escape through a hole dug out from under a high concrete wall like one associates with prison grounds. And, not unlike the myth of Persephone, just as the girl was about to reach the other side to freedom, an unseen force pulled the child back.

The force of the dark unconscious, the archetypes and personal complexes, continued to hold its power: the redemption of the feminine principle into ego consciousness is followed by the loss. The dynamics of the tension of opposites, enlightenment followed by regression, are evidenced here. It is not without a constant struggle to hold the tension of opposites. One must hold equally in consciousness the confrontation with the negative (not to repress it) and the receptivity of the new symbolic images, thus allowing the third element, the transformative factor, to enter in.

This psychic dynamic is illustrated in the Grimm's tale *Rapunzel*. The story tells of a couple who were so desirous of a child. The mother had a ravenous desire for a particular herb that grew in a garden she spied from her window. To appease this hunger, the father went to steal it, but just as he did, the owner, an evil enchantress, caught him. In her wicked plotting, she granted him the herb, for she knew that once the mother had eaten it, she could lay claim to the child and take her as her own. In order to have complete power and control over the girl, the witch locked Rapunzel in a tall, stone tower. Throughout the years her hair grew very long and strong, so long that a prince charming was able to climb up her hair. The end of the tale celebrates the now-grown young maiden being rescued from her prison tower by a brave prince. We find this happening in the dynamics of our psychic life as well. The negative feminine force (which operates out of wile and deceit, quite the opposite of Eros) as well as the negative masculine (as symbolized by the phallic-shaped stone tower) must be confronted with great effort. It is then that ego consciousness becomes more fully integrated and stronger in order to withstand the force of the unconscious that imprisons a life of wholeness. With these stronger new attitudes (Rapunzel's hair), transformation can take place.

A following dream:

> I am going to adopt a daughter and I feel wonderful about it. There are many girls here (ages 10-12 years old), but the one who is to be my daughter is beautiful and has black hair. She is slender and her presence is somehow different from the other girls. My mother and I are discussing her name and trying to pronounce it correctly. I say her name, Astarte. I love to say her name and to hear it.

Delores was not familiar with myths of Astarte, yet through the wondrous and mysterious workings of the archetypal unconscious, this strange name came to her in her dream. Astarte, goddess of love and fertility, was the primary deity worshiped throughout the eastern Mediterranean lands dating back to as early as the Bronze Age. Even without cognizant knowledge of Astarte, Delores was adopting and assuming as her own, that is, integrating into consciousness, the archetypal energy attributed to the feminine principle. No longer are the strongholds of the negative masculine archetypal force the dominant ruling factor of her psyche. The feminine principle is redeemed and upheld as divine. The divine nature is indicative of the feminine component in the Self, the archetype of wholeness.

With the redemption of the feminine principle now more firmly integrated into consciousness, Delores experienced distinct attitudinal changes. She valued herself; she experienced herself as one who was worthy of love and who could relate to others with care and love. The strength of ego consciousness allowed further development to take place, as is found in the following dream:

> I am sleeping and then awakened by someone coming into the door. I see that a young man has come in the front door. He is carrying a stack of books bound with a leather strap. I suppose that he is a student. He is gorgeous. He has brown skin and thick beautiful black hair and appears to be from the Middle East. He walks over to my side of the bed. I am wondering how he unlocked the door. He shows me that he has two keys; both are silver. One looks like a bank deposit box key and the other looks like a door key.
>
> The young man seems to want to make love to me. I think that he must be mistaken. I am wearing an old tee shirt, am overweight, and have morning breath. Now he is lying on the side of the bed. He says, "Salim." I say, "Is that your name?" With quiet passion he says, "Salim means 'God.'" I feel his passion and know that he does want to make love. Between my cradled hands, I feel the strong beating of his heart. The beat seems in concert with his passion, at times taking a different rhythm. I want to make love to him but I need to go to the bathroom. I go to the bathroom and then brush my teeth. It is still hard to believe that he wants to make love to me. I am crossing the room and am almost back to the bed. Then my alarm clock beeps, and I awake dismayed at least!

Delores is now awakening to, that is, becoming conscious of, a new factor. No longer the negative archetypal forces that sacrificed or held captive the feminine, a new masculine energy is present. The silver key, the metal of Venus, Roman goddess of love, facilitates entrance of this young, virile, masculine symbol. Salim, the divine masculine component of the archetype of the Self, wishes to "make love," as compared to "having sex." He also symbolizes a positive animus, the masculine principle of Logos, and is recognized as spirit, who indeed inspirits life. He is the source of inspiration. Now the psychic field is sufficiently developed for uniting of the masculine and feminine principles. Dr. Jung referred to this dynamic as the Sacred Marriage or the *Hieros Gamos*. A term used by the early alchemists, the *Hieros Gamos* indicates the joining of opposites.

Although in the dream the uniting of the masculine and feminine principles is not yet consummated, the potential for this wholeness is present.

Through the series of Delores's dreams we find the conscious development of Eros, the feminine principle. First we become very aware of the sacrifice and debasement of the symbolic feminine principle. This is followed by a new valuing of the feminine principle as seen in a concerted struggle to redeem and to protect Eros. This then leads to an integration of Eros into ego consciousness and the potential of unity and wholeness. How does this relate to the World Soul? It appears that the same steps are necessary. We find that, not unlike Delores's early personal life, collective consciousness in our world has abused and negated the feminine principle. Women and men alike remain unconscious to this necessary element for psychological health and wholeness. Without the concerted effort of confronting the negative archetypal forces within, not necessarily projecting them onto "the other" without, enlightenment is impossible. In such cases, there remains only the dire condition where ego deems itself to be the center of the universe, fully unaware of a much greater design. As each individual becomes more conscious of the feminine principle, not only does this have a dramatic effect on others, but it also increases that necessary filament which leads to the enhancement of the greater design, the World Soul. As the modern-day philosopher, Eckhart Tolle, wrote, "You are here to enable the divine purpose of the universe to unfold."[9]

Notes

[1]   C . G. Jung, "The Meaning of Psychology for Modern Man," vol. 10, par. 304–305.

[2]   Author's note: I found it an exciting syncretistic event that, at the time of writing about World Soul, the announcement and celebration of the Higgs boson had been manifested in the CERN laboratory. The God particle, as it is called, is described as a bonding agent found in all things throughout the universe.

[3]   Francis Cornford, *Plato's Cosmology: The Timaeus of Plato*, 40.

[4]   CW 13, par. 263.

[5]   CW 8, par. 931.

[6]   CW 14, par. 372.

[7]   The Black Eyed Peas. "Where Is The Love?"

[8]   CW 7, par. 78.

[9]   Eckhart Tolle, *The Power of Now: A Guide to Spiritual Enlightenment,* p. 1.

References

Cornford, F. *Plato's Cosmology: The Timaeus of Plato*. Indianapolis, IN: Hackett Publishing, 1997.

Jung, C. *Collected Works*. Princeton: Princeton University Press, 1953–1979.

The Black Eyed Peas. "Where Is The Love?" *Elephunk*, 2004.

Tolle, E. *The Power of Now: A Guide to Spiritual Enlightenment*. Novato, CA: New World Library, 1999.

Wild Cats and Crowned Snakes
Archetypal Agents of Feminine Initiation

by Nancy Swift Furlotti

Introduction

Dream animals lurk in the background of our psyches, growling, barking, hissing from our deep, dark recesses, reminding us of their presence and of the fact that we, too, are animals. We live with our pets, tamed and domesticated as they are, which have learned to serve us in all the ways they do. We love their personalities, their natures, and the attention they pay us. But what about the animals that are not domesticated—the wild animals, the ones that can hurt us, the ones that don't care about serving us but serve another master—raw, pure, instinctual life itself? These are the animals that cause us to scream when we see them. We run from them in fear and do not understand their message when they appear in our dreams. They are inscrutable, unpredictable, primal. These are the dream animals that carry the potency of the archetypal symbol, the numinosity of a god-image. What might it mean when we have an encounter with such an animal?

In this chapter I explore two dreams of wild cats and two dreams of snakes that occurred at important transitions in a woman's life. Each animal acted as an agent of initiation representing the need for a reconnection to a deeper part of her instinctual nature. Initiations take women down into the body, into the deep nature of their femininity and sexuality, their instinctual animal nature and connection to soul. The deep feeling experience in the body acts as glue to bind a woman to her opposites. It generates the strong erotic attraction that leads to the focused exploration and development of the personality through relationship. This relationship moves her from being alone and undifferentiated within herself, to being "two" in the presence of the inner other—and perhaps of the real-life other as well. With the coming together of the two, a new force emerges, the "third," which Jung refers to as the transcendent function. We transcend ourselves in the meeting with the other, not only through the development of a real relationship, but in relation to the greater Self and the cosmos, opening the door to a spiritual realm beyond the temporal. This is the goal of initiation that may begin with the beckoning of an animal.

What Is Initiation?

Mircea Eliade defines initiation rites as "second births." These rites entail "ordeals and symbolic death and resurrection, that were instituted by gods, culture heroes, or mythical ancestors; hence these rites have a superhuman origin, and by performing them the novice imitates a superhuman, divine action."[1] Furthermore, "Initiation is a revelation of the sacred, of death, and of sexuality."[2] Throughout history many cultures' initiation rites for females began with the onset of menstruation. Elaborate rituals accompany this transition from childhood to womanhood, just as they do at each new initiatory stage.

The mythological ancestors who reside in the underworld are the keepers of the knowledge of initiation. In these rites, initiates may be tortured, cut to pieces, boiled, or roasted. Knocking out of teeth, amputation of fingers, circumcision, subincision, which is the lengthwise slicing open of the underside of the penis, tattooing, or scarring are performed in the ritual process of death and resurrection. Initiatory death can include a return to chaos, initiatory sickness, or insanity. "Access to spiritual life always entails death to the profane condition, followed by a new birth."[3] Candidates are given new names and may often don the skin of an animal as a way to connect with their newfound totem, a guiding animal that will accompany them on their journey. These rites and mysteries create deeply spiritual experiences, offering access to the sacred.

Eliade believes that psychoanalysis is a modern form of the initiatory pattern:

> Just as the initiate was expected to emerge from his ordeals victorious—in short, was to "die" and be "resuscitated" in order to gain access to a fully responsible existence, open to spiritual values—so the patient undergoing analysis today must confront his own "unconscious" haunted by ghosts and monsters, in order to find psychic health and integrity and hence the world of cultural values.[4]

The dream is considered to be the royal road to the unconscious. It leads us down into the introverted world of the psyche where the path of initiation lies ready to be taken, or not. This path appears before us a number of times during our lives to further expand our relationship to more parts of ourselves and to open the door to a deeper knowledge of the profundity of life. Dream animals are important as a way to further wholeness and balance within the personality. They also represent a collective longing for a healthy connection to the natural world. Animals are crying out for recognition as they head for extinction at the hands of humankind disconnected from its inner nature as well as from the natural world.

A Case History of Initiation

The following two dreams of wild cats emerged at important crossroads in the life of a female patient and served the function of grabbing her attention and leading her down into the initiatory work that was required at those times. Each one revolved around an animal that brought attention to an unknown part of herself and facilitated a reconnection to the instinctual world of the feminine in her, which was strong, self-determined, and spiritual. Von Franz tells us that "the redemption of the feminine means not the redemption of the flesh; it means the redemption of the divinity of the flesh, of the divine, archetypal, godlike aspect of the flesh."[5]

For a woman, the spiritual path descends into the body, into instinct and sexuality. The striving of the feminine psyche through individuation is towards the *mysterium coniunctionis,* the internal unification of opposite principles or aspects, including the feminine and masculine within. This *coniunctionis* involves a reuniting as one, a rediscovering of the original wholeness of creation that includes the world, psyche, soul, and spirit. The outer world is by no means left out of the process. Projection of our inner aspects onto friends, lovers, and enemies brings these figures face to face with us in real world interactions. It is the conscious interweaving of this inner and outer complexity that leads one to a fulfilled life. However, this type of journey can be guided only from within.

Dreams are the language of the psyche, and amplification is the process of deciphering this very special language to understand the messages from within. Here, I confine the amplifications to the archetypal level, with just enough personal information to show the movement, over time, of these dream animals: how they emerged from the woman's psyche to initiate change at significant stages in her life. The dreams are personal to her but can also be viewed as an example of the process of feminine development in general.

At the time of the first dream my patient, "Anna," was a pre-adolescent twelve-year-old beginning to leave the world of childhood. She had been a tomboy all her life, with two self-possessed brothers, a sister, and a very strong mother with little feminine compassion. Her father had committed suicide a few years earlier, suffering from bipolar disorder. Anna's *real* mother was nature itself, the great mother, to whom she escaped as often as she could.

The First Dream

> A black jaguar appeared before me, staring at me with its penetrating green eyes. I was its prey. Terrified, I grabbed a gun and shot the cat through the head, opening a perfectly clean, round hole, large enough to look through, as if it were a window into another realm. It did not die, nor did it seem to be affected by the shot. It kept coming after me, unstoppable. I was left terrified, and have carried the vivid image of this encounter with me my whole life.

Twelve is a highly significant time in a young girl's life. It requires of her that she leave behind the sheath of childhood that she wore and now begin to differentiate herself into a woman. With the commencement of menstruation, she would have to learn to interact with boys in a new way. Initiation begins at menstruation. Life becomes sharper, and her instincts need to be honed to help her adapt to this phase. New archetypal energies emerge out of the unconscious, in raw forms as they first appear, terrifying and dangerous. Over time, as they become more consciously integrated into the ego, they lose their frightening appearance. This dream jaguar was no exception. It grabbed her attention and, unbeknownst to her at the time, signaled the onset of a new phase of her life and a lifelong journey.

The psyche does not select images capriciously. The black jaguar of Anna's dream very specifically pointed to what she needed to become aware of: an animal of the realm of the dead or underworld. Its specific form carried the unknown in her and was presenting itself in such a frightening way that she knew she had to understand it. There was no possibility of hiding from it; it was magical and "unstoppable."

It was clear that Anna had to deal with the loss of her father, a wounded soul wandering the halls of the underworld. He did not shoot himself, but his death was equally violent to her psyche. At twelve as she was about to step into adulthood, to become a woman, without her father's guidance, she needed this dark animal to help her make sense of this tragic loss, to process all the feelings left behind, and then to help her learn to become a woman. Needless to say, Anna missed her father terribly and felt abandoned by him. The depression that led to his suicide did not die with him but instead settled in her, demanding she live his unlived life. Unaware of this, Anna saw him as the ghostly good parent while her mother remained the adversary, the target of all her anger and sadness. Her traumatic loss not only created a split between the masculine and feminine in her but closed the door on her own life.

A gun shoots projectiles that create holes. Bullets are penetrating like the arrows of old. A bullet stops us, draws blood, life's essence, and forces change, much like thoughts that force their way into our reality. Anna could not stop this messenger from the depths with her thoughts, her thinking ability, nor could she escape through her intuitive function. The bullet blew a huge hole in the thinking mind. She had to find another way. The experience brought her down into her feeling and sensation self. The black jaguar beckoned her into the underworld to converse with its inhabitants, both helpful and destructive, to make peace with the loss of her father, and to find her own feminine instinct that had been wounded and left inaccessible to her up until then.

The dream cat represents feminine independence and individuality, the instinct to sniff out what is genuine and what is not. Anna would need these sharp instincts to usher in an awareness of the darker sides of life and of human nature. This awareness was offered to her through the panther's invitation to initiation.

To understand why the psyche selected a jaguar for this initiation, it is helpful to explore its representations in mythology. The black cat is an underworld creature, a shamanic agent comfortable in both nocturnal and earthy realms. What is important to remember is that deities depicted in mythology are archetypal and are therefore whole in themselves. They contain opposites—as, for example, masculine and feminine, creation and destruction. The gods have goddess consorts, and vice versa, that represent their opposing sides. The archetypal dream jaguar also contains the unity of opposites. It may be perceived as good or bad depending upon the face it currently turns toward us as well as the face we turn back in response.

In Mesoamerican mythology the black jaguar is the totem animal of a powerful god named Tezcatlipoca, the underworld god whose name means "*smoking mirror*." He is a mercurial, Dionysian god of madness and ecstatic transformation, an old nature god connected to the realm of the great mother and the moon. Whereas a mirror offers self-reflection, a *smoking mirror* offers an entrance into the depths, the source of both destruction and creation. Both Tezcatlipoca from Mesoamerica and Dionysus from Greece are associated with panthers. They are both known to descend as shamans into the underworld during their rituals to recover what is lost and forgotten, precious, and needed at initiatory moments in life. The creative potential for change and transformation originates in the underworld. Anna needed the invitation of an underworldly god in the form of a panther to escort her.

Jaguars are the largest and most powerful cats of the Americas. In Mesoamerica they were creatures of shamanic transformation and were frequently seen shifting form from one god to the next. Identified with the sun and its nighttime form, as the jaguar god of the underworld, the jaguar is fierce, independent, and creative—the dark side of the Great Mother. These black cats possess the foresight and insight needed at initiation. Von Franz points out that, "If she is meant to be a cat, that would mean she is meant to be an individuated woman, a personality in her own right."[6]

The Second Dream

The second dream came when Anna was in her forties:

> I was led into a sacred temple, dressed in a long white gown by an older priestess who was preparing me for an initiation. When I was ready, I was led into the center of a very large room and was told to lie down on the floor at the base of an altar facing it. The room was lit by candles and I waited. Soon a huge tiger entered the room and laid down on top of me, placing its paws on either side of my head with its face directly above mine. I was to have sexual intercourse with this tiger. I was terrified.

At the time of this dream, Anna was married with two children. Her daughter was age twelve, the same age she had been when she had the black jaguar dream. Through her, Anna was taken back to the memory of her own adolescent transition. She had learned well after her dream initiation at twelve, healing the wounds left by the death of her father and the lack of connection to the feminine in her family of origin. She was finding her way, although still wavering between the feminine and masculine parts of herself. By this time, Anna was developing a career, taking a step out into the world after focusing predominantly on nurturing others. She knew all along that something in her life was missing. As an appropriate time in life to begin to shift the focus back to herself, this dream called her to a sacred initiation with the deity of transformation, this time in the form of a tiger.

This is a strikingly powerful dream reflecting a combination of animal and spirit— of spirit released through the animal. No longer the dark cat of the underworld from her pre-adolescent days, but now what was appropriate for her at this time in her life: the gold-and-black-striped majesty of the tiger. Interestingly, though, both tigers and jaguars come from the same species, *Panthera tigris*, the largest of the cat species. It is only in the safe *temenos* of the temple that she could be pushed to the extreme limits of her instincts and emotions, to the ritualized experience of life and death. What remained of her dark emotions that had not been transformed through the initiation with the black jaguar were now brought to consciousness.

Symbolically, tigers carry powerful, dangerous, destructive emotions that need to be tamed, and if they are not, they can tear apart one's consciousness. When tamed, however, the power of this animal can be incorporated as a source of strength and protection. Ritual union with a tiger-god necessitates consciousness of the reality of creation and destruction, the temporal and spiritual within, and the need for the ego to mediate between these opposites. The color of the cat, gold and black, points to a union of these opposites. All the dark underworldly cat energy that helped Anna survive was unleashed in a confusion of affect as she stepped beyond her role of mother into herself. The spiritualized priest-priestess tiger was a reminder that she needed to consciously contain and humanize this potency in order to have it available for her further development, while at the same time not destroying others in the process. It was time for her to release herself from her father's depression, the affect surrounding it, and his unlived life once and for all so that her life could be her own.

Many potent deities throughout the world are connected to tigers, and many of those are also represented by the jaguar. In Hindu mythology, Kali, the goddess of creation and destruction, rides on a tiger, whereas the tantric god, Shiva, wears a tiger skin in his form as the destroyer. He is the god who teaches the basic unity of all things, a god that bridges the outer and inner, the large and small, spirit and matter, the macrocosm and the microcosm. "He is naked, libidinous, and preaches rapture, love, detachment, and friendship with nature. God of Sensual Pleasure and of Death… Shiva is at the same time benevolent and terrible."[7]

Shiva's enlivening side, Shakti, embodies the active feminine primordial energy needed to awaken Shiva to his dance of creation. Shakti is the Great Divine Mother. The way of initiation through this deity in tiger form, embodying both Shiva and Shakti, brings the awareness of spiritual awakening through the body and sexuality. This is the way of Tantrism and Kundalini, the awakening of the female Shakti energy in the form of a serpent that begins the development of the relationship to the suprapersonal within the individual. The energy resides in the root chakra and ascends up through the chakras and then descends in a circular pattern throughout the body, activating emotions, soul, and spirit. It is for this reason that the ritual necessitated Anna having sexual intercourse with the tiger, to ignite the Kundalini energy through affect and sexuality. Interestingly, at this same time, Anna experienced tremendous energy coursing through her body, feeling as if she were a live electrical current.

Daniélou helps to make sense of this experience: "Tantrism exploits and utilizes the physical, subtle, and spiritual possibilities of the human being… The body is the basis, or instrument of all realization. No life, thought, or spirituality can exist independently of a living body."[8] What was being asked of Anna was to first recognize her tiger potency, both what was constructive and destructive, and then to open to the realities of her spiritual nature in conjunction with her instinct, sexuality, and body. As a child Anna had been sexually molested, and her connection to her body shut down. The initiatory cats returned this potency by awakening her body. After the tiger dream, not only did she say her final goodbyes to her father, but she reconnected to her own creative life and sexuality.

Dionysus frequently shows up in dreams as the dark masculine other for women of this age, offering an ecstatic ritual experience of renewal to remind them of the deep creative potential that comes from truly living *in* the body, *with* the body. When this dark god shows up, the sparks of sexuality are ignited, and the flame that has dwindled to embers burns once again with the force of youth. This flame of creativity is not intended for procreation this time but for the birth of one's inner spiritual child that will help give meaning to the second half of life. This dream represents the sacred marriage, or *hieros gamos,* of the mortal with immortal, reminiscent of the initiations that took place at the ancient sacred temples in honor of the feminine goddesses. "Within the erotic life a power of insight is working. The erotic seems a way into insight into the nature of things, and that grows into the spiritual aspect above."[9]

The Third Dream

After two dreams of wild cats, Anna's psyche brought forth serpents. The third and fourth dreams came when she was sixty, a time that ushers in the last third of life. Over the twenty years between her second and third dreams, Anna continued to successfully differentiate the many aspects of herself, including the feminine from the masculine, consciousness from shadow. She was the mother of grown children, had a successful and satisfying career as an artist, yet over time she and her husband's differing interests caused them to grow further and further apart. They became more alienated, angry, and dissatisfied in the marriage. With this dream she is pushed to an important cross-roads, for another initiation:

> I was in the backyard of my house with my husband and family, having a barbeque gathering. I saw a small gray snake slither towards the house and enter. I told my husband, and we both went into the house to look for it. We found it in our dressing room. I was terrified and climbed up on a square pedestal that was an island of draw-ers in the center of the room and laid across it facing down while my husband stood on the floor on right side of the pedestal. The snake circled counterclockwise around the pedestal and as it did, it grew huge in size and transformed into a golden yellow color. As it arrived at and moved past my husband on the right side, it shrank back down to its original size and gray color. Once it moved passed him, it again resumed its large size and beautiful golden color. The serpent circumambulated around the two of us four times.

This dream depicts the movement away from family, from the backyard where Anna was living a part of her life, perhaps on auto-pilot mode as the nurturing mother and wife. Since the children were grown, the focus now shifted to her husband. The small gray mercurial snake catches her vision and penetrates into the privacy of her house. As a newly emerging and highly potent symbol from her psyche, she must follow. Going into her house is going into herself, where she resides psychologically with her husband and with her animus, her inner masculine. They find the snake in their dressing room, the most intimate and private area of their lives and of their relationship. There is a square pedestal in the center of that small room, which points to the Self at the center of her being. Anna lies across it while her husband stands to one side. This metaphor points out that he is not at the center but off to the side, perhaps that they have taken different paths. Indeed, this is the case as the snake circumambulates around them, growing large and golden as it passes her and returning to a small and gray form as it passes him. One is called to initiation; the other is not. The snake moves in a counter-clockwise direction, suggesting the movement towards the unconscious, again down into initiation. Her husband stands to her right, remaining in the objective world of reality, where a snake is just a snake. Anna sees that she may have to leave him, symboli-cally or in real life, to further her own call to individuation.

"When a serpent appears in a dream or active imagination, he often represents the utterly unexpected solution, something we could never think of consciously in a thou-sand years."[10] The magical, golden snake is a shamanic, spiritual teacher, manifesting in animal form, representing the deep creative potential that wants to incarnate to es-tablish relationship with her. Phallic as it is, it brings spirit—the spirit of the chthonic realm. It is from deeper layers in the psyche than the wild cats. It does not *descend into* the underworld, it is *of* the underworld, yet it is also a bridge to the realms of earth and heaven. Snakes represent both the negative and the positive mother, because they carry the potential for creation and destruction. They are both feminine and masculine, bringing fertility and death. They manifest the innermost truth of the body and are a symbol for the unconscious psyche that strives for consciousness.[11]

The fact that the serpent is golden points to illumination, clear insight; that there has been an extraction from instinct to consciousness, just as the gold is extracted from the *prima materia* in alchemy. The gold is what is precious and whole. It is a luminosity that emerges from the dark, an underworldly chthonic wisdom that brings soul and spirit. It is totally other, which refers to what is divine, therefore representing both the god-image and the human soul. As the Kundalini snake, the sun serpent, it has access to absolute knowledge and energy that begins at the earth root and moves to heaven, from sexuality to wisdom.

The Fourth Dream

The last dream took place shortly after the third, as the meaning was becoming more understood:

I dreamed that the same golden snake turned into a boy about twelve with a beautiful crown on his head. He was seated on the floor next to a wall in a room much like the dressing room of the original dream.

The golden snake is an archetype that humanizes itself by becoming real, as it has in the form of a young inner masculine figure, an animus with authority. It is Anna's own authority now that manifests, not custom or convention. The crown is round and bejeweled, an image of the Self, of wholeness worn on the head, on the crown chakra, of this transformed boy. He is twelve, the age at which her initiation journey began when she faced the black jaguar. It is a significant number, but more than that, it carries the archetypal energy of completeness, of an ending and a beginning at the same time. It is the apex of one stage and the initiation into the next. As the product of the multiplication of three times four, it contains both trinity and quaternity. Our counting system is based on twelve: a dozen, twelve inches in a foot, twelve hours of the day. This number measures out the passage of life.

The young boy stands at the crossroads in Anna's life, bringing the realization of the divine other within herself. In essence, he is soul that has come to meet her. Within him are combined chthonic sexuality and instinct, soul and spirit. From here her task is to take hold of this new authority that is both feminine and masculine. "[She] who is able to do this and so to face reality, becomes consciously immortal, or perhaps it should read 'conscious of immortality.'"[12] This brings Anna to the ultimate reality of her own unique nature—and to the nature of the psyche itself.

Conclusion

Anna struggled with and learned from her initiation at age twelve, instigated by the black jaguar, and found her strength, power, and independent voice. It served her well, but by midlife something else was needed; she was asked to tame and complement those attributes, to let her father go and let her mother in. She was called to recognize the darker side of her cat nature, her lower chakras, containing her ferocity, which could be as dangerous and ruthless as the tiger that lay down on top of her. She needed to domesticate her animal instincts and transform them into a spiritual ferocity that would give meaning to her life. It was only by connecting to the positive aspect of her animal ferocity that she was able to let go of relationships that did not support her soul, spirit, and body. From wild cats to golden serpents, all representing aspects of her life energy, these creatures have called Anna from the dream world to her initiations along the path of her life's journey.

The psyche will lead us through the ups and downs of life's travails if we listen to its guidance through our dreams. These dreams give us the necessary insight into significant initiations that were collective experiences in ages past, but have been lost to us today. Amplifying the images and symbols in dreams turns up the volume of the psyche beyond a whisper, opens them into a full bloom so that we are able to smell the powerful and alluring fragrance of the past, present, and future of humanity, and glimpse into the wholeness of life, to what is universal. Without the deep resounding connection to our body and sexuality, we would not have the glue that holds us fast to this mysterious process, the *mysterium*, that bring us to a place of wholeness.

Notes

1   Mircea Eliade, *The Sacred and the Profane: The Nature of Religion*, 187.

2   Mircea Eliade, *The Sacred and the Profane: The Nature of Religion*, 188.

3   Mircea Eliade, *The Sacred and the Profane: The Nature of Religion*, 210.

4   Mircea Eliade, *The Sacred and the Profane: The Nature of Religion*, 208.

5   Marie-Louise von Franz, *The Cat*, 100.

6   Marie-Louise von Franz, *The Cat*, 63.

7   Alain Daniélou, *The Gods of Love and Ecstasy: The Traditions of Shiva and Dionysus*, 50.

8   Alain Daniélou, *The Gods of Love and Ecstasy: The Traditions of Shiva and Dionysus*, 148.

9   C. G. Jung, *The Psychology of Kundalini Yoga: Notes of the Seminar Given in 1932 by C. G. Jung*, 102.

10 Barbara Hannah, *The Archetypal Symbolism of Animals*, 225.

11 James Hillman, *Dream Animals*, 25–26.

12 Esther Harding, *Woman's Mysteries Ancient and Modern*, 238.

References

Caspiri, E. *Animal Life in Nature, Myths, and Dreams.* Wilmette, IL: Chiron Publications, 2003.

Daniélou, A. *Gods of Love and Ecstasy: The Traditions of Shiva and Dionysus.* Rochester, VT: Inner Traditions, 1992.

Eliade, M. *Shamanism: Archaic Techniques of Ecstasy.* Princeton, NJ: Princeton University Press, 1974.

_____. *The Sacred and the Profane: The Nature of Religion.* New York: Harcourt, 1987.

_____. *Rites and Symbols of Initiations: The Mysteries of Birth and Rebirth.* Putnam, CT: Spring Publications, 2009.

Harding, E. *Woman's Mysteries Ancient and Modern.* New York: Harper Colophon Books, 1971.

Hannah, B. *The Archetypal Symbolism of Animals.* Wilmette, IL: Chiron Publications, 2006.

Hillman, J. *Dream Animals.* San Francisco, CA: Chronicle Books, 1997.

Jung, C. *Aion.* Princeton, NJ: Princeton University Press, 1978.

_____. *The Structure and Dynamics of the Psyche,* Princeton, NJ: Princeton University Press, 1981.

_____. *The Psychology of Kundalini Yoga: Notes of the Seminar Given in 1932 by C. G. Jung.* Princeton, NJ: Princeton University Press, 1996.

Ronnberg, A., and Martin, K., eds. *The Book of Symbols.* New York: Taschen, 2010.

Von Franz, M. *The Cat.* Toronto: Inner City Books, 1999.

A Dream in Arcadia

by Christian Gaillard

Translated by Anita Conrade

Upon discovering this essay, the reader may be surprised, since I do not intend to lead readers into my office and suggest that we explore and interpret one of their dreams. And I shall not share one of my own dreams, although I dare to hope that might also interest readers. Nor have I any intention of taking us into the library of innumerable and always fascinating writings on the subject of dreams, or of suggesting one of the no less innumerable methods or theories developed over the centuries to help us find our way.

Instead I am going to suggest that readers and I take a journey to a distant place in both time and space. Let us travel to Italy, to Pompeii. Actually, our destination is a nearby city, Herculaneum, at a time in the distant past, over two millennia: the first century B.C.E. Our goal is to discover, or rediscover, a work of art, rather than the story of a dream. A painting.

This work was hidden from view for a long time … for nearly nineteen centuries. Long buried under the lava and ashes of Vesuvius, it was discovered in the eighteenth century, during the archeological dig in the Basilica of Herculaneum. Note that, according to the specialists of Roman culture, a basilica was not, strictly speaking, a religious edifice, as in our Christian culture. Instead, it was the most public space in any town, where people could meet to discuss town affairs or politics.

The work, currently hanging in the National Museum in Naples (see fig. 6.1), was painted under the reign of the Emperor Vespasian. Ever since its rediscovery, it has elicited both great admiration for its quality and the greatest perplexity as to its meaning. In his account of his travels in Italy, Goethe remarks how amazed and enthralled he was to see it.

Figure 6.1
Hercules recognizing his son Telephus in Arcadia
National Museum of Naples, photo by AGD

It is a fresco painting, measuring 1.71 metres by 2.02 metres. These impressive dimensions are important because they determine our initial physical and emotional relationship to the work. We must therefore take the time to absorb the work, as it is presented to us, as a whole and in each of its parts. To do so, we should adopt a simple, open, perceptive, and exploratory attitude. We should also pay attention to our position in relation to the painting, and to the emotional impact seeing it and being around it has upon us, along with the questions that might arise from those observations.

Here you can see a woman reclining. Supporting her head with her arm, she is almost lying down. Her body, draped in white, creates the diagonal line of the painting—a diagonal line barred by the staff she is holding in her left hand.

A man is walking towards her or has stopped in front of her. He is crowned with ivy. Holding his right hand behind his back, he has a hunter's quiver and arrows slung over his shoulder and a fur cloak over his left arm. At the edge of the scene we can see a young boy laughing and playing pipes, a bowl of fruit, a doe suckling a child, an eagle, a lion, and a young winged woman whose outstretched arm points back to the doe suckling the child.

We ask ourselves what is going on or what is about to happen. The scene is highly enigmatic.

At First Glance: An Initial Reading through the Lens of Mythology

Perhaps, like me, my readers are analysts. But we are outside the ordinary circumstances of our clinical practice, and even outside the setting of an exchange between clinicians. We are confronting a work of art. How should we hold ourselves? How should we proceed?

Of course, it is rarely a good idea for an analyst to approach a work of art without any guidance. We need the help of art historians, who obviously know more than we do about their field of research, which is, moreover, often highly specialized. So we need to use their knowledge. And I would add that we need to work largely under their supervision—until the moment, as we will see, where we go on alone, with our own hypotheses and interpretations, beyond their knowledge and their own work methods.

What can historians of Roman art bring us concerning this work? Art historians tell us that it is what they call a *megalograph*—that is, a painting of large dimensions that pictures several contemporary mythological characters, represented more or less at the scale of humans.

Which mythological characters? This man walking towards the woman, with his quiver and arrows slung over his shoulder, and the fur cloak over his arm, is *the half-god Hercules,* they tell us.

And what is he doing here? He is looking at a child, in fact his son, who is called *Telephus.* Hercules is greeting him, recognizing him as his own.

Art historians who are also mythologists can fill us in on the background. It was quite well known that little Telephus, Hercules's son, was abandoned in the mountains of Arcadia, in Greece, where a doe saved him by suckling him with her own milk, until the moment when Hercules, his father, finally found him and recognized him as his son.

So we know that the man moving towards the woman is the half-god Hercules. But what about this woman, this lady, whose body is half-reclining across the picture, so impressive in that pose, in her drapes and her restraint … who is she?

Here our art historians seem rather perplexed. This woman, so important in the composition of the scene, is manifestly an obstacle for them. Apparently, it is much more difficult for them to identify her, to recognize her by their own means.

The art historians have consulted with each other, discussing the female figure at length. And finally, for the most part, they conclude that this woman could well be an allegorical representation of *Arcadia*, the happy, early mythical land. According to the well-known myth of that time, it was in Arcadia that the little Telephus was abandoned, then taken in by a doe, and finally found by his father, Hercules. What is more, they add, perhaps to convince themselves of this interpretation, the fruit basket next to this allegory of Arcadia would be there in order to evoke, in its own way, the fertility and wealth of this mythical land, where nature was always said to be ideally protecting and perfectly generous.

So we have an initial interpretation—or rather an initial reading—of this work that is classically mythological. Allegedly, this is *a representation of Hercules recognizing his son Telephus in Arcadia*. In fact, *"Hercules recognizing his son Telephus in Arcadia"* is the title that is generally given to this painting.

A Second Approach, More Sociopolitical

But, one might ask, what was this painting doing in Herculaneum? What meaning could it have there? This brings us to a second attempt at interpreting the work—a less knowledgeable interpretation than the first, but this time more sociological, and indeed, as we will see, more political.

This fresco, we are reminded, was in a privileged position in the Basilica in Herculaneum, a place in the town where it was fitting to celebrate the cult of the Roman emperor, in this case the Emperor Vespasian. Now, we know that Vespasian was very keen to spread the knowledge, or at least the popular belief, that he was of the noblest ancestry. He claimed to be descended from the Etruscan kings, who themselves were supposedly descended from Telephus, the natural son of Hercules. So Vespasian himself wanted to be recognized as a descendant of the half-god Hercules!

According to this social and political interpretation of the painting, in addition to being a representation of a well-known episode of Greek and Latin mythology (of Hercules recognizing his son Telephus in Arcadia), this fresco is also, and perhaps more importantly given the period in which it was painted, a political means of celebrating the cult of the Roman emperor.

This is very interesting and very instructive. But can we leave it at that? Can we be satisfied with these mythological, sociological, and political interpretations? What about the female figure, this lady, with her body heavily reclining across the painting? She is very sure of herself and her pose, but it seems to me that she is also *curiously defensive*, drawn into herself, protected by the staff she is holding firmly in her left hand. Strangely, her eyes are open wide upon the man walking towards her.

How can we see this woman, this lady, as simply an allegory representing a place, Arcadia? And how can we see this work, this scene, as simply a celebration of the emperor and his noble descent? What is more, this man we see going forward is perhaps the half-god Hercules, but is he not himself too human, too fleshly, too truly present, to be simply a mythological figure that serves only to flatter the emperor?

Our way of seeing is surprised. And we protest. *In fact, the painting protests.* It cannot, and does not want to, be reduced to a simple illustration of a myth or a political instrument.

Not Just Reading but Seeing Differently

This way of seeing, in which we acknowledge our surprise and protest, moves away from ready-made interpretations that are too sure of themselves. It is open, questioning. Most importantly, it is a way of seeing that involves learning *to be overawed.*

So let us recapitulate—*da capo.* This woman, this "Arcadia," is sitting, half-reclining, before the man, standing, we call *Hercules,* who is moving towards her. The diagonal line of her body overawes the onlooker.

And we are also astonished, afterwards, by the other diagonal line that crosses that of the woman's body, created by the hand gesture of the winged young woman. It also crosses the painting, leading us to the other corner of the painting, to the scene of the doe with the child.

Our way of seeing has changed. We no longer seek what we know already—the myth of Hercules recognizing his son Telephus in Arcadia, the cult of the emperor at Herculaneum. Now that we let ourselves be overawed, we can perceive and feel the *tension created by the composition of this work*, by the diagonal lines that cross at the very center of the painting, at the very center of the body of the woman who sits still while a man walks towards her, or stops before her, his weapons under his arm.

We can now better perceive and feel *the tension, the suspense*, created in us by this work that was supposedly a banal allegory or political illustration: We perceive and feel the *suspense* of an expected and imminent encounter, manifestly very centered, but held up: *a suspended encounter.*

What kind of encounter? What kind of *suspense?* What is about to happen?

To See Is Also to Recall

As we open our way of seeing, letting ourselves be overawed and becoming rather dreamy, we recall *other poses, other compositions, other analogous structures* in the art of the same era … just as, I think, the men and women of the time could recall them … at least those who allowed themselves to go beyond the literal meaning of such a scene, here the mythological illustration, or its immediate political meaning—those, then, who knew how agreeable and interesting it is to welcome the *associations* and *amplifications* that come to us when we are overawed by an encounter with a work of art.

Figure 6.2
Hercules and Augé, in S. Reinach
Repertorio dei dipinti greci e romani,
Rome, L'Erma di Bretschneider, 1970

We recall this scene *in the house of the Vettii in Pompeii.* Of course, we recognize Hercules. And we see him struggling with a young woman whose body is also lying across the painting.

Here, in Pompeii, as earlier in Herculaneum, *an encounter is staged.* But while in the Basilica in Herculaneum (fig. 6.1), the so-called "Arcadia" remains firm and steady like a landscape; here, in the Vettii house, the woman is almost on the ground. She is wavering and falling, already down on one knee. We are shown the same situation, *but it is quite another story.* Which story? Which other moment? Which other episode in Hercules's adventures?

Contemporaries of this work, in the first century B.C.E., knew very well that this is where Hercules meets a young woman, or rather a girl, whom we also know well; her name is *Auge.* Perhaps you know this story. It is a nasty story.

For here, in Pompeii, in the Vettii house, the scene depicts the famous episode where Hercules, who was traveling round the world to prove his strength, was invited to the court of the king of Arcadia. The king had a daughter: young Auge. He loved and adored his daughter so much that he wanted her to remain forever a virgin. And the best way he had found to keep her a virgin was—of course—to dedicate her to Athena. So marriage was completely forbidden.

But Hercules is Hercules. Invited to eat and drink at the king's table, he imbibes without restraint. Inebriation ensues. And the story would have it that in his drunkenness, he threw himself upon the king's daughter and raped her.

This is the scene we can see here: *Hercules throwing himself upon Auge to rape her*—a scene that is not in suspension like that of the fresco in Herculaneum. But it is a dramatic and tragic scene. Because we know that not only was poor Auge raped by Hercules, she became pregnant afterwards. As a result, her father banished her from his court, sending her into exile—whereupon the child, in fact little Telephus, was abandoned in the mountains and owed his life to a doe who found him and took care of him by suckling him with her own milk.

At Herculaneum (fig. 6.1), we find ourselves before the enigma of a suspended encounter. Here (fig. 6.2), we are right in the middle of the tragedy … the tragedy of a girl, a young woman, savagely raped, then rejected and exiled … and the tragedy, too, of an abandoned child. Our way of seeing the painting at Herculaneum (fig. 6.1) becomes more complicated, more troubled and worried.

Yet Another Affair

But here again, supported by our attention to composition and therefore to the structural dynamics of this painting, our way of seeing becomes yet more complicated. For yet another scene is associated in the same way to what we have seen in Herculaneum.

Figure 6.3
Dionysus and his retinue discovering Ariadne sleeping
in S. Reinach, Repertorio dei dipinti greci e romani,
Rome, L'Erma di Bretschneider, 1970

Here the man is standing up, like the Hercules in Herculaneum. And the woman is now lying down on the floor in front of him. We can see that she is asleep. But the woman here is not Arcadia. And she is not Auge either. Now we are confronted with another well-known figure of the mythology of that era: *Ariadne.*

Ariadne, you will recall, is also a girl, a young woman, who also lived a strange story. She was *the daughter of the king Minos*, who had had the famous labyrinth built where no one was to enter, under pain of death. But the hero Theseus was passing that way.

Ariadne, out of love for him and betraying her father—like poor Auge—gave him a thread, so that he could enter into the forbidden labyrinth and come out again safely. But Theseus, who owed her so much, later pathetically abandoned her. You know about the tears of Ariadne, and her despair.

Here we can see *Ariadne, abandoned on the bank of the island of Naxos*, where she has finally fallen asleep, having cried all her tears. The subject is again an encounter between a man and a woman. And again it is a tragedy, the tragedy of an abused and then abandoned woman.

Except that here the man who is walking towards her is not Hercules, as in Herculaneum or in the Vettii house. This is not a warrior thirsty for wine and for victory. It is a totally different character from Greek and Latin mythology: *Dionysus*. We recognize him by his young good looks and almost feminine attitude, and also by his accompanying retinue, the Pans, more or less youthful, playful, and bestial, and by the thyrsus one of them is carrying.

This Dionysus is not going to throw himself upon the woman, as Hercules did in the Vettii house. We know—as did all the contemporaries of these paintings, of course—that, quite on the contrary, *he will be seduced by the beautiful sleeping woman*, that he will take her to Olympus, the home of the gods, and the myth tells us how he *marries her* in due form, thus making up for her having been abandoned by the traitor Theseus. It is even said that they had three children. We are contented. This time, it is a happy ending.

In this way, the brutality of Auge's rape by Hercules and the abandoning of little Telephus in the mountain are answered by the ideally restoring story of Ariadne found by Dionysus, who then married her on Olympus.

Poor Auge (fig. 6.2), with her terrified eyes and divided gesture—with one hand she defends herself against Hercules, yet she is already on the ground—is hurried into tragedy by the violence of the almost parallel diagonal lines we can see in this painting. Whereas Ariadne (fig. 6.3), who too has been abused and abandoned, is now sleeping and dreaming of the ideal happiness that is waiting for her, and that will finally be realized by the gentle Dionysus.

And now we can see what the fresco in Herculaneum (fig. 6.1) was holding in suspension. We can see, or perceive, what creates its *suspense*: This painting, through its composition, its structural dynamic, *contains*, in an enigmatic but pressing way, *at once the scene of the rape of Auge* and *that of Ariadne being found and then married on Olympus.*

Now we can see "Arcadia," the woman whom we call *Arcadia, also becoming Auge and Ariadne.* This Arcadia is reclining as the man walks towards her. Yet she has her eyes wide open, and at the same time she is drawn into herself, her body barred by the staff that cuts off this encounter. *She knows, or at least she shows us through the painting, that she is both Auge and Ariadne.* For Auge, the going is tough: rape, banishment, exile. But as *Ariadne,* she dreams of the ideal accomplishment of her dream on Olympus.

This Arcadia is also Auge. And she is also Ariadne. Through the painting.

The strength of this painting in Herculaneum, its creative strength, is that it both covers and encloses the Pompeian scenes: It contains them. Freud would say that it *condenses them*—here Freud uses the very evocative German word *Verdichtung,* which means that we are confronted by a complex, composite reality, organized in layers, each covering over and including the others.

The creative strength of this work is to *remain enigmatic,* to *remain in suspension,* to *keep us in suspense,* so that at first glance we do not know all that it has to show us. But now we can perceive it. And more importantly, we experience it. We experience the terribly dramatic and equally ideal eroticism of this scene.

We were told that this painting served to tell a well-known story, a mythological story of another era … and that it served to support the cult of the emperor. But this painting evidently has a quite different strength, a quite different quality, and different scope. Here we are not dealing with anecdotes, with what has been said and known before. I have just mentioned *condensation.* We must go one step further. In fact, I would call this work *symbolic.* Through its strength and its uncanny composition, it tells us—on many levels, it shows us, or rather makes us see, perceive, *and most importantly experience*—both what we want and do not want to know about relationships between a man and a woman, between a woman and a man.

We live the tragedy and the dream of this woman who is at the same time Arcadia, Auge, and Ariadne—an *Arcadia-Auge-Ariadne*—who is no longer only made up of distant characters, cast in mythological narrative space, but close to us, ourselves as we are today, strangely close to us, to the scenes, tragedies, and dreams of our everyday lives. *For such is the strength of symbolic life.* This strength that touches us is a *questioning force*—and first of all, of course, an enigmatic questioning.

From Freud to Jung

You will have noticed that our approach to this work has passed progressively from Freud and Freudian psychoanalysis, when I was talking about *condensation*, to Jung and Jungian psychoanalysis, when I talked about *symbolic life*. We passed from observing the work of condensation brought about by this painting to the live perception of a scene, at first enigmatic, but actually highly charged with emotion.

Freud showed us the way and led us to Jung—as is often the case in the clinical practice of psychoanalysis. It remains to move forward in this direction because this work asks for more, through yet more elements that are decisive in its composition and effect.

Starting first of all with the character of Hercules: This Hercules is quite surprising. We have been accustomed to seeing him everywhere else, in Pompeii, Stabies, and Herculaneum; in his role as a conqueror, often violent, always hurried, passing from one victory to another with the ardor of a gladiator.

Yet here he is, not throwing himself upon the woman who is just in front of him. Quite the contrary, amazingly, we see him stop in his tracks. What then could have stopped Hercules here and rendered him so deep in thought?

The answer to this question is given by the painting. It replies with the presence in the composition of *the young winged woman* we can see just behind him. It is manifestly her presence and her hand gesture that stops Hercules in his tracks. It is she who intervenes in the encounter *between the man and the woman*, an encounter that might have turned out badly, as did the encounter between Hercules and poor Auge.

So who is this young winged woman? The mythologists tell us that they can identify her, that she even has a name. The Romans call her *Virgo*. And the Greeks call her *Parthenos*. That is to say, *she is the virgin*—a figure, a character that was so revered at the time that they made a kind of angel of her and cast her up into the heavens, so that she became a constellation of stars known today as Virgo, the constellation of the virgin.

This well-known figure of Greek and Roman mythology is made concretely present in this painting, very beautiful in her features, her skin, touching and promising with her spray of grain in the crook of her arm. Yet she is high up in the sky. What is this "virgin" doing here?

We can see that, not only does she stop Hercules in his tracks, where he could have become violent and even raped, but with her diagonal gesture, insistent and gently imperative, *it is she who leads his, and our, attention to the doe and child.*

This scene of the doe and child is an event in the art of the era. It is no doubt the most successful and accomplished, and the happiest scene in this painting. This is the scene that so enthralled Goethe during his travels in Italy. It is like a painting within the painting. Have you ever seen a scene so accurate in its depiction of the sensation and emotion, the happiness of the perfectly confident and reciprocal attachment between child and doe, or doe and child?

We have been told that Hercules recognized his son Telephus in Arcadia. That was rather abstract. Here, truly, he *looks at, and discovers this child*, his own son, whom he recognizes, in whom perhaps he recognizes himself. Who knows? Perhaps now that he is touched by this shared tenderness, this reciprocal attention that the painting renders manifest and palpable, Hercules goes so far as to remember what he experienced as a child.

Could this doe be something other than prey for this hunter? For this man, this hero, could a woman be something other than an Auge he wants to rape? Is it possible to experience an encounter in such a relationship to the other, in such a confident and tenderly reciprocal relationship as that manifested here between the child and the doe?

It is the young woman behind his head who leads him this far—this *virgo*, this *virgin*, who stops him in his tracks and speaks to him, to whom he listens and by whom he is transformed. To the extent that he not only comes to forget his morals as a hunter, warrior, or gladiator, he not only leaves his weapons slung over his shoulder, but what is more, he forgets the eagle and the lion—the insignia of his strength. They are on the ground, rather frightened and useless.

Might not this figure, this feminine presence, this girl or young woman, be a beautiful representation in the painting of what Jung would call the *anima*? Might not this figure, this presence, be the voice of the feminine inside us, who would like to reach us from our own childhood, and to whom we often fail to listen?

Does this painting not make us see and perceive and understand, in its own way, and does it not make us experience, in the end, what Jung will teach us two thousand years later?

But What Does She Have Behind Her Head?

Let us look once again at the painting. This work makes us see and perceive something else again. What indeed can we see behind Arcadia's head? What is *this funny creature* doing behind her with his pointy ears, a bit furry, half wild, playing the pipes and manifestly enjoying and mocking everyone and the whole scene?

The mythologists, of course, will tell us that this half-human, half-wild creature is a *young Pan*. Pan, as we know, is a peculiar god or demon. In Latin he is often called *niger* (black), *rusticus* (rustic, crude), *lubricus* (lustful), *nocturnus* (nocturnal). Funny devil. They say he is always ready to leap upon any girl, or even a goat. Here we cannot see them, but we know that he has a goat's trotters.

Now our Arcadia-Auge-Ariadne has this devil of a Pan right behind her head. And I ask myself whether she is not lending him a complacent ear … this devil of a Pan is whispering who knows what into Arcadia-Auge-Ariadne's ear. She is pretending she does not know him, of course. But we can see that she is nonetheless very close to him.

This painting shows us that behind Arcadia-Auge-Ariadne's head, there is this Pan—this *animus*, we shall say with Jung—that could well tell us, in fact, of the hidden, intimate complicity this woman has with the man against whom she seemingly defends herself. As if, in fact, this woman, despite her shy grand-lady air, secretly, deep down, were hoping for something from this man we can see moving towards her—even if he might show himself to be a bit brutal, a bit wild, and, who knows, even a bit bestial.

It is quite possible that this Arcadia, whom we have seen to be also Auge and Ariadne, is not as innocent as she likes to appear. At least in her dreams.

Decidedly, our amplification of this painting—with its figures and presences, the symbolic life it stages and shows in interaction, through its figuration, dramatization, and condensation, as Freud would say, and especially through the internal and structural dynamics of its composition, as we say after Jung—has taught us a lot, long before Freud and Jung, about what can go on in the background of an encounter between a man and a woman, between a woman and a man.

There you have my contribution—or rather, the contribution of some paintings from long ago—to our thoughts today about dreams and their amplification.

References

Barbet, A. *La peinture murale romaine,* Paris, Picard, 1985.

Castiglione Morelli, V. *Pompei. Abitare sotto il Vesuvio,* cat. exhibition Ferrara, 1996.

de Caro, St. *Il Museo archeologico di Napoli*, 1994; *Pompei. Un art de vivre,* Paris, Gallimard, 2011.

Frachi Dell'Orto, L. *Rediscovering Pompeii,* cat. exhib. New York, Rome, 1990.

Gaillard, C. "La femme et la loi," in "La Villa des Mystères à Pompei," *Cahiers de psychologie de l'art et de la culture,* n° 7, 1981–1982.

"Et in Arcadia ego. Un rêve pictural à Herculaneum," *Cahiers de psychologie jungienne,* n° 46, 1985.

avec G. Sauron, "Propos croisés sur la fresque de la Villa des Mystères à Pompéi," *Cahiers de psychologie de l'art et de la culture,* n° 11, 1985.

avec C. Bourreille, "Le giron d'Arcadie," *Cahiers de psychologie de l'art et de la culture,* n° 12, 1987.

"Le rêve est-il créatif?" in *Des interprétations du rêve. Psychanalyse, Herméneutique, Daseinanalyse,* H. Mésot, ed., Paris, Presses Universitaires de France, 2001.

"La psychanalyse jungienne," in *Psychanalyses, psychothérapies: les principales approches,* M. Elkaim, ed., Paris, Seuil, 2003.

"The Arts," in *The Handbook of Jungian Psychology*, R. Papadopoulos, ed., London/New York, Routledge, 2006.

Jung, Paris, Presses Universitaires de France, 2013 (6th edition).

Goethe, W. *Ueber Kunst und Altertum*, 1818.

Kraus, Th., L. von Matt, *Lebendiges Pompeji. Pompeji und Herculunum. Antlitz und Schiksal zweir antike Städte*, Köln, Dumont/Shauberg, 1973.

Navan, M. L. *Pompeiano. La decorazione pittorica nelle collezioni del Museo di Napoli*, cat exhib. Roma, 2007-2008.

Reinach, S. *Repertorio di dipinti greci e romani*, Roma, L'Erma di Bretschneider, 1970.

Sauron, G. "Nature et signification de la mégalographie dionysiaque de Pompéi," Académie des inscriptions et Belles-Lettres, Paris, de Boccard, 1984; *La grande fresque de la Villa des Mystères à Pompei*, Paris, Picard, 1998.

Shefold, K. *La peinture pompéienne*. Essai sur l'évolution de sa signification, Brussels, 1972.

Simon, E. "Deutung and künsterische Herkunft der Geflügelten," in "Zum Fries der Mysterien Villa bei Pompeji," *Jahrbuch des deutschen archäologischen Institut*, n° 76 1961.

Veyne, P., F. Lissarague, F. Frontisi-Ducroux, *Les mystères du gynécée*, Paris, Gallimard, 1998.

Zuntz, G. "On the Dionysiac fresco in the Villa dei Misteri," *Proceedings of the British Academy, 49*, 1963.

Muse of the Moon
Poetry from the Dreamtime

by Naomi Ruth Lowinsky

> The moon in the east grows ever fuller …
> Her belly swells, full of moon children …
> as soon as the sun comes up in the east,
> He … pierces the moon's flesh with his knife …
>
> "Sun, leave my children, leave them alone!
> Your knife is murdering my unborn moon-children
> The blade of your light stabs our light to death …
>
> —Bushman myth[1]

A Poet's Credo

Dreams are the guiding words of the soul.[2]

Long ago and far away—when time was a circle—the dream and the poem were kin. Poetry was conceived in the belly of the moon, close to the unconscious, where dreams live. This was the time of the Shaman and tribal consciousness. Yet the Bushman myth of how the moon tried to protect her babies is familiar to anyone who has woken from a dream and tried to rescue it from the piercing knife of the sun, for the battle between the moon and the sun belongs to us all.

In the time before linear time the moon had a bigger say in the affairs of humans than she does today in our light-dominated, digital world. In that time the shaman and the poet, the dancer and the drummer, the healer and the artist were one being, whose function was to invoke the gods and animal spirits, to induce visions, to dance and chant the collective myths, to go into trance and retrieve the soul of a person or of the whole tribe. The poet Robert Bly remarks that the poet of ancient times "flew from one world to another." This involved a "long floating leap… from the conscious to the unconscious and back again."[3]

My credo is this: I believe in the poetry of the dreamtime. I believe it is essential that our poetry reach back to the roots of human consciousness and retrieve our collective soul. I believe poetry is one way we bring ourselves back into relation with the moon, animals, plants, and ancestors. Of course, not all poets would sign on to my credo. But I believe it is the job of those poets who honor the moon and her babies to give voice to the realm described by the Mexican Mazetec Shaman Maria Sabina, who said,

> There is a world beyond ours, a world that is far away, nearby and invisible. And there it is where God lives, where the dead live, the spirits and the saints, a world where everything has already happened and everything is known. That world talks. It has a language of its own. I report what it says.[4]

Wild Horse Girl

> We see houses in our dreams that need to be repaired
> And horses that no one has fed for three weeks.[5]

The moon and the sun have been battling it out in my life since I was a girl. I was a moonchild—full of reverie, pipe dreams, wool gatherings, and bird's nests. The sun broke through from time to time, often in school. I loved learning—mostly I loved reading. When I was a young adult the sun found me and demanded to know how I planned to make a living. I said I was a poet. "I repeat," said the sun, "how do you plan to make a living?" Luckily I stumbled into a Jungian analysis during that time and began to learn the Jungian dance, which meanders from the moon tree to the sun tree and back. I found my calling, or so I thought, in Jungian psychology, and entered what the Hindus call the house-holding phase—developing a profession, raising a family, tending a marriage. But the moon kept singing to me. Her voice got louder and louder. It was her time, she said—now that I had a day job and the sun was satisfied. She demanded I reclaim the poet I'd been as a young woman and as a child. And so it was that I found a poet I admired to be my teacher. In the manner of an initial dream in analysis, I had the following dream before our first meeting:

My poetry teacher and I are standing in a meadow. Behind us there is a large book-shelf, full of black and red ledger books, the kind I used as notebooks when I was writing poetry in my 20s. Suddenly a horse, straight out of a Paleolithic cave painting, gallops across the meadow. It is so beautiful, so vivid; it takes my breath away.

The teacher promises to help me with my books. And so she does.

Had I known the Navaho praise song for the horse when I woke from that dream, I would have chanted it, to honor so powerful a visitation from a spirit animal:

> My horse with a hoof like a striped agate,
>
> with his fetlock like a fine eagle plume:
>
> My horse whose legs are like quick lightning
>
> whose body is an eagle-plumed arrow:
>
> My horse whose tail is like a trailing black cloud.
>
> The Little Holy Wind blows thru his hair.[6]

When I was a girl I spent a considerable amount of time as a horse. I pawed the ground and whinnied. I tossed my head. I trotted. I galloped. I pulled on my reins, shouting "Whoa." I was both horse and rider. The horse was the magical steed of my imagination. I began writing poems during those horse-girl years. I learned to ride the tension between wildness, sheer animal power—"my horse whose legs are like quick lightning"—and human control—to ride the leaps of my imagination. Like the Navaho poet I felt the breath of the divine in the company of my horse—"the little holy wind blew through his hair."

The dream of the horse from the Paleolithic remembered me as a wild horse girl and announced my mature calling as a poet of the dreamtime and the primordial. The Muse of the Moon requires the capacity for shamanic descent, which, according to the late Don Sandner—a Jungian analyst who knew the shamanic realm intimately—"unfocuses the mind, loosens the ego from its rigid outward ties, and allows it to descend… to the depths, richness and perspectives of an open universe populated by animal and human forms …"[7]

Almighty Sun

> I am weary, my soul, my wandering has lasted too long, my search for myself outside of myself … I found you when I least expected you. You climbed out of a dark shaft. You announced yourself … in advance in dreams.[8]

In the collective drama between the sun and the moon, the sun has gained ascendancy in human affairs. The sun is a great god—we'd have no life on earth without him. But the knife-edge of his clarity can do terrible damage to our moon babies. With Bly, I have mourned our "demythologized intelligence, that moves in a straight line made of tiny bright links, an intelligence dominated by linked facts rather than 'irrational' feelings."[9] With Jung I have mourned the loss of soul suffered in a time that has "condemned us to haste"[10] and deprived us of access to the "spirit of the depths."[11]

When the sun claimed poetry as his baby, it became more rational, told epic histories, obeyed complex rules, turned into an elegant form of argument. Even then it was considered dangerously lunar by those, like Plato, who wanted to ban the poets from *The Republic*.[12] Bly complains of the long dry centuries of poetry created entirely by the "efficient workaday conscious mind" and of American poetry written, he claims, "essentially without the unconscious."[13]

Poetry has been a battlefield for sun and moon, with sun being mostly ascendant until, just over a hundred years ago, Freud and Jung took their dive into the dream-time. The surrealists leapt into the depths alongside them and began writing poems and painting imagery from dreams and fantasy. They opened "the gates of the soul to let the dark flood of chaos flow into" all that "order and meaning."[14]

Romanticism's Prehensile Tail

> The creative process … consists in the unconscious activation of an archetypal image… The artist translates it into the language of the present, and so makes it possible for us to find our way back to the deepest springs of life.[15]

The French poet André Breton, who wrote the "Manifesto of Surrealism," considered the surreal "a *dialogue* with the other (with what is encountered by way of dreams, coincidences, correspondences, the marvelous, the uncanny; a reciprocal exchange connecting conscious and unconscious thought)."[16] That's a pretty good description of a classical Jungian analysis, whose purpose is to give voice to the other—the marvelous, the uncanny, the shadow—as it is revealed in dreams, synchronicities, and active imagination. It is the job of a good analysis to revive those damaged moon babies, with their weird images, their animal natures, their ghosts and ancestors, their wild and unexpected romps through our civilized consulting rooms.

Psychoanalysis was a major influence on Breton and Surrealism, supporting their "quest for an art connected to the unconscious."[17] Both depend on the associative leap from one realm to the other. During the period when Jung was confronted by the shattering series of visions he recorded in *The Red Book*, poets and painters began to cultivate the weird, the irrational, the paradoxical, the disorienting. And Breton declared that surrealism was the "tail" of Romanticism, but a "strongly prehensile tail."[18] A prehensile tail, like a hand, can grasp. Surrealism grasps the world in a fierce and provocative way. It is a kind of divine madness which, to borrow from Jung's *Red Book*, "is nothing other than the overpowering of the spirit of this time through the spirit of the depths."[19] Consider these lines from a poem by Breton:

> My love whose hair is woodfire
>
> Her thoughts heat lightning …
>
> My love an otter in the tiger's jaws …[20]

These images make no logical sense. But they elicit a powerful feeling of danger, of threatening heat, of the violence of the animal world. They burst through the realm of rationality into a deeper, wilder terrain that we recognize from our dreams. The prehensile tail of the surrealists shatters the day world, opens the mouth of the cave into the underworld.

In mid-twentieth century America, Robert Bly was an advocate for the moon's babies. Influenced by the Surrealists and by the Spanish poets Lorca and Machado, he was part of a movement against the tyranny of the sun that included the Beat poets, the Black Mountain poets, and others. Bly argued for a poetry of the "deep image." The image, writes Bly, "is an animal native to the imagination."[21] "If there is no image," he wonders," how is the unconscious going to make its way into the poem?"[22] Bly decried the formal poetry then (and now) in vogue, created entirely by the "efficient workaday conscious mind… Our poetry has been a poetry essentially without the unconscious."[23] The image, writes Bly, "is a house with a room for the light world and the dark world, for the conscious and the unconscious, for the world of the dead and the world of the living."[24] That is the house I live in as a poet and as an analyst.

Faust Woman

> Dreams pave the way for life, and they determine you without our understanding their language.[25]

Some years ago I had a dream that has been working on me ever since. It has been the catalyst for a poetic sequence—*The Faust Woman Poems.*[26] In the dream a woman from long ago, dressed in long skirts, with a mauve shawl and a baby on her hip, arrives at the Sanctuario of Chimayo in New Mexico—a place that is sacred to me. This lovely little adobe church has been called the "Lourdes of America" because of the legendary healing properties of its "holy dirt." It was built in a place sacred to the local Indians, where in 1810 a priest found the miraculous crucifix of Our Lord of Esquipulas. It has been a pilgrimage site for almost 200 years. There is a room adjoining the Sanctuario whose walls are covered with the cast-off crutches and radiant photos of the healed, the saved, the transformed. I have often gathered its "holy dirt" and taken it home with me. The atmosphere is thick with suffering, prayer, yearning, ghosts, release.

In my dream the woman from long ago who is also me, is met at the door of the church by a priest, who gives her a brooch in the shape of Mary—carved in amethyst. He pins it on her shawl, at her throat. A voice from the altar calls out: "Faust Woman."

Why would the voice of the Self call me "Faust Woman?" Is that a curse, an accusation, a blessing, a simple truth? In the years since this dream has been working on me, it has told me many things. The woman from long ago who is also me is given an image of Mary to wear at her throat. Who is Mary to me, a Jew?

Mary, to whom I have spoken often, tells me that she knows the divine in her body; she is a "House of God." She is also an ordinary woman who knows the gifts and the suffering of a woman's life. She says I am given an image of her to wear at my throat because she embodies the essential themes of my life work—my opus—which is to give voice to the experience of women, in my family and in the collective, and to track the reemergence of the goddess. She reminds me that Jung recognized her as an incarnation of the great goddess; he made note of the fact that her elevation to the status of a

Goddess was affirmed by the Catholic Church itself in its Dogma of the Assumption of the Virgin.[27]

My dream, however. is more than a personal dream. It is an expression of my generation of "Faust Women." We women who carry the moon in our bodies, who measure circular time with our periods, have lived too much in the narrow realms of domesticity. We've needed exposure to the sun. The Women's Liberation Movement of the 1960s and 1970s took us by storm, flung us out of our homes into the market place, opened our crown chakras and let the fierce sun shine in. Suddenly we were astronauts, lawyers, senators, belly dancers, goddess worshippers, divorcés, single mothers, accomplished lovers, even poets. Like Goethe's *Faust*, we gained great power over the things of the world and over our own lives and bodies. Like Faust, we wanted everything—having the sun, we wanted the moon. We leapt into the depths of the collective unconscious, into the realm of circular time—the realm of "The Mothers" where Faust embraced Helen of Troy—and brought back ancient images of the feminine—the feminine face of the divine—the goddess in her many forms. Like Faust, we gained our libidos and risked our souls. Like Faust, we caught glimpses of the mystery and the eternal feminine. Here is the poem that tells the dream:

The Dream

> You arrive at the church in long skirts
> mauve shawl   the baby
> on your hip
>
> Light from the eyes
> on the altar
> touches your throat
>
> Maria carved in amethyst
> sing to us
> sing to the wooden Santos
>
> We have come to be
> healed   Reveal to us
> your next incarnation

Look at you

in your red power suit

your pointed shoes

amulets tucked

between your breasts

Changed woman

what have you done

with the baby?

What will you do

with hot blood

hard currency

the smell

of new cars?

A voice from the altar calls you

Faust Woman

I sat in the Sanctuario at Chimayo recently and meditated on my generation of "Faust Women." We have been given so much choice, so much possibility, so much worldly power, poetic license, and spiritual sustenance. But we have had to suffer the tension of extreme opposites within ourselves and the culture: our Mary vs. our "Faust Woman" natures, our moon natures vs. our sun natures, our families vs. our professions and/or creative callings—gender issues that bedevil the American polis to this day. The dream of the woman from long ago who is also me insists we acknowledge the damage we've done as well as the glories we've known. The process has given me many poems and has been a healing. It has brought my life as a Jungian and my life as a poet together in our common ancestor, Goethe. Here is the title poem of the sequence:

Faust Woman

There are goddesses throned in solitude, outside of place,

Outside of time….. They are the Mothers. [28]

You didn't know the taste
of your own honey   didn't know
willow thighs   delta song

until that cast out She
materialized in your kitchen   A dazzle of dust
ridden light   a voice   a hand
offering you the world

Do you want power among city towers, purses of gold, flashy transport?
Would you prefer a country lane, green glow of vineyards, summer breasts?
What about lovers? A stormy character playing the flute?

A silent guy with dreads? Maybe a talkative lover who'll promise
to publish you   if only you'll break out
of your kitchen cage   take a hammer
to the dishes   an axe to the door!

This is not your elegant traveling scholar   *Grandfather Goethe*

     But She's from your own realm
     you've handed her down to us

this home wrecker   this bearer of light
daughter of Mothers who've been treading
     the untrod untreadable

     empty of voice   empty of prayer
          since Troy fell…[29]

What Oracle Speaks in Our Dreams

> Whoever speaks in primordial images speaks with a thousand voices… and evokes in us those beneficent forces that ever and anon have enabled humanity to find a refuge from every peril and to outlive the longest night.[30]

I have learned, over a lifetime of working with my dreams, that some demand more of me than that they be written down or told to another. They need to be made into poems. Such a poem does not necessarily explain the dream, dissect it, or make sense of it. It translates the dream into another medium—a process which requires conscious and unconscious to talk to each other. The poem, when it works, is a creation of the Jungian dance from the moon tree to the sun tree and back. The dreams that have shaped my life, and shape-shifted into poems, are lily pads across the pond, stepping stones across the "untrod untreadable," a plumb line to the fall of Troy and to the cave paintings of the Paleolithic.

I am one of many poets in the "Lineage of the Prehensile Tail and the Deep Image," who feel the intense pressure of the ecological danger in which we now live. It is urgent that we reweave our human connections to the moon, to the realm of plants and animals, and to the dreamtime. Like the Shaman of old, we do this for the sake of our souls and for the collective soul. Like the prophet of old, we do this by talking to the divine, listening to our dreams, honoring the mystery and transmuting "our personal destiny into the destiny of mankind."[31]

Poems, like dreams, don't usually make external things happen. They don't change events, save the polar bears, stop the plunder of the rain forests. But if we pay attention, if we listen with the part of us that belongs to the Paleolithic, that remembers the holiness of plants, animals, stones, dirt, that feels the little holy wind blow through our horse's mane, that is both Madonna and "Faust Woman," home wrecker and light bearer, the moon may—if we are lucky—lend us her old black magic, grant us prophetic vision, shamanic voice. Here is a *Faust Woman* poem in that mode:

Sisters of My Time

What became of our fierce flowering? Don't you remember
how that Old Black Magic revealed Herself to us—gave us the fever
the crazy nerve to burn bras, leave husbands, grow animal hair?

We knew Her belly laugh, Her circle dance
Her multiple orgasms—It was Our Period.

What became of us—Our Period long gone—stuck
in traffic jams, eaten by Facebook—gone stale
amidst the unwept unsayable? Some of us burst
our vessels. Some of us descended into root cellars—
ghosts among the apricot preserves.

Meanwhile our bones thin, our skin loosens, our hands
can't handle a mason jar. And our Red Queen, what of her?
Her rain forests bleed out. Her corn won't tassel,
Her cattle are dying of thirst, Her Ivory Billed Woodpecker—
that God Almighty Bird—has not been heard for a generation.

Our Lady of Ripening's gone on a rampage—hot flashes
in the heartland, fire in the forest, flood
in the bayou, weeping
ice caps. Our grandchildren starve
for Her belly laugh, Her circle dance.

Now is the time, Sisters, to gather
what spells we know, what seeds we've cultivated
what Oracle speaks in our dreams, for the root cellars
of memory, the mason jars of prayer—emergency rations—
for the daughters of the daughters of our daughters

long after that Old Black Magic

has spirited us away …[32]

Notes

[1] Stephen Watson, *Song of the Broken String*, 12.

[2] C. G. Jung, *The Red Book*, 233.

[3] Robert Bly, *Leaping Poetry*, 1.

[4] Donald F. Sandner and Stephen H. Wong, *The Sacred Heritage*, 11.

[5] Robert Bly, *Meditations on the Insatiable Soul*, 8.

[6] Jerome Rothenberg, *Technicians of the Sacred*, 40.

[7] Donald F. Sandner and Steven H. Wong, *The Sacred Heritage*, 10.

[8] C. G. Jung, *The Red Book*, 233.

[9] Robert Bly, *Leaping Poetry*, 4.

[10] C. G. Jung, *The Red Book*, 253.

[11] C. G. Jung, *The Red Book*, 229.

[12] Alex Preminger and T. V. F. Brogan, eds., *The New Princeton Encyclopedia of Poetry and Poetics*, 912.

[13] Robert Bly in Donald Hall, ed., *Claims for Poetry*, 27.

[14] C. G. Jung, *The Red Book*, 235.

[15] C. G. Jung, *Collected Works 15*, par. 130.

[16] Mary Ann Caws, *Surrealism*, 15.

[17] Fiona Bradley, *Surrealism*, 31.

[18] Penelope Rosemount, *Surrealist Women*, xlvi.

[19] C. G. Jung, *The Red Book*, 238.

[20] Mary Ann Caws, *Surrealism*, 30.

[21] Robert Bly in Donald Hall, ed., *Claims for Poetry*, 26.

[22] Robert Bly in Donald Hall, ed., *Claims for Poetry*, 27.

[23] Robert Bly in Donald Hall, ed., *Claims for Poetry*, 27.

[24] Robert Bly in Donald Hall, ed., *Claims for Poetry*, 45.

[25] C.G. Jung, *The Red Book*, 235.

[26] Naomi Ruth Lowinsky, *The Faust Woman Poems*.

[27] C. G. Jung, *Collected Works 11*, par. 469.

[28] J. W. Goethe, *Goethe's Faust*, trans. Barker Fairley, 106.

[29] First published in *Spoon River*, under the title "The Visitor."

[30]   C. G. Jung, *Collected Works 15*, par. 129.

[31]   C. G. Jung, *Collected Works 15*, par. 129.

[32]   Naomi Ruth Lowinsky, "Sisters of My Time" in *The Book of Now*.

References

Bly, R. in *Claims for Poetry*, edited by Donald Hall, Ann Arbor, MI: The University of Michigan Press, 1982.

_____. *Leaping Poetry*. Pittsburgh, PA: University of Pittsburgh Press, 2008.

_____. *Meditations on the Insatiable Soul*. New York, NY: HarperPerennial, 1994.

Bradley, F. *Surrealism*. Cambridge, U.K.: Cambridge University Press, 1997.

Caws, M. *Surrealism*. London: Phaidon Press Limited, 2004.

Goethe, J. *Goethe's Faust*, trans. Barker Fairley. Toronto: University of Toronto Press, 1970.

Hall, D. (ed.) *Claims for Poetry*. Ann Arbor, MI: The University of Michigan Press, 1982.

Jung, C. *Collected Works 11*, New York, NY: Pantheon Books, 1958.

_____. *Collected Works 15*, Princeton, NJ: Princeton University Press, 1966.

_____. *The Red Book*. New York, NY: W. W. Norton & Company, 2009.

Lowinsky, N. *The Book of Now*. Edited by Leah Shelleda. Skiatook, OK: Fisher King Press, 2013.

_____. *The Faust Woman Poems*. Skiatook, OK: Fisher King Press, 2013.

Rothenberg, J. *Technicians of the Sacred*. New York, NY: Anchor Books, 1969.

Sandner, D., and Wong, S. *The Sacred Heritage*. Abingdon, UK: Routledge, 1997.

Preminger, A., and Brogan, T. (eds.). *The New Princeton Encyclopedia of Poetry and Poetics*. Princeton, NJ: Princeton University Press, 1993.

Rosemount, P. *Surrealist Women*. Austin, TX: University of Texas Press, 1998.

Watson, S. *Song of the Broken String*. Rhinebeck, NY: Sheep Meadow Press, 1991.

Dreaming the Face of the Earth
Myth, Culture, and Dreams of the Maya Shaman

by Kenneth Kimmel

For me, only Dios ... I sing to God, I sing to the Lamp, I sing to the moon, the star, I sing to the angels, I sing to the world, I sing to the sky, I sing to everything ... and all the saints ... the ancient ... only Dios ... only Dios the Sun, the Sun ... the day, the day....

A shaman-priest's song in praise of creation, inspired by a dream

Introduction

In 1974, at 23 years of age, I traveled to the remote village of Santiago on Lake Atitlan in the Highlands of Guatemala, gathering first-hand accounts of dreams of divination, healing, and initiation reported to me by Maya-descended shamans. This was part of the research for my graduate thesis in psychology. I was fortunate to have witnessed a distinct way of life that only five years later would become irreparably changed by seventeen years of renewed civil war and government counterinsurgency directed against the indigenous people in the highlands of Guatemala.[1] The survival of Maya culture is due in no small part to the strength and resilience of its people and the enduring traditional life that sustains them.

Santiago is situated on the shores of Lake Atitlan, surrounded by volcanoes. It is commonly held that supernatural guardians—"los duenos de cerro"—dwell within these mountains. To the devout, "duenos" inhabit everything—rocks, rivers, springs, hills, etc.—what we might call "a world ensouled." For the shamans, "dreams function as cultural representations analogous to myths and rituals ..." and not simply as manifestations of one's individual psychology.[2] Dreams are often viewed as visitations from ancestor deities that demand rituals in sacred earth shrines or enactment of healing ceremonies.[3]

Those destined to become healers may come upon special rocks, shells, or fragments of archeological figures that speak for supernatural beings.[4] Dreams invariably follow, offering prayers and cures to the ones called by the "duenos" to serve them. Other healers receive dream after dream, calling them to mountaintops to receive sacred knowledge from the supernatural beings there.

The people that I encountered in the village of Santiago were warm and welcoming. When you looked into their eyes they held your gaze. They smiled broadly when you smiled. Many still lived in homes made of volcanic rock walls and thatched roofs. Their traditional woven garb was bright and colorful, adorned with images of birds and animals. Once I came upon one of their splendid weaving looms that filled an entire house. Women washing clothes peacefully shared the rocky water's edge with *very large* vultures. These are some of the lasting images from thirty-eight years ago that have stayed with me—and will always stay with me.

The Maya people of the Highlands of Guatemala live in apparent peace with the great ambiguities surrounding their spiritual beliefs and practices. The rich heart of ancient Maya ceremonialism beats beneath their worship of Jesus, Mary, and the Catholic saints. Their pantheon of earth and sky gods has simply taken on the names of the saints to appease the Spanish friars and conquistadors, continuing their unbroken worship of the ancient ones. They have incorporated the new teachings into a whole cloth of scarcely visible seams, without losing thread, texture, or color of either, despite the forces from outside that have tried and failed through the years to erode the Maya faith in their enduring earth traditions.[5] As in many cases of Spanish conquest, the Church of Santiago on Lake Atitlan is built over the remains of an ancient place of power to the people of this area—the Maya Center of the World.

They hold their principal healing god *Maximon* above Jesus, for he is incarnated from their own dying and reborn Maya hero/demigod *Hun Hunahpu*. Yet he carries the mantle of darkness as well as light. If one's "dream soul" encounters *Maximon* on the road at night, he often induces terrible fright in the dreamer—"susto"—causing illness from "loss of soul." Yet, it is *Maximon* the priests call upon to retrieve the dreamer's soul and restore the person back to health.

Some consider him to be the "father of Judas," the Betrayer. Others call him "Grandfather," "the fourth brother of Jesus," and "San Simón"—which derives from "Simon Peter," "Don Pedro," or Saint Peter. He is known by many names, but one is significant—*Mam*, for it translates from the Mayan language to "Sun," the fiery orb of creation. His shaman apprentices are called, "young suns." In some stories it is *Maximon*, while in spirit form, that carries the sun to its highest point in the heavens at the holiest time of the year and draws its heat down to earth to ripen the fruit of the harvest. The mythic and ceremonial significance surrounding *Maximon* is the core to understanding the dream culture of the shamans of Atitlan, and is therefore central to this inquiry.

The Beginning Point

The following dream comes from a personal journal entry from March 15, 1974, one week after arriving in Santiago. It was a long, rich, and multi-faceted dream, and in one part of the narrative I sketched a picture depicting a ritual scene in the village:

> I walk outside of a bookstore in a town nearby Santiago and encounter a beautiful woman who feels familiar to me. She is versed in Greek mythology. She invites me to enter a drawing contest. The drawing must begin from *a natural flowing line* which soon evolves into a *tree*—the most beautiful tree I have ever drawn. *This is the beginning point.* Next to the tree I sketch a *shaman* standing before his *table* used for *divination*. Upon the table is an emblem of the *sun*—a golden circle with rays emanating from the center; then two *flaming white candles* and *burnt offering* of copal incense, the smoke wafting up from the pot; lastly, I draw two eggs signifying *rebirth*.

I find out later, much to my disappointment, that a young girl has "won" the competition by simply walking on the beach and finding a rock. I later came to discover that the dream had rendered the predominant images of Maya ceremonial shamanism in my drawing of the ritual scene.

Upon reflection, I interpreted the bookstore and "contest" as something to do with my graduate degree; the competition was probably related to my drivenness and need to control the feelings of uncertainty—of losing myself in a strange land. The need for control isolated me from a deeper connection to the rich cultural and emotional life around me. The girl who found the rock strolling along the beach, however, acted effortlessly. Could her rock have been endowed with an indwelling spirit, as the Maya believe, and not just a cold, inanimate object? Perhaps her achievement was reassuring to my own fears of losing my culture—my core of self. I realized upon awaking that I had to simply let it go. Subsequent to the dream I experienced an openness and a more "natural flow" to my life in the village, and I attribute that to the dream, whether conscious or not.

With this experience we come to the "beginning point" of this exploration. Given my dream's articulation of my intuitive immersion in the culture of Santiago, the Tree is a good place to begin.

The Dreaming Tree

Journal entry, Santiago, Atitlan, March 17, 1974:

Today the guide I hired escorted me up into the hills above the village of Santiago. Our destination was a tree sacred to the people here. They call it *Arbol de Palo de Pito*—the Tree of Divination. It bears the bright red beans or seeds that shamans use in their "mixes," to divine through dreams, to cure, to foretell the future, to lift spells, or to cast them. There is an altar with fragments of copal incense, half-melted candles, pottery shards, and the red beans of the *Palo de Pito*, scattered beneath its boughs.[6] This is the place where the apprentice shamans have come for centuries to sleep and dream. My guide tells me this is where "their dreams come true," where they learn shamanic knowledge only their dreams can reveal. The shaman practitioners come here to ask for healing dreams for the sick and sometimes they bring them here to do ritual and spend the night. This is the tree from which the wooden body and mask of the shaman god *Maximon* was originally carved. I am told Shamanic healers have been trekking up here long before conquest times. But nowadays, my guide says, not so much, for "there are not many people who wish to [do the curing] work."

As I sat beneath the *Arbol de Palo de Pito*, my guide recounted the story of the first carver of *Maximon's* effigy:

There was a shaman in ancient times. A man called "First in the Road" did things in our village. He went by the sea. So this man came here, he made the image of *Maximon*. So he made the image of *Maximon*, and ... they played drum for him, they played drum for him ... *Maximon*. Yes, then, done, the world worked, sun after sun, sun after sun ... the face of *Maximon* ... Then they put *Maximon* in the temple, in the Cofradia Santa Cruz (religious house).... He is ancient; he has been here a long time, formed.

From the tree roots of *Maximon's* "birthplace," legend has it, the wooden body and mask of "Mary Kastalyan" was formed. She is dual-natured, carrying the name of the Mother of Christ on the one hand while bearing the mantle of the Maya Moon Goddess and patron deity who brings the lake and volcanoes into being. She is mother, twin, and lover to her "divine son," *Maximon*, alluding to their roles as Great Mother and dying and resurrecting god of fertility, who are celebrated in the great agricultural civilizations through the mysteries of death and rebirth.

My benefactor, Linda, who generously shared several of her anthropological contacts with me, first came to Santiago as a nun. The people would tease her and say, "Poor Sister Linda, she knows only *half* the truth." Eventually she left the church and returned to Santiago as an ethnomusicologist to record songs of the *sanjorines*—the healers who sing songs for curing and love. The people then told her knowingly, "Now Linda knows the *whole* truth." Nature and Spirit, sorcerers and healers, patriarchal and matriarchal deities, all seemed to abide together here.

Dreams of Healing and Divination

As we began the descent down the hillside, to my good fortune, we encountered a man on the footpath—a reputed shaman on his way up into the mountains. He carried in his bag a small *mesa*[7] and sacred implements for divination purposes, as well as a vulture feather that was used, he explained, to speak with the souls of the dead. He stopped to talk with us, and I asked if he would explain to me how curing dreams came about. He was amazingly forthcoming:

> There must be a dream, one dream. But it means you have faith ... The dream gives a reason or explanation.... So it means if one believes in his heart, [the dream] gives you an explanation and speaks to you. If not, then no. It won't speak to you if you don't value it ... if you don't take account of it. Only thus.

The shamans of Santiago are diviners, soothsayers, and "Daykeepers"—those who divine by keeping count of the days in the sacred 260-day divination calendar through their *palo de pito* seed mixes. The interpretation of dreams take into account the meaning of the day in which it was dreamt. The day of one's birth determines the "face of one's day," that is one's character, which they name *nawal*. The *nawal* is also one of the names given to that part of the dreamer that leaves the body and travels in the world at night.

Shamans born on certain days of the Maya calendar are given a type of soul that they call a "body soul" or "heat lightning" which resides in their blood and muscles, enabling them to receive messages in their body from the supernatural and natural worlds. Those who possess the body soul consult it for proper dream interpretation.[8]

Anthropologist Bill Douglas describes a healing ceremony where a shaman's patient was suffering from fever and swelling throughout his body. The shaman consulted the three primary divining implements on his table. Perhaps it was through the "heat lightning" in his body that he sensed a vibration from one of the divining objects speaking for the ancestor spirit of *Rey Mantequetan*. This indicated that the cure would be divined to him through a dream. Subsequently the shaman had a dream, and addressed his patient in a mediumistic style, speaking *as* the voice in the dream. "Don't worry, sit on my back and in fifteen days I will cure you. You will see your body just as it was before."[9] The shaman dreamt of a large flat rock that would cure his patient. He instructed him to sit naked on the "back" of a rock he had found for fifteen consecutive days, during the hottest time of the day. The swelling slowly sweated from his body and his health returned.

In Maya religious view the dream voice was that of the earth deity inhabiting the rock, speaking to the patient through the shaman who was himself in a state of mystical identification. From this shared dream of doctor and patient an intuitive, novel, and creative interpretation could arise. The shaman's ceremony represented a cultural framework for the creation of what we might think of as a transcendent field for the curing dream to emerge, while the patient's enactment of it could then amplify the "prescriptive dream."

Douglas reported another healing session where the spirit of the divining table, *Pascual Avaj* (the god of earth sanctuaries), indicated that the patient was sick *from* a dream. In this case *Maximon* had encountered his *ajelbal*—his dream soul—on the road and had frightened it.[10] This called for a special ceremony at the "Cofradia Santa Cruz," the religious house of *Maximon*. It was *Maximon* who caused "fright" and loss of soul to the patient, but paradoxically, it was he who had to retrieve it and bring the soul of the patient back to him.

At this point it is important to describe the religious house of *Maximon*. The first time I entered the "Cofradia Santa Cruz," darkly illuminated by candlelight, I was overcome by the thick smell of frankincense and myrrh that permeated the room. A shaman deep in prayer swung an ornately sculpted copal incense bowl back and forth. Hanging dried fruits decorated each of the walls. Rhythmic sounds of a strumming guitar filled the house, combined with the soft prayers of a healer "begging for a miracle," kneeling before the altar of *Maximon*. The wooden effigy was seated on a chair, dressed in shirt, coat, pants, and shoes. Silken scarves adorned his neck—offerings for his blessings—and two wide-brimmed hats sat atop his head. A *gourd* wrapped in cloth, I was told, served as his "head" and lay behind his wooden facemask, a detail that will in time prove to be significant. He had a long protruding nose and wide round hole for a mouth where countless bottles of "aguardiente"—ceremonial cactus liquor—were poured down his metal-lined "throat." Other bottles were passed around the congregation. A lit cigar was always in his mouth. A painted life-size carving of Jesus lay to the left side of the altar, in an open wooden coffin with carrying poles, between two effigies of the crucifixion that hung on the walls behind it. On a smaller table white prayer candles burned.

To return to Douglas's report, the patient who was sick from his dream went to the "cofradia" bringing ceremonial offerings of "aguardiente" and cigars for *Maximon*. The shaman began his "costumbre"—his ritual prayers—and when he felt that "Mam" was in a receptive mood, he took the wooden statue's coat off of him and wrapped it around the shoulders of his patient, who was deep in prayer. The sickness of "soul fright" was "absorbed" into the coat and the soul of the patient was returned to him, restoring his health. When *Maximon* "took his evening walk" the illness diffused into the night air.

Maximon's Priest-Shaman

Bearing gifts for Nicolás, chief prayer-maker for the Cofradia Santa Cruz, renowned dream healer and table diviner, my translator and I were invited into his home and granted a private audience. Nicolás, nearly seventy years old, stood before his divining table and began a long oration of blessings and prayers to his protecting gods. Afterward we sat and talked. Over the course of several hours, he showed great patience in answering my many probing questions pertaining to his shamanic practices. (The brash exuberance and naiveté of youth was my only saving grace.) He was generous and authentic in his responses. Originally, Nicolás had no intention of becoming a shaman.

He had a lucrative family business, but, as he said, *Maximon* had other ideas in mind for him. He came to him many times in his dreams and would not leave him alone. I asked him how he had come to acquire his knowledge, and these were his words:

> I used to be a merchant, and I traveled far to other towns selling vegetables, every week, week after week. And then *Maximon* came to me: "Why don't you get a table? Why don't you get a chair? I will give you good prayers." I said, "No, I won't do that. I don't want to be a prayermaker." But *Maximon* came and insisted, knocking at the door at night [in my dreams].[11]

Maximon's "vigilance" finally convinced Nicolás of his calling and he assented to undertake shamanic training in service to *Maximon*. Because Nicolás had come to serve *Maximon* as his Chief Prayer-maker of the *Cofradia Santa Cruz*, he acquired no ordinary *dream soul* during his training. His own *soul*, he confided, took form in dreams as no less a personage than *Maximon* himself!

"Popol Vuh"—The Maya Book of the Dawn of Life

Some believe the origin of *Maximon* is traced in the *Popol Vuh* to the two oldest Maya deities—"Grandmother of the Dawn" and "Grandfather of the Day," known as the "master of seeds." The first of two creation myths in which they are featured states:

The "Heart of Sky," who were the makers and modelers of all the Worlds, invoked Grandmother and Grandfather to assist in the creation of the Third World of *Wooden People*. Through their powers of soothsaying, the first grandparents consulted their divining "mixes," comprised of seeds from the *Palo de Pito*[12] and corn kernels, just as the Maya priests of today use these same "mixes" to invoke the name of *Maximon* in their divining rituals. Hewn from the same kind of tree as *Maximon*, the *Wooden People* were brought into animate being when the grandparents "spoke" to the seeds and corn. Their race multiplied and spread over the world, but they had nothing in their hearts or minds; they had no memory of their builders, the "Heart of Sky." So the world of manikins was destroyed when a great flood was brought down upon them.[13]

In the next stage of creation, the makers brought about the age of the Hero-twins. They were *Hunahpu* and his brother, *Xbalanque*, born from the magical spittle of their father's severed head that hung in the sacred *calabash* tree. Their father, *Hun Hunahpu* and his twin brother, *Seven Hunahpu*, were born themselves in the blackness of night to their parents, Grandmother of the Dawn and Grandfather of the Day. As we will see, both *Hun Hunahpu*, his two twin sons, and *Maximon* all endure sacrificial deaths, dismemberment, and rebirth in typical shamanic fashion, and each brings light from out of the darkness.

The elder twins descended down to the Underworld of *Xibalba*, having been challenged to a ball game by the Lords of the Land of Death. It was simply a ruse, for the Lords meant to sacrifice them. Their mother, Grandmother of the Dawn, wept bitterly at their departure, perhaps divining the true fate awaiting them. Having failed the tests put before the brothers, the head of *Hun Hunahpu* was cut off, his body buried in the "Place of Ball Game Sacrifice." Then his brother was killed and buried there as well. When *Hun Hunahpu's* head was placed in the crook of the *calabash* tree, abundant fruit miraculously began sprouting from every branch. His head could not be distinguished from the other gourds.[14] The Gods of the Underworld were so astounded by this event that they forbade anyone from coming near the tree or picking its fruit.[15]

One day the moon goddess, *Blood Moon*, came to the tree desiring its "forbidden fruit." The head of *Hun Hunahpu* spoke to her. Holding out her palm he spit into it. His saliva, he told her, was like his son, and because of this, the father would never disappear, "but [would go] on being fulfilled."[16] The saliva had impregnated her with *Hun Hunahpu's* twin sons. She traveled to the house of Grandmother of the Dawn through a hole onto the earth. Announcing the coming of a second incarnation of Grandmother's sons, she proclaimed, "They have merely made a way for the light to show itself...."[17]

Blood Moon's twins were called little *Hunahpu* and *Xbalanque.* When they grew up, they too were summoned down to *Xibalba*, vowing to redeem their fallen father and uncle. They passed through all the trials set by the *Xibalbans*, but in their moment of triumph they willingly sacrificed themselves in the great stone oven, and their burnt bones were finely ground and thrown into the river. There they were magically reconstituted. They became masters over death and rebirth. They came before the Lords of *Xibalba*, who demanded that one brother kill and dismember the other and bring him back to life as a show of their power. Witnessing the miracle, the Lords of Death desired to know the feeling of death for themselves, and the hero-twins killed them. Forevermore the power of *Xibalba* was diminished. Their work complete, the twins ascended into the light of heaven, with the sun belonging to *Hunahpu* and the moon to his brother.

One ceremonial Maya bowl depicts their father reborn as the God of Corn, "sprouting" from a cleft in the shell of a turtle, the symbol of mother earth, following in the mystery traditions of countless fertility deities the world over.

Maximon's Underworld Descent During "Semana Santa"

The death and rebirth of the *Popol Vuh's* hero-twins and their father is reflected in the pageantry and ritual in Santiago, Atitlan, during Easter Holy Week—"Semana Santa." This uniquely syncretistic[18] "ritual time" re-enacts the mysteries of both shamanic and Christian sacrifice and resurrection. Here two "other brothers" play out the drama— *Jesucristo* and *Maximon*.

The major Maya calendar conceives of the yearly cycle as eighteen months spanning twenty days in each month. At the end of the year are the five terrible "days of the dead" needed to keep the world in balance with the natural cycles. The Maya fashioned Easter week to fit in with this ceremonial time. To the Maya of Atitlan, the first Sunday after the first full moon following the vernal equinox is the time of the greatest heat of the year. One story describes a yearly fertility ritual that commences one week before Easter, where a special envoy of religious men travel to a town on the way to the coast to bring back fruit to the village. On their journey back to Santiago they dress as women, *Maximon's* "mares" that he rides up from the coast. Meanwhile *Maximon* is "sacrificed," his effigy dismembered, coinciding with the end of the solar year which is roughly at the beginning of the "five terrible days." On the next day the "mares" arrive and the fruits are laid out to adorn the church square—their Center of the World, according to Maya beliefs. *Maximon's* dismembered effigy is laid among the fruits, while his spirit flies to the zenith of the World Tree to bring the sun to its highest point in the heavens after the time of the vernal equinox. He draws the heat down from the sun to ripen the fruit on the hottest day of the year. He resides at the zenith point in the "center of the cross" of the four roads that lead to the four corners of the world. Completing his task, he descends the axis of the World Tree and returns to earth.

During the year a wooden block is placed over a hole on the center of a tile floor in the church—a hole reputed to be at the very Center of the World. (If you recall, the church was built over a Maya sacred place.) Its opening connects the earth with the awesome power of the Underworld. On Good Friday, however, the block is raised, ceremonial "aguardiente" is poured into the hole, and incense is burned to purify the space. It is a terrifying thing to expose the opening, for it is a place where the dead come up and materialize. *Maximon's* spirit, like *Hun Hunahpu* and his sons, travels down through the hole to the Underworld to communicate with the dead. A large wooden cross is then wedged into the hole, bringing to mind the image of the axis of the World Tree.[19]

Mam has returned from the zenith of the sun's path in the sky and descends to the depths of the Underworld as Lord over darkness and the dead. His rebirth comes about on this saddest of days in the Catholic year—Good Friday. He is delivered back to life by the sacrifice of his own brother, the Sky God— *Nahaul Jesuscristo*,[20] who is hung on the tree of life while *Mam's* "body" is reassembled in the town square. On Easter Sunday their effigies are paraded through the town, with great rejoicing in their resurrection.

The Maya Center of the World, the soul's "ascent" of the World Tree to bring down the ripening heat of the sun, elements of sacrifice, the Underworld, and renewal are all widespread motifs reflected in shamanic traditions, myths, and mysteries. They are the living symbols for the people of Santiago, renewed over countless centuries through ceremony and myth, enacted upon sacred earth sanctuaries.

Reflections and Conclusions

This brings to a close this all-too-brief exploration. We return to where we began—with the beautiful image of the Shaman's Tree from my initial dream, recorded back in the village of Santiago in 1974. The stunning art that emerged from the dream was executed with a mastery that transcended my own conscious abilities, as if psyche's "unseen hand" were guiding my own. The tree stood at the center of the picture I had drawn, looming above the shaman and his divining table, implying that this sacred tree was the very center—the beginning, end, and beginning again—of that which connects all things. In the mind and heart of the Maya shaman, the "roots" of the Dreaming Tree, World Tree, and Tree of Sacrifice are all deeply embedded in the sacred earth, in the embodied cultural experience, and in the imaginal realm of dreams, visions, and myths. Living in the paradox of these seemingly distinct worlds, the hard edges that define their differences come to be indistinguishable in the mind of the shaman. This construct of a "participatory universe," where the shamans' dreams mediate between seen and unseen realms and the natural and human worlds, is a construct shared by the earliest people and in the remotest areas of the world today. Their vestiges still thrive among the Maya people of Guatemala. Levy-Bruhl describes a kind of mystical identification between psyche and the world—where one can be both he and another thing simultaneously. He calls it "prelogical." Here logic is suspended—not undeveloped—in these mystical states of mind where, like in dreams, the fixity of conscious Cartesian logic loosens and gives way to a kind of thinking capable of holding paradox in mind.[21] My dream alludes to it, as well, in the scene where the girl finds a rock while strolling on the beach. The Maya shaman might interpret this to mean that the sacred earth being who inhabits the rock has called the soul to it. Jung describes it in his own way in *Psychological Types* as "esse in anima"—*to be in soul*, that is, to be in a non-dualistic relationship between psyche and the world.[22]

In my view the dreamer's dreams signify our singular place in the world as well as our cultural and historical place in time. We are born into a symbolic, changing, historical world, there before the infant speaks its first words. Our traditions emerge and evolve from this archetypal matrix. Dreams of healing, initiation, and divination in the Maya shamanic tradition are the primary means of transmission of a way of life over a continuum of thousands of years, a civilization that has endured times of enormous suffering, loss, and change throughout its history. The dreams emerge out of the context of this social and historical tapestry comprising great beauty and sorrow, woven from remembered myths, venerated, grieved, and renewed through yearly ceremonies and personal rituals. The single individual cannot separate himself fully from it, only add his distinct differences to the rich weave of culture to which he is a part.

In this fragmented and alienating modernity in which we live, we would do well to cherish those rare moments of surrender of our illusions of isolation from the world— "to be in soul," as Jung describes it. Like the twenty-three-year-old psychology student, we might all glimpse a trace of ourselves embodied in *the face of the earth*.

Notes

1 There were roughly three periods of civil war beginning in 1960 and ending in 1996. It is estimated two hundred thousand people were killed—mostly indigenous—and over one million were displaced until the dictatorship fell. The war spread to the highlands during the last phase of the civil war beginning in 1979, and Santiago was a major center of resistance. More than a thousand Maya from Santiago were killed by the military. The horror and gravity of this relentless attack on their very survival prevents any idyllic portrayal of a paradisiacal existence.

2 Barbara Tedlock, "The Role of Dreams and Visionary Narratives in Mayan Cultural Survival," 467–468.

3 Shamanic traditions in highland Guatemala descend from the ancient Maya agricultural mysteries involving cycles of sacrifice and rebirth—the way of the seeded earth. Like all shamanic traditions, it traces its origins to prehistory and the way of the animal powers among the hunter-gatherer tribes.

4 Bill Douglas, *Illness and Curing in Santiago Atitlan*, 134–141.

5 Since the 1950s there have been movements that have come and gone, launched by Protestant evangelicals and certain Catholic orthodoxy, to teach the separation of soul from the body. The Maya Sacred Earth was demonized as a place of sin and the domain of the Devil. The dreams of new converts or "catechists" actually began changing, where the Christian God would appear, calling them to destroy the earth shrines sacred to the Maya. (See Benson Saler, "Religious Conversion and Self-Aggrandizement: A Guatemalan Case," 110–111.) Since the post-war years rapprochement with the catechists has led to their renewed honoring of the earth's shrines connected to a change in their dreaming. The catechists came to realize that the traditional Maya were not their enemy, but rather the government whose sinister aim was to destroy Maya culture. (See Barbara Tedlock, "The Role of Dreams and Visionary Narratives in Mayan Cultural Survival," 470.)

6 I learned from scientific papers subsequent to my visit to Guatemala that consuming the seeds of the *Palo de Pito* has been known to induce narcotic effects, sedation, mild inebriation, and deep sleep. These effects may all play a part in shamanic belief in the bean's "divinatory" properties. Women consuming them for aphrodisiac effects reported erotic dreams occurring while in deep sleep. (See Christian Ratsch, *The Encyclopedia of Psychoactive Plants: Ethnopharmacology and its Applications*, 238.)

7 A table containing sacred objects and religious implements used as mediums to commune with spiritual forces and to divine cures.

8   Barbara Tedlock, "The Role of Dreams and Visionary Narratives in Mayan Cultural Survival," 466–467.

9   Bill Douglas, *Illness and Curing in Santiago Atitlan*, 378.

10   The *ajelbal* may take the form of a dove or a dog in dreams. I was told that the villagers began to fear *Maximon's* growing power to cause "Susto," or fright, in the people, so they cut off the statue's legs to limit his power.

11   *Maximon* was imploring Nicolás to get a divining table and chair to perform ritual and prayers.

12   The *Popol Vuh's* English translation uses the name of the coral tree, but, according to ethnobotanists, they are the same species, one being the Spanish translation, the other, English. In Quiche Maya dialect, it is called Tzite.

13   *Popol Vuh: The Definitive Edition of the Mayan Book of the Dawn of Life and the Glories of Gods and Kings*, 70–71.

14   Recall that behind the mask of *Maximon* his "head" is formed from a *calabash* gourd.

15   In the shamanic culture of the Warao Tribe of the Venezuelan Amazon, only shamans are permitted to pick the gourds from the *calabash* tree to fashion their healing rattles.

16   *Popol Vuh*, trans. Dennis Tedlock, 99.

17   *Popol Vuh*, trans. Dennis Tedlock, 103.

18   "Syncretistic" refers to the reconciliation of different systems of belief or religion, especially when they are diverse in character.

19   Personal communication with Linda O'Brien.

20   *Nahaul* translates as "shaman."

21   Refer to Robert A. Segal, "Jung and Levy-Bruhl." *Journal of Analytical Psychology*, 637–638.

22   C. G. Jung, CW 6, par. 46–64.

References

Douglas, B. *Illness and Curing in Santiago Atitlan*. Ph.D. Dissertation, Stanford University, 1969.

Jung, C. *The Collected Works of C. G. Jung*. Vol. 6A. Princeton, NJ: Princeton University Press, 1970.

Popol Vuh: The Definitive Edition of the Mayan Book of the Dawn of Life and the Glories of Gods and Kings, translation and commentary by Dennis Tedlock. New York: Touchstone, 1996.

Ratsch, C. *The Encyclopedia of Psychoactive Plants: Ethnopharmacology and its Applications.* Rochester: Park Street Press, 1998.

Saler, B. "Religious Conversion and Self-Aggrandizement: A Guatemalan Case." *Practical Anthropology 12*(3), 1965: 105–114.

Segal, R. "Jung and Levy-Bruhl." *Journal of Analytical Psychology* 52, 2007: 635–658.

Tedlock, B. "The Role of Dreams and Visionary Narratives in Mayan Cultural Survival." *Ethos 20*(4), 1992: 453–476.

Coal or Gold?
The Symbolic Understanding of Alpine Legends

by Gotthilf Isler

Translated by Mathias Rosenthal

Where legends were still told, the Alpine people lived in a meaningful world, embedded in outer and inner nature. The contents of the collective unconscious are constellated in these popular legends. They compensate for the Christian attitude of the conscious mind, as shown in this chapter with examples of treasure legends. The treasure is hidden and hard to find, and often it seems to be mere charcoal. But brought home or seen through the eyes of an innocent child, it is revealed to be shining gold, a symbol of god in man:[1] the self. The question remains: Could the coal, seen from the outside, be the gold seen from the inside? Are such legends a hint to the *unus mundus*?

There is a famous book by Eduard Renner, *Goldener Ring über Uri [The Golden Ring over Uri]*, that opens a chapter with an outrageous popular legend:

> In Rinderbüel in the Maderanertal an entire Alpine pasture lies buried under rocks. One evening, when the herdsmen were milking the cows, a voice was heard from the sheer cliff above the huts: "I must let go!" The chief herdsman put his hands to his mouth and called out: "You can hold it still longer!" The next evening the voice was heard again: "I have to let go!" Once again the fearless herdsman answered: "You can hold it still longer!" The third evening had drifted over the quiet pasture, the last cow was being milked, and the entire herd was standing together, masticating, when the threatening, almost pleading voice was heard again from the overhang: "Yes, I must let go!" The herdsman pushed the milking stool out from under the cow, and with the full milking bucket in one hand, called out: "So let it come down!" At that very moment the rock burst apart and came crashing down, sparks flying, burying the entire beautiful pasture with all the animals, the farmer, and his servants under boulders and debris. Only a cow herdsman and the red cow of a widow escaped. By chance the cow had wandered on down to the creek at the end of the pasture.

This legend juts out into our flat, reasonable world like a monument, a witness of a holistic experience of nature and spirit. Man faces nature—it is alive, has a voice, and he has a relationship with it, fights it, implores it—and is always defeated. Man is part of a much larger context that far exceeds personal will and planning. The legend reminds us of the medieval philosophy of the interconnectedness of all things, *corre-spondentia*.[2]

The embeddedness of human life in a larger context of meaning is clearly captured in a short legend from Silenen (Uri):

> There was a place in Frentschenberg near Bristen where a light was seen every night for many years. Later on, an ash tree grew there, and the light was seen as before. Thirty years later, a child climbed up into the ash tree and died in a fall. Since that time the light has not reappeared.

"Uncanny and large," Renner writes,

> this legend rises up in front of us and puts an entire fate under a spell. For years, perhaps centuries, a place has been waiting for this fate to be fulfilled. The way the tree buds, grows, waits is very metaphorical, and far away from it the fruit, which will once fall out of its crown, ripens in the womb of primal mothers, grandmothers and its mother. The life and the death of a human being have already happened in the big plan before this child's birth, and death seems to mark only the beginning of this plan.

These two tales are not tales of personal experience, since the storytellers make no such claims. But it is possible that the tales are based on others' experiences. The perception of such an interconnectedness seems to match a primal state of mind that Lévy-Bruhl calls *participation mystique*. As Jung explains in his lecture, "Archaic Man,"

> Thanks to our one-sided emphasis on the so-called natural causes, we have learned to differentiate what is subjective and psychic from what is objective and "natural." For primitive man, on the contrary, the psychic and the objective coalesce in the external world. [...] His country is neither a geographical nor a political entity. It is that territory which contains his mythology, his religion, all his thinking and feeling in so far as he is unconscious of these functions. His fear is localized in certain places that are "not good." The spirits of the departed inhabit such and such a wood. That cave harbours devils who strangle any man who enters. In yonder mountain lives the great serpent; that hill is the grave of the legendary king; near this spring or rock or tree every woman becomes pregnant; that ford is guarded by snake-demons; this towering tree has a voice that can call certain people. Primitive man is unpsychological. Psychic happenings take place outside him in an objective way. [3]

For us modern people the world has been largely demystified, except for those rare events in which such a connectedness suddenly appears, or when a dream or a vision occurs near a corresponding event in the outside world—for example, when a death is "announced." Even educated people from the city have told me of such experiences; once the cracked upper rim of a water glass even "announced" the birth of a child. Such experiences—announcing a person's death, an accident, or a change in weather in a "spooky" way—are frequently documented in legend collections.

The legend of the "Nightly Light and the Ash Tree" corresponds with the reliable report of a 68-year-old woman, noted by Josef Müller. Probably sometime in her youth she saw, two years in a row, a nocturnal light at a certain place on a mountain. The woman's employers were unable to see it. At this very place a boy who herded the goats later fell to his death.

Voices warning of an accident or a fall in the mountains can be found in many legends. In 1857 the shoemaker Alexander Gort, from Klosters (a mountain village), recounted the following experience to Nina Camenisch, a legends collector:

> In the mine of Davos I often heard a strange knocking in the rock. Sometimes it sounded like someone knocking on rock, sometimes on wood. It was supposed to be the little mountain men, little creatures, dwarfs, with long, gray beards.

If they knocked on stone, it was a good sign and then the work would go well. If it sounded like they were knocking on wood, it meant that the little ghosts were angry and the workers would labor in vain:

> Once I was working alone in a shaft when I heard a loud whistle above me. It was one of the little mountain men who was whistling, looking at me in a curious way and waving. I got scared and ran away. A short time later a heavy rock fell where I had been working. The little mountain ghost had wanted to warn me.

The first part of the story contains elements of the folk beliefs about dwarves that were probably widely known. The collector must have been moved by the second part, the experience of the storyteller, because she added, probably to assuage her own doubts and those of others: "From the old man's mouth this story sounded so real and full of life that one could tell he believed it himself."

Jung viewed such events as told by Alexander Gort as synchronicities, as expressions of a kind of knowledge that is independent of the consciousness of the person who has the experience. In our above examples, the light that is visible for two years and the little mountain man's whistling and waving signify a foreknowledge that something is going to happen in those locations. Jung speaks of the absolute knowledge of the collective unconscious that is independent of the conscious mind. These are inexplicable events, but they probably have an *a priori* meaning that exists outside of humans. Synchronicities give the person who has the experience the impression of a meaningful connection with the world; they are manifestations of the *living spirit.*[4]

It seems to me that this "spirit," this other dimension, accounts for the essence of all legends, not just of the experiential ones. In all real legends another world—a mythical dimension—reaches into our world, which is ruled by our senses. Wilhelm Grimm compared the mythical element of the fairy tales with "small pieces of a burst gem which lie scattered on a ground covered with grass and flowers; only an eye with a sharper gaze can detect them." With this comparison Grimm characterized the nature of all religious stories—and folk legends are religious tales.

From a modern psychological perspective this mythical element is an expression of the archetypes of the collective unconscious. Whereas Grimm assumed that the mythical is the "residue of a belief that reaches down into the most ancient time," a belief "which expresses itself in a metaphorical understanding of supernatural things," Jung saw that the psyche, inasmuch as we are conscious of it, generally manifests itself in images, that the soul lives in images.

Our dreams give us the most precise knowledge of the unconscious, a knowledge not influenced by the conscious mind. Dream research has shown that there is a meaningful connection between our dreams and consciousness. Most of the time, we understand their motifs because they arise from our lived experience; they are mostly memory images. But their selection and arrangement, their combination in an individual dream, are determined by autonomous factors of the unconscious psyche. Experience shows that dreams can compensate for the attitude of the ego, which is to say that dreams confront the conscious mind with such contents of the unconscious that enable the ego to conduct its life in a way that is "more correct," more appropriate to the facts of life. It is as though the "maker of dreams" possesses some superior knowledge, which is why we are often under the impression that *somnia a Deo missa*—that dreams were sent to us by God. They enable us to gain an overarching perspective of our inner psychic nature as well as of our external life circumstances.[5] Ordinary nocturnal dreams tend to address everyday questions, whereas the great "archetypal" dreams mostly address the religious attitude of the individual or fundamental problems of the dreamer's time.

Folk legends behave in a similar way. When we examine the legends of a valley or a larger region, we find out that they compensate for the conscious attitude of the population. The motifs of the stories embody psychic contents. Most motifs, as well as entire story types, have been known for centuries, but what really remain alive and are remembered in the act of storytelling (often in new combinations) are the contents that the conscious mind should take into consideration in a religious way. The legends can be compared with dreams, although they do not reveal very many individual characteristics; rather, the legends reveal the *contents of the collective unconscious that concern the entire culture in which people live*. The legends of a certain region are, in a way, the dreams of the people. Since our great cultural problems no doubt hang together with the unsolved problems of Christianity, many folk legends are still relevant for us moderns; like dreams they are "sent by God" and must be taken seriously.

I demonstrate this point by means of a few treasure legends. The meaning of the stories is not always easy to see. The unconscious often speaks with a soft voice—as, for example, in the popular legend of the dwarf midwife. In the town of Brienzwiler in the Haslital (in the Bernese Oberland region of Switzerland), an elderly wood carver told the following story:

> It was in the middle of the night when a little dwarf came to a woman and asked her to come along because his wife was in bed needing help. She quickly put her clothes on; the little dwarf led the way and she followed. They got to the wife, and when all was done the woman got ready to go home. But the little dwarf told her to wait a moment so that he could get her payment; it wasn't long before he returned with a handful of coal, which he placed in her apron. The woman looked at the coal and thought, "I already have this at home," and as she was walking home she didn't even turn around when a piece of coal fell from her apron and to the ground. The dwarf saw the piece of coal fall and called after the woman:
>
> "The more you lose, the less you have!"
>
> The midwife acted as if she was hard of hearing and continued walking. In her kitchen she angrily threw the coal on the stove lid, went to bed and slept until late in the morning.
>
> It was late when she came into the kitchen in order to start the fire. She saw something glittering on the stove lid: wherever she had thrown the coal there was a little heap of gold! Now she understood what the dwarf had meant; she rushed down the

stairs and wanted to look for the lost coal, but she wasn't able to find even the smallest piece.

As long as we can see only a lovely children's story in this legend, it remains strange and does not move us. But as soon as we see it symbolically, it takes on a different look. Then it reads like this: In the darkness and tranquility of night a creature from another world comes to a woman; she helps that creature and receives a "highest value" as a gift, but does not realize the value of the gift until it is too late.

As Jung has pointed out, symbols are not signs for something known, but the best possible expression of an unknown psychic fact.[6] Symbols cannot be simply explained; rather, their meaning is found in a careful amplification—that is, by comparison with historical symbols such as those found in alchemy or in the various religious systems.

Dwarves are often "subterraneans": They do not live in the everyday world of the conscious mind, but psychologically in the unconscious. They are spirits of nature. In the Alpine region they appear often as little wild men or wild women who live in remote areas. But unlike the dwarves of the popular Nordic belief, they are neither goldsmiths nor blacksmiths, but helpful creatures who assist a peasant in the stable and with herding cows, or help his wife in the kitchen. In the Alpine region dwarves are mainly believed to be creatures who possess a secret knowledge, who know more than ordinary people. In myths, fairy tales, and dreams, the inferior function, which always represents the unconscious, often appears in an unsightly form such as a dwarf. In his seminar on "Nietzsche's Zarathustra," Jung said, "the dwarves know the things that are hidden […], these little gods […] have since time immemorial been supposed to have the secret knowledge."[7]

In the feminine psyche dwarves are associated with the creative unconscious as embodiments of helpful ideas and thoughts. As experience shows, dwarves appear more often in dreams of women than of men. A young mother had an impressive dream of a squirrel that cried golden tears. She had to store these tears carefully. In the course of the dream, the squirrel turned into a dwarf. In the midwife legend the dwarf—this creative side, this aspect of the peasant woman's unconscious—seeks her help and she gives it freely; she departs immediately to visit the realm of the "other side" and to assist in bringing forth new life: A dwarf child is born. In conscious terms this means that now a new aspect of the unconscious wants to become conscious. And the unconscious, the spiritual and creative side of the woman, gives her a generous reward—gold, the highest, the most precious, the most prized—but the conscious mind does not understand, is blind to the value, sees only black coal, and disregards the precious gift.

A poor woman of Laufenburg once dreamt that she would be able to find a large treasure at the Habsburg castle on Good Friday at noon. But at that time all she saw was a fleeing black cat and a pot full of shards. She told her tale of woe to a Capuchin monk, "who reproached her heavily and blamed her doubting mind for the glaring transformation of the treasure." Certain legends state quite clearly that the devil blinds people (or conceals the treasure itself) so that they are unable to see the treasure or the preciousness of the treasure. For the alchemist Gerardus Dorneus the devil was the *binarius*, the number two, the "doubter."[8] A childlike mind is needed to recognize the treasure, the highest value of the soul. In the "pure" hand of a four-year-old child, the painted porcelain chips and pieces his mother had found turned into pieces of gold in his eyes. Innocent children "see even ghosts," a peasant from Siat says, concluding with a story about a boy who reported seeing "a golden saw in which dwarves, little men, sawed crystals in the water of a creek. He said he had seen the crystal sawdust lying in the sun, in and on the banks of the creek. Both the creek and the water wheel the creek was driving were full of crystals." There are many legends in which children have seen a treasure; these are often reports of remembered childhood experiences.

Naturally, the treasure of the legend, the gold, must be understood symbolically. Gold—which can appear as coal or leaves or slabs of slate or cherry pits with holes in them, and disappears after the smallest error in behavior—is no ordinary gold, much like the gold of the alchemists. It has more to do with the treasures of heaven than with earthly wealth, but many stories take the element of gold quite concretely, as ordinary matter rather than symbolically, such as this one from Vrin:

> A student of the black arts asked an ox trader who was driving his cattle down to Lugano . . . why he was coming here with his cattle. He said that on his wild meadow on the Maiensäß mountain there was a gold pit. This meadow now belongs to us, but I've never found any gold there. A niece who was listening [commented] ". . . but you've never dug there (*laughing*)—you should dig!"

Perhaps the niece noticed that another kind of gold might be meant, but we do not know this for sure. In the legends of the Alpine region, there are often "Venetians" who know where gold sources can be found or who collected precious stones in their sacks and carried them to Venice. The saying of one such Venetian is well known; he used it to scold the peasants: "The stone you're throwing after your cow is often worth more than the cow itself." This is an enigmatic idea, of course, and gives rise to many speculations and hopes. Josef Müller reports a supposedly true incident in which the archaic mentality of a person from the Swiss canton of Uri clashed with the reasonable attitude of modernity:

> The belief in the miraculous city of Venice once had deep roots in the people of Uri. A few decades ago, a mentally handicapped man from Bauen [on the Lake of Lucerne] collected all kinds of crystals and crystal-like stones, until he had almost filled his room with them and no longer had any space for himself. "If I took those crystals to Venice, I'd be a rich man," he believed unshakably and, indeed, he had the intention to travel to Venice with them. Once the commissioner responsible for the orphans stopped by in the man's absence and, in a bureaucratic fit, not seeing the value of the stones, equal to the Nibelung's treasure, dumped the precious gold into the deep lake. This made the man so angry that he refused to work and became a burden of the welfare office.

The man projected his highest value—it is not very difficult to recognize that it was a psychic one—into the stones (the *philosophical stones*!) and with their loss, lost the purpose of his life. What might look like an insignificant incident on the shore of the Lake of Lucerne by a simple man has been happening on a large scale for more than two centuries: Collective enlightened blindness (i.e., blinded by the light of "its" own mind) is dumping former religious values into the lake. Such ideas embody psychic truths, as all religions have their origin in psychic necessities. When these truths are lost, the individuals lose their roots—lose connection with all those things that enable them to lead a meaningful life and then get lost in the limitations of their own judgment and reason. In this way the loss of the Christian world of images, as Jung writes, "has created millions of impoverished minds, forcing them to use miserable and poisonous substitutes, a process for which our time delivers disturbing proofs."[9] The only way to regain the connection with the past and our "inner ancestors"—and to salvage these irreplaceable values—is for us to understand what these ideas mean in psychic terms. In a letter of 1955 Jung wrote: "One could well say it is a problem of our time whether our mind is capable of developing itself so that it can understand the symbolic point of view or not."[10]

The symbolic meaning of gold is manifold. In addition to its lasting value, its *incorruptibilitas*, its association with the sun is an important aspect: Since ancient times, both have been characterized with a circle—O. The scholar and alchemist Michael

Maier (around 1600) saw gold as an image of the sun, as "*deus terrenus*" (the god in the earth).[11] The sunlike quality of the gold has to do with its nature as light, *lumen*. It is, quite obviously, an image for the light-bringing, consciousness-creating quality of the collective unconscious, for illumination from the unconscious. In his theoretical writings "On the Nature of the Psyche" Jung shows that the archetypes, in addition to their numinosity, have a luminosity; that is, they have "about them a certain effulgence or quasi-consciousness."[12] In this respect, the gold of the legends is equal to Paracelsus's "light of nature," that is, the absolute knowledge of the collective unconscious. It is reasonable to assume that the treasure is a symbol for the archetypal structure of the collective unconscious, for the innate and autonomous faculty of the objective psyche to create fantasies. Paracelsus himself called the *lumen naturae* "the first and best treasure the rule of nature comprehends."[13] *The illumination from the unconscious brings meaning that emanates from one's own soul.*

When the peasant woman from Brienzwiler mistakes the gold she received from the dwarf for her midwifery for mere coal, she is unable to see that "in the hidden place" inside herself, she has an ability of the soul, something like a divine spirit that knows more than she does herself. As a lot of treasure legends say, to possess this spirit constitutes the happiness and the wealth of life because it is identical with the meaning of life. In dreams this light of nature, the inner symbolic gold, appears as the star-strewn heavens, as stars reflected in dark water, as nuggets of gold or golden sand scattered in black earth,[14] as stars gradually emerging in the sky, as a Christmas sky that signifies all the happiness and the suffering of the world. Such dreams give us the hope that life, beyond all earthly limitations, has an "eternal" meaning.

Paracelsus saw that the *lumen naturae* can be found in man himself. "It is enkindled by the Holy Spirit"; it is found in our innate "*astrum*" or "*sydus*," the star in man. It is the dream spirit that speaks to us in dreams.[15] For Dorneus it is the image of God inside of man:

> The life, the light of men, shineth in us, albeit dimly, and as though in darkness. It is not to be sought as proceeding from us, though it is in us and not of us, but of Him to Whom it belongeth, Who hath deigned to make us his dwelling place. [...] He hath implanted that light in us that we may see in its light the light of Him who dwelleth in light inaccessible, and that we may excel his other creatures. In this especially we are made like unto Him, that He has given us a spark of His light. Thus the truth is to be sought not in ourselves, but in the image of God [*in imago Dei*] which is within us.[16]

129

There is a type of legend that demonstrates more clearly than others that the treasure is the precious secret of the individual. In one such legend, "The Dream of the Treasure on the Bridge," the following story was told in Visperterminen, in the canton of Valais, Switzerland:

> A peasant from Findelen [a village about 6,500 feet above sea level, where peasants could stay only in summertime] dreamt that he would make his fortune if he went to Sitten [the capital of Valais]. He had this dream three times in a row; the dream was so clear that he made a plan to go and see if it would come true. When he stepped on the large bridge in Sitten, he met a man who asked him where he was going. He said that he had dreamt three times that he would make a fortune by coming to Sitten, and he wanted to see if it was true. The other man laughed at him and called him a fool, because he, too, had had a dream that he would find a fortune in the house at the upper end of the village of Findelen, but that the dream had left him cold. The peasant went back home and said: "What was it the other man said? In the house at the upper end of the village! That's my house! I should look around a little!" He dug and dug and found a pot full of gold. He had made a fortune in Sitten after all.

It seems that a man must first go out into the world, if only to discover that happiness cannot be found there. There he meets "the other inside himself": his own disbelief. In this type of legend, the treasure is always found in one's own house or garden, on one's own land. But even this treasure must be guarded as a secret.

"Finding yourself" does not lead only to happiness, but also to suffering, to crucifixion. Also in the legend of "The Dream of the Treasure on the Bridge," in a variant from Naters, a village in Valais, a previously poor man was "accused of witchcraft or theft" and tortured because of his newfound wealth—and finally released upon the testimony of the man on the bridge—"and carried home in a trough, broken and cracked, where he died three days later."

The gold of the legends, the treasure, has nothing to do with the Christian idea of God, but rather with the *deus absconditus*, the God hidden in matter. He seems to belong to a counter-world of Christianity. The treasure is often guarded by animals, or by an unholy virgin in the shape of a toad or a snake who wants to be kissed, or by the devil himself. Or, the treasure appears only on Christian holidays—for example, on Good Friday during "the Passion" or during midnight mass on Christmas Eve, when all the pious and the faithful sit in church. The treasure—the *lumen naturae* that emanates from the center of one's personality—signifies a revelation from below, and if one wants to possess the treasure, one must confront one's own animal, instinctual side; one's own feminine side; and, in principle, evil as such. The new light always comes from the despised place, where nobody thinks to look for it.

Even in our seemingly harmless motif involving the dwarf, the male or female dwarf sometimes first appears as an ugly toad to two poor women or girls working in the field. The woman who spares the toad or treats it loyally in some other way is then asked to help with a birth or asked to become the godmother of the dwarf child. There are also variants in which the woman appreciates the value of the gift of the dwarf and finds herself richly rewarded by the coal, which is transformed into gold. As in the treasure-keeper legends, here, too, the highest value, the new consciousness, comes from the disregarded realm of human instinct—from man's animal soul—and the toad symbolizes a rejected aspect of maternal instinct.[17] The renewal comes from the "lowest" female nature itself. The gift of the dwarf, the coal itself, also belongs to this lowest nature. In many treasure legends, the primary matter of the treasure, the alchemical *prima materia*, consists of coal. In Kästris (a town in Grisons, a canton of Switzerland), a woman told the following story:

> Every hundred years a crowned snake appears lying on a linen cloth below the castle, named *Chisti sut*. On the cloth there are glowing coals. The snake has a key in its mouth, and the person who takes the key away from the snake would redeem the snake, and then the coal would turn to gold.

Since carbon is the main chemical element of the physical organism, the deeper question is whether the coal could be the physical aspect of the same unrecognizable reality, which, on the psychic side, appears as the archetype of wholeness. Then, these legends would convey a reference to the hypothetical *unus mundus*, which might contain the ordering principle of matter and psyche.[18] The dwarf's midwife would then represent the "materialistic" view of the world. The treasure of legends always comes from those realms of man or nature that have been outcast by the Christian consciousness and have yet to be redeemed; that is, we have to establish a conscious relationship with them. In the legends this task is often a matter of life and death.

When we view many legends together, we see that those elements live on in them that are archetypally valid at the time of their recording. Generally speaking, the legends compensate for the limitations of Western Christian consciousness: They contain references from the unconscious about the direction in which Christianity ought to develop; the treasure and redemption legends, in particular, portray how immensely difficult this differentiation of consciousness is. To stay with the imagery of the dwarf legend, it is wise not to disregard the legends as worthless coal, but to attempt a careful understanding of their meaning. Those who can see only coal will not be able to understand that the legends are actually quite valuable, not worthless. Whoever can at least feel the gold might begin to ask: What are those highest values that want to be seen? These individuals may embark on a quest, an adventurous search, where everything is still open and final answers are not to be expected. It is those whom I would like to encourage with these thoughts.

Notes

1 The word "man" and gender-specific terms are used through out the paper at the request of the author rather than using the more current gender-neutral language.

2 Cf. C. G. Jung, "Synchronicity: An Acausal Connecting Principle," CW 8, par. 924.

3 C. G. Jung, "Archaic Man," CW 10, par. 128.

4 On the topic of synchronicity, cf. Jung, "Synchronicity: An Acausal Connecting Principle," CW 8. See also, Marie-Louise von Franz, *Psyche and Matter.*

5 Marie-Louise von Franz, "The Individuation Process." In *Archetypal Dimensions of the Psyche*, 294.

6 C. G. Jung, *Psychological Types*, CW 6; a definition of symbol is found in par. 814–829.

7 C. G. Jung, *Nietzsche's Zarathustra: Notes of the Seminar Given in 1934–1939* (Vol. II). Edited by James L. Jarrett, Bollingen Series XCIX, 1239.

8 C. G. Jung, *Psychology and Religion*, CW 11, par. 104. See also, "A Psychological Approach to the Trinity," CW 11, par. 180.

9 C. G. Jung, *Mysterium Coniunctionis*, CW 14/I, par. 338; cf. CW 14, par. 347.

10 C. G. Jung, *Letters*, Vol. II, 229 (Letter to Edward Vernon Tenney, Feb. 23, 1955).

11 C. G. Jung, *Psychology and Alchemy*, CW 12, par. 445.

12 C. G. Jung, "On the Nature of the Psyche," CW 8, par. 338.

13 The "*primum ac optimum thesaurum, quem naturae Monarchia in se claudit.*" Quoted in Jung, CW 8, par. 390.

14 C. G. Jung, CW 8, par. 396.

15 C. G. Jung, CW 8, par. 390*f*; see also "Paracelsus as a Spiritual Phenomenon," CW 13, par. 148.

16 Gerardus Dorneus, quoted in Jung, *Mysterium Conjunctionis*, CW 14, par. 48.

17 "The toad [...] generally signifies an anticipation of the human being on the level of coldblooded creatures, and actually stands for the psyche associated with the lower spinal cord. Like the snake, it is a symbol of the creative unconscious." C. G. Jung, *Letters*, Vol. I, p. 213. (letter to Wilhelm Laiblin, April 16, 1936). In the case of uterine ailments, toad devotionals are common.

18 On carbon and its four valences, cf. C. G. Jung, *Psychology and Alchemy*, CW 12, par. 327. On the topic of the *unus mundus*, cf. *Mysterium Coniunctionis*, CW 14, par. 759 ff; von Franz, *Psyche and Matter.*

References

More sources can be found in the original German version of this text: Gotthilf Isler: Kohle oder Gold. Zum symbolischen Verständnis einiger Alpensagen. In: *Lumen naturae. Zum religiösen Sinn von Alpensagen.* Vorträge und Aufsätze. Jungiana, Beiträge zur Psychologie von C. G. Jung, Reihe B, Bd. 5. Küsnacht 2000, 292–309.

Grimm, J., and Grimm, W. *The Complete Grimm's Fairy Tales.* New York: Pantheon Books, 1944.

Jung, C. *Alchemical Studies. Vol. 13. Collected Works of C. G. Jung.* Translated by R. F. C. Hull. Bollingen Series XX. Princeton, NJ: Princeton University Press, 1983.

_____. "Archaic Man." In *Collected Works of C. G. Jung. Vol. 10. Aion.* Translated by R. F. C. Hull. Bollingen Series XX. Princeton, NJ: Princeton University Press, 1959.

_____. "Concerning Mandala Symbolism." *Archetypes and the Collective Unconscious. Vol. 9.I. Collected Works of C. G. Jung.* Translated by R. F. C. Hull. Bollingen Series XX. Princeton, NJ: Princeton University Press, 1981.

_____. *Letters, Vol. 1: 1906–1950.* Bollingen Series XCV:1. Princeton, NJ, Princeton University Press, 1973.

_____. *Letters, Vol. 2: 1951–1961.* Bollingen Series XCV:2. Princeton, NJ, Princeton University Press, 1976.

_____. *Mysterium Coniunctionis. Vol. 14. Collected Works of C. G. Jung.* Translated by R. F. C. Hull. Bollingen Series XX. Princeton, NJ: Princeton University Press, 1971.

_____. *Nietzsche's Zarathustra: Notes of the Seminar Given in 1934–1939. Vol. II.* Edited by James L. Jarrett, Bollingen Series XCIX. Princeton, NJ: Princeton University Press, 1988.

_____. "A Psychological Approach to the Trinity." In *Collected Works of C. G. Jung. Vol. 11. Civilization in Transition.* Translated by R. F. C. Hull. Bollingen Series XX. Princeton, NJ: Princeton University Press, 1970.

_____. *Psychological Types. Vol. 6. Collected Works of C. G. Jung.* Translated by R. F. C. Hull. Bollingen Series XX. Princeton, NJ: Princeton University Press, 1971.

_____. *Psychology and Alchemy. Vol 12. Collected Works of C. G. Jung.* Translated by R. F. C. Hull. Bollingen Series XX. Princeton, NJ: Princeton University Press, 1971.

_____. "Psychology and Religion." In *Collected Works of C. G. Jung. Vol. 11. Civilization in Transition.* Translated by R. F. C. Hull. Bollingen Series XX. Princeton, NJ: Princeton University Press, 1970.

_____. "On the Nature of the Psyche." In *Collected Works of C. G. Jung. Vol. 8. Structure and Dynamics of the Psyche*. Translated by R. F. C. Hull. Bollingen Series XX. Princeton, NJ: Princeton University Press, 1960.

_____. *Nietzsche's Zarathustra: Notes of the Seminar Given in 1934–1939 (*Vol. II). Edited by James L. Jarrett, Bollingen Series XCIX. Princeton, NJ: Princeton University Press, 1988.

_____. "Synchronicity: An Acausal Connecting Principle." In *Collected Works of C. G. Jung. Vol. 8. Structure and Dynamics of the Psyche*. Translated by R. F. C. Hull. Bollingen Series XX. Princeton, NJ: Princeton University Press, 1960.

von Franz, M. *Archetypal Dimensions of the Psyche*. Boston: Shambhala, 1997.

_____. *Psyche and Matter*. Boston: Shambhala, 1992.

Sophia's Dreaming Body
The Night Sky as Alchemical Mirror

by Monika Wikman

There is a Secret One inside us;
the planets in all the galaxies
pass through Her hands like beads.
That is a string of beads one
should look at with luminous eyes.

—Kabir

Fig. 10.1.
From the feature film, *Avatar*,
directed by James Cameron and
produced by 20th Century Fox, 2009

The Star-Strewn Sky

For us humans throughout time, *universal* is the experience of awe when we look into the night sky. Our little earth from which we gaze, as the indigenous soul sees it, is more than an objectified object in space. To many indigenous Native American people, such as the Iroquois, the earth is sky turtle discovering new substance in the creation matrix to put on its back—*ah, earth!*—to catch *first woman*, falling out of the sky. And onto turtle's back she lands, and first woman rides the earth world as turtle spirit through the cosmos.

The Sufi tradition likewise emphasizes an attitude of inquiry that opens consciousness to the *felt presence* of the divine in and beyond form, simply advising when relating to the natural world and the many other dimensions of existence, "Don't ask *what* or *why*—ask *who.*" This attitude of "I–thou" curiosity helps awaken us to the unique unfolding presence in all things, the felt presence of the macrocosm in the microcosm.

Living in northern New Mexico, where the stars are searingly bright due to such low moisture and nearly nonexistent light pollution, experiencing the night sky continually shocks one into a sense of awe. Going out to feed horses before dawn and after sunset, I am grateful for these moments as the stars seem to come down from the heavens shining brightly on the low horizons right over the horses' backs, and in *this way* I feel myself daily as blessed.

I know as a child this was for me the single greatest wonder: to sleep outside in the oak tree fort and gaze all night from my cozy sleeping bag into the starry void. Through the night while dreaming and waking, I felt the presence of the canopy of stars relating back and forth with me, and somehow the great ache I carried as a child came into some new balance.

Years later I was touched by another woman's childhood love of the stars. In the early 1990s I asked Gret Baumann, Jung's daughter and an astrologer, about her dearest memories of her father. She said unequivocally that what came to mind was being with her father outside at night under the stars around the campfire. These were the moments that impressed themselves into her, and she spent her adult life practicing astrology as a result. This has been true for me too, and I imagine, for many others interested in astronomy, astrology, star myths, and the star body/subtle body mysteries.

We just have to recall the image from the film *Contact* for a perfect portrayal of the poet as the valuable lens through which to take in the mysteries of the night sky and many worlds. Jodie Foster as scientist is rocketing through the wormholes into other dimensions, and as she is shot into the awe of it all, she mutters to herself in a confession of conversion, "They should have sent a poet."

When we look mythopoetically into the names and myths of current night sky discoveries, synchronicities and meaning may arise and open us to the changing god image in the human soul, to the unfolding cosmic myth of our time. Jung, of course, was deeply interested in this phenomenon and explored extensively the mythic meaning in the changing god image as we move through the precession of the equinox into the Aquarian Age.

More recently, Richard Tarnas's book *Cosmos and Psyche*[1] tracks this phenomenon through the discovery of the major planets in our solar system with tremendous research and ingenuity. And Melanie Reinhart's work on Chiron[2] and other asteroids and planetoids, such as her recent work on Orcus, is seminal for depth psychology.[3]

The Gnostic Myth of Sophia: The Divine Feminine Emerges

The recently discovered (and astronomer-named) dwarf planets and planetoids reveal faces of the divine feminine that parallel the Gnostic myth of Sophia that resides at the foundation of Western alchemy.

To drop into this myth, we'll go by way of the backyard garden of some friends of mine in Devon, England. About ten years ago, Julian David and his wife Yasmin hosted a week-long gathering for analyst friends with their creative works. On the opening night, gathering in the exquisite hand-hewn garden, tended completely by Yasmin for decades, the candles were lit, the banquet table set, the central fountain aglow in the moonlight. Introverted Yasmin was nowhere to be found, having grown shy and weary of company. I hoped that her sense of being overwhelmed would subside and I would get a chance to connect with her.

A few hours into the gathering, a little face peeked around a post in the kitchen. Yasmin said, "Monika, *psst*. Be careful of falling into the organic beauty of things!" And then off she went back into the quiet. Even in this brief encounter, I felt profoundly visited by a nature spirit: with her artist's eye and gardener's heart and hands, she had spent her life deeply loving the beauty of the particulars in the natural world. When

Yasmin died years later, she was fittingly buried in a sheet in her own garden among the flowers.

This statement by Yasmin stuck with me and is echoed in the Gnostic myth of Sophia: *"Be careful of falling into the organic beauty of things!"* In the myth, the divine, in creating the manifest world, falls in love with creation. The divine's feminine half, Sophia, looking in on the newly created world of spirit, is so attracted to the world that she leans forward so far she finds herself falling into creation. As she tumbles via love and attraction into the manifest world, she enters all forms, every sentient being. In the world of form, she partly gets trapped in matter. Sophia is simultaneously in her divine spirit form, in perfection, and also in matter, in every cell of creation in the time-space world.

Now importantly, along with Sophia, human consciousness in the time-space world tends to forget its origins and become fixed, limited, encapsulated, or cut off from the flow of the eternal. And so here in the embodied world, Sophia seeks the presence of humans who cultivate the expanding field of awareness that unites her upper and lower selves in a third field, her subtle body.

Salve e coagulatio, separatio e coniunctio (dissolve and coagulate, separate and join, differentiate and unite)—the alchemists say that this paradoxical process is the heart of the great work that grows the third field, a mysterious unifying field of the subtle body between polarities, between personal and impersonal worlds, where healing, vision, wholeness, creative generation, and fresh infusion from and insight into the larger cosmos opens to us.

We can see from the point of view of Gnosticism that the manifest world is the playground for the divine's own awakening, and the field of imagination is where she plays, suffers, heals, creates, and grows her subtle body with the help of humans. The Sufi creation myth sees it this way also: The manifest world is the *Tajalliyat*, the mirror for the divine to find its own face.

So the night sky, with discoveries of new planetoid bodies being named for the divine feminine, in a way shows us particular faces of the divine feminine personified in the imaginal field with us. With the discovery of Eris in 2003,[4] and then with Ceres promoted from asteroid to dwarf planet, children nowadays grow up learning the planetary pattern as including both Eris and Ceres as part of our solar system, with the "largess" of Eris's discovery having also dwarfed Pluto. The Western sky as we know it is changing![5]

140

Sedna, Indigenous Shamanic Goddess of the Inuit

In November of 2003, a new minor planet was identified in the sky circling our sun at the furthest known regions of our solar system and named for an indigenous goddess of the oceans, Sedna, or *Mother of Deep*, as she is called. The astronomers (Brown, Trujillo, and Rabinowitz) who discovered this minor planet named her Sedna. The official astronomical classification for Sedna as a trans-Neptunian object, cloud object, or dwarf planet is still to be determined, with evidence for each held by various astronomers since her discovery. Trekking the farthest edge of the known and unknown of our solar system, its icy body navigates the coldest regions; thus the Inuit goddess of the deep, cold arctic oceans seemed a fitting name to them for this new discovery.

There are many versions in Canada, Greenland, and Alaska of the creation story of Sedna, but they all share the same archetypal pattern and ending. In one version Sedna is dissatisfied with men and so marries a dog. Her father is so angry that he throws her into the sea, and when she tries to climb into his boat, he cuts off her fingers. Her fingers become the walrus, seals, whales, dolphins, and other creatures of the deep. And she becomes a mighty sea goddess who roams the deep arctic oceans; her hair is entangled with the seaweed and the "sins of humanity." Sedna carries the grief of the world in her hair as she swims the depths. Shamans know it is to her they must go when a member of the tribe requires healing, or when food is sought from the ocean world, or when they are in need of direction, energy, and guidance from the spirit world for the well-being of themselves and tribal life. And so, trekking into the ocean worlds in subtle body states the shamans go, knowing to bring with them compassion and a comb. For when they meet up with her, if they offer to comb out the sins of humanity from a few strands of her tangled seaweed hair, she may become appeased and hear their requests.

In some versions she is a rejected orphan who meets the same fate with her hands, which are dismembered by the village people, and she sinks into the sea and experiences the same fate as a sea goddess, *Mother of Deep*.

In the great depths, Sedna takes up residence as a shamanic goddess.

If we descend with compassion for our intertwined plight and bring a comb to untangle a few strands of Sedna's hair tangled with our fateful troubles, we may give an offering to the spirit of the depths. In turn the "mother of the deep" may be appeased and give with both hands for the healing of many worlds.

Cosmologically and psychologically Sedna holds a wounded healer archetypal pattern in the depths of the psyche in which *the divine seeks visitations, or co-participation with humans, in healing and visionary states of consciousness.* This requires a dismemberment sacrifice of our old consciousness so the new can be re-membered in union with the spirit of the depths.

Recently in a Canadian gallery for Inuit stone carvers, I saw images of Sedna in black stone portraying her many forms, including what the Inuit see of her as we meet up with her and comb out the transgressions of humanity from her hair. As the people learn to honor her, meet her, and feel with her, she heals. Her hair is braided and Sedna's mirrored grief becomes sonar ocean songs as she swims the icy depths with melodic resonance emanating love for all creatures. She never loses her capacity to discover new songs in the icy oceanic netherworlds. Her resonant tones of blues and blacks in the unfathomable depths are like no other being, they say.[6]

This indigenous feminine "mother of the deep" portrayed in our night sky changes the pantheon, changes the face of the divine for our current times—a face of the divine swimming in the nethermost regions, an indigenous, shamanic, divine feminine face who holds the dissociative icy depths of the psyche, the cutoff feeling and suffering that, when faced, potentially may lead to healing and the recovery of soul among the human, plant, animal, and archetypal spiritual worlds.

Sedna's presence also strikes to the heart of the importance of the indigenous soul in our times. Westerners in the Americas have the fate of bridging the intellect of the West with the soul of the indigenous *that lives in the land itself.* And so much health for our planet depends upon this bridge.[7]

Awakening to the World Soul

To work our own wounds that intermingle with the greater grief of the world soul links us to the flow of life. There are mysteries inherent here that bring to light the human and archetypal co-created field of healing and realignment, as we give back our healing to the *anima mundi.*

The ecological myth of our time seems to me to be mirrored in Sedna's pattern. To open our eyes to the suffering in the world and to its beauty is often something the psyche just plain insists on during individuation. Sedna feels to me to be part of this awakening to the world soul. Felt experiences of inclusivity, subtle body states of healing and visioning, and a vibrant healing song at the bottom of creation are her gifts.

I had a dream four years ago that illuminates this awakening on the web of creation to the felt experience of the world soul. In this dream,

> I was standing with the inner teacher who said to me, "I am here seeking to put super glue in your eyes." And as I contemplated what that might mean, and how strange it seemed, I agreed and said, "Well, ok." The teacher put glue into my right eye and my left and then showed me that one eye was for the inner world and was oriented inward to that, which seemed normal to me in the dream. What was a huge surprise is that one eye with this super glue was oriented to the outer world of forms. The teacher told me: "One eye will be kept to the inner world and one to the outer. You are to identify with neither, and with the one to the outer, you are to witness both the beauty and the suffering with their distinct particular manifestations that are in the world."

Since that time I have literally had my eyes opened to the revelation of the beauty and suffering of the divine in the natural world. There is a spirit of the in-between, of the third world, accompanying this eye-opening experience. Von Franz found that the individuated person lives in a state of active imagination in which outer and inner reality have become one. Here the intensity of the ego decreases and the wisdom of the collective unconscious flows through.[8] Jeffrey Raff likewise states that the conscious ego, which is united with the manifest self, experiences life from a central position that is based in the imaginative worlds and that neither identifies with the outer life events or with inner archetypal states. The ego's union with the self would not simply be expressed in a state of awareness, but in an ongoing creative and imaginative experience.[9]

This vision born of the third world is actually ages old. As Rumi saw it, "… and though we seem to be sleeping, there is an inner wakefulness that directs the dream and that will eventually startle us back to the truth of who we are."[10] The age-old alchemical myth is turning in our times toward current-day mysteries. What *is* this new myth that requires our eyes to open in ever-new ways and pushes now for us to live more and more awake in the psychophysical unitary reality, and more and more capable to feel the soul of the world?

Something in the heart of creation in our post-postmodern world loves to reveal itself to us, to have us co-participate with it and find inclusivity and mutuality with all sentient beings.

Recently I had the good fortune of teaching with Andrew Harvey, and something he said stuck with me. He asked participants to look at what, in relationship to the world, breaks their hearts, and then to let it—the heartbreak—break their hearts open to the flow of love in the psyche, in the world. I carry that as a gem, a prayer bead now, and it feels linked to the medicine of Sedna and to connecting to the realms of the deep that know archetypal grief. We are all aware one can drown in these depths, but when the spirit of the deep and our dreams assist us, we also may find another way so that the deeper music informs and enriches our human lives.

Feeling the presence of Sedna within and without, and using the eyes of the imaginable, I turn toward something in the world soul that breaks my heart, the life of our literal oceans.

So much changes during a lifetime. My grandmother remembered horse-drawn carriages that carried the milk to her door. What will we say at the end of our lives as we look back at what came into our manifest world? In a recent podcast interview on the *anima mundi*, I brought this topic up.[11] I imagine myself looking back and saying to the next generations: "I remember when we had this archaic toxic material called *plastic*, and we used it in everything for convenience without thinking! We finally realized there was no 'away' to throw plastic to, and our earth cannot take it back. We polluted our oceans with plastic, killing animal, plant, mammal, bird, and plankton, without thought or feeling. This dissociative state collectively was mirrored in our oceans. At one time we even had two huge vortexes in the oceans the size of Texas, and plastic soup so pervasive that sea animals could not avoid it and died horrendous deaths in numbers too large to calculate."

During the times we are currently in, remarkable people rise up in the face of the impossible collective blind zeitgeist and address this collective possession. One filmmaker, Chris Jordan, stands out with his film on the animals of the oceans. He opens our eyes to their plight.[12] Patrick Furlotti is another example of creative, youthful energy that is unable to turn a blind eye to this collective dissociative psychosis. His aim with his foundation (Global Mana), his research, and his films is to help catalyze humans to awaken their ability to *feel* and *act on behalf* of the health of our oceans. Patrick is working toward finding solutions to clean up the vortex of plastic garbage in the South Pacific, a problem that the collective sees as too big to solve. One of these acts in the face of this collective problem is an enormous specialized ship set to venture out into these vortexes to suck up plastic and take it ashore, where it can be recycled.

He also brings awareness of the dangers of plastics for all living beings by swimming long ocean distances, from island to island, through these polluted waters to help illuminate the problem.[13]

Plastic is a symbol, of course. Overly processed petroleum leads to a substance the earth cannot take back, which can be seen to represent false self-attitudes and substitute gods that need to be dealt with so that the religious attitude of life lived close to the soul may grow instead.[14]

While writing this essay, my own unconscious responded powerfully and with humor. I had just been to see the film *Lincoln*, with its portrayal of the legislated eradication of slavery. In my dream,

> I am talking about what we will see when we look back over our lives, developments of human beings able to feel and act for the world soul. And as I am speaking, the voice of a wisdom figure beside me on my right touches my arm and says, "Yes, remember there was a time when blacks could not vote, and there was a time when women could not vote! And there was even a time when animals could not vote!" And with that the scene opened to a round table where the animal spirits each took their seats. They had out their voting ballots, and each was actively voting with its fins, paws, hooves, etc. One of the animals there, a female dolphin, looked at me as she voted and gave me a smile that radiated happiness and some spirit of recognition between her and me.

I awoke with a laugh. Psyche has such a sense of humor amidst these processes of awakening. "Remember a time when animals couldn't vote!" Of course, this is true on an inner level; animals as instinctual allies in the human psyche do vote within us at every turn for the shape of the life to be lived, if we will only listen and take their votes into account. And when we tune in to the voices of the outer-world sea creatures, clearly we know they do vote "no" for toxic plastic that decimates their worlds and lives. There can be dream and vision experiences, too, of seeing how decimated species and peoples go on to live in wholeness in the realms of the psychoid. These dreams evoke a felt sense of the larger cosmos and bring us back to daily life with open eyes and hearts more capable of love for this world, among the many realms of existence.

New Unities with the Divine Born from Darkness

Years ago I experienced an important crisis and eventual healing during a divorce process that involved the presence of one of these dark goddesses, or "mothers of the deep." I was just coming to terms with the fact that my long marriage was over. A descent into the unconscious made itself known in the grief, and down I went, step by step, as the sacrifice was demanded of the life and identity I had formed. I suddenly became very ill, and I nearly died. The ordeal turned out to be an incarnational choice point at the crossroads between life and death.

After weeks of recovery, when I finally returned home that first night, I recall lying alone in bed feeling immense vulnerability—*how precarious my tiny little human life truly is*. I lay shivering under the covers with this felt realization. Then suddenly in the dark alone, I began to feel like I was in a psychic free-fall into greater darkness. It took my breath away. I heard clearly that I was to go with it, and I did. Free-falling into the great blackness I went. I fell and fell, and finally the darkness itself caught and held me.

The darkness became a Presence, a feminine Presence that was Blackness. As she held me, the "me" disappeared, dissolved. She had no face, and neither did I. I could feel my essence become one with Her Presence of blackness. It was an utter death, and in the surrender there was cool, calm, abject peace with all that is so and not so, and with living or dying. I then sensed Her face emerging in the blackness, some sense of Her eyes and Her compassion emerging into features in and of the blackness. Her face became my face in this utter darkness. And my face was somehow both mine and Hers. With this moment of re-creation something deep, deep down among the many worlds sighed a sigh of compassion and release. And with this spirit of love I was released back into my bed, into the time-space world, and I was changed, utterly.

A few months later, my friend Robin van Löben Sels introduced me to the myth and image of Aditi. Aditi is a Vedic goddess whose name means *free, unbound*. She is the boundless heaven compared with the finite earth. She is the primeval generator of all that emanates, the eternal space of boundless whole, an unfathomable depth signifying the veil over the unknown. She is the mother and father of all gods, as the *Rig Veda*, a collection of ancient Vedic hymns, describes her. Aditi is implored frequently for blessing children and cattle, for protection and *forgiveness*.

There are images of Aditi as the throne of darkness. Supplicants or initiates approach icons of her throne of blackness, and upon it there is a veil. If one pulls back the veil and looks into her dark body, a mirror is there, and she may or may not show you your new face from her dark mirror. Her mystery is at the heart of the alchemical mysteries of the *nigredo*, the black alchemy, in which alchemists exclaimed, "If your stone goes black, rejoice, for this is the beginning of the work." The spirits of the *nigredo* that come to meet us during times of great change, individually and collectively, appear with grace in the alchemical mirror of the night sky, within and without, with new star nurseries birthing. These new unities born from the great void, as Jung states, represent "the metamorphosis of the gods" and of our humanity.[15]

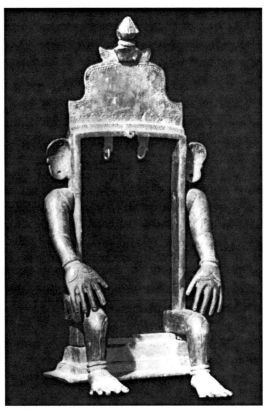

Figure 10.2. Aditi, Hindu goddess of the void, statuette, iron, 19th century.
From *The Tantric Way*, p. 124. Used with Permission of Thames and Hudson.

I hope you, dear reader, recognize your own story/Aditi's story in this offering.

Notes

1   Richard Tarnas, *Cosmos and Psyche: Intimations of a New World View*.

2   Melanie Reinhart, *Chiron and the Healing Journey*.

3   Melanie Reinhart, *Orcus, Companion of Pluto*.

4   Named for the goddess of strife and discord (Eris is excluded by Zeus from a wedding feast because she is "unpleasant"; in retaliation she throws in her nasty apple to the wedding, which brings out the worst in everyone and eventually leads to the Trojan War), she seems to me to be a face of the feminine inside postmodernism.

5   New children's books were quickly published to help children learn the new planetary pattern, and *National Geographic* children's books had a contest for a new verse that would help children remember the planetary pattern. Maryn Smith, age 11, from Montana, came up with this: "My Very Exiting Magic Carpet Just Sailed Under Nine Palace Elephants" (Mercury, Venus, Earth, Mars, Ceres, Jupiter, Saturn, Uranus, Neptune, Pluto, Eris).

6   Interview in 2011 with an Inuit stone carver, Ikirnujik.

7   I recall Jung addressing this in his writing but have not relocated the exact cite since.

8   Marie-Louise von Franz, *Alchemical Active Imagination*, 147–148.

9   Jeffrey Raff, *Jung and the Alchemical Imagination*, 62.

10 Coleman Barks, *The Essential Rumi*, 113.

11 http://www.shrinkrapradio.com/2012/11/09/325-reflections-on-the-animus-mundi-with-jungian-analyst-monika-wikman-phd.

12 For Chris Jordan's film, see http://www.midwayfilm.com.

13 See Patrick Furlotti's foundation (http://www.globalmanafoundation.com/index.php) and his activist efforts on YouTube (http://www.youtube.com/watch?v=H1dTE_rQi Gs&list=UUADUyAOC2DcJKV05pVgZGYQ).

14 See my book *Pregnant Darkness: Alchemy and the Rebirth of Consciousness*, 49 and 197. Also, see Hallie Iglehart-Austin's innovative non-profit work on behalf of the oceans, on the web at http://www.alloneocean.org.

15 C. G. Jung, *The Undiscovered Self: The Problem of the Individual in Modern Society*, 110.

References

Barks, C. *The Essential Rumi.* New York: HarperOne, 2005.

Furlotti, P. *Global Mana Foundation and ocean life activist efforts.* Accessed January 20, 2013, from http://www.globalmanafoundation.com/index.php and http://www.youtube.com/watch?v=H1dTE_rQiGs&list=UUADUyAOC2DcJKV05pVgZGYQ.

Iglehart-Austin, H. *Heart of the Goddess.* Berkeley, California: Wingbow Press, 1991.

Jordan, C. *Midway: Message from the Gyre.* Retrieved January 20, 2013, from http://www.midwayfilm.com.

Jung, C. *Aion: Researches into the Phenomenology of the Self. Vol. 9.ii. Collected Works of C. G. Jung.* Translated by R. F. C. Hull. Bollingen Series XX. Princeton, NJ: Princeton University Press, 1979.

_____. *Memories, Dreams, Reflections.* Edited by Aniela Jaffé. New York: Random House, 1965.

_____. *The Undiscovered Self: The Problem of the Individual in Modern Society.* New York: Signet, 2006.

_____. *The Red Book.* New York: Norton, 2009.

Mookerjee, A. and Khanna, M. *The Tantric Way.* London, England: Thames and Hudson, 2003.

Raff, J. *Jung and the Alchemical Imagination.* York Beach, ME: Nicolas Hays, 2000.

Reinhart, M. *Chiron and the Healing Journey.* London: Starwalker Press, 2010.

_____. *Orcus, Companion of Pluto.* Accessed January 20, 2013, from http://www.melaniereinhart.com/melanie/Orcus_000.htm.

Tarnas, R. *Cosmos and Psyche: Intimations of a New World View.* New York: Viking Press, 2006.

Wikman, M. *Pregnant Darkness: Alchemy and the Rebirth of Consciousness.* York Beach, ME: Nicolas Hays, 2005.

_____. *Anima Mundi.* Retrieved January 20, 2013, from http://www.shrinkrapradio.com/2012/11/09/325-reflections-on-the-animus-mundi-with-jungian-analyst-monika-wikman-phd/.

von Franz, M. *Alchemical Active Imagination.* Boston: Shambhala, 1997.

The Dream Always Follows the Mouth
Jewish Approaches to Dreaming

by Henry Abramovitch

Introduction

In this chapter, I provide a brief overview of Jewish attitudes to dreaming. I begin by briefly discussing Biblical dreams and go on to present a Rabbinic view of dreams and their interpretation. I conclude by presenting details of a contemporary Israeli dream pilgrimage tradition.

> When we shut our eyes, from all parts of the body energy travels to the heart and this is like animals going to Noah's ark.... The waters rise and the ark begins to float. Then the dove leaves and finds its ways to visions and dreams.... One should tell dreams only to one who loves the dreamer.
>
> —*The Zohar, The Book of Splendor*

Biblical Dreams

Jewish tradition is strongly ambivalent toward dreams.[1] On the one hand, the rationalists were extremely suspicious of dreams, claiming that only a sixtieth part of dreams was prophecy and that they never fully came true. They claimed that dreams are always combinations of truth and illusion, and the prophet Zechariah (10:2) even claimed that dreams are simply lies. On the other hand, dreams and dream interpretation played an enormous role in the lives of many figures in the bible: Abraham, Jacob, Joseph, Solomon, Ezekiel, and Daniel all have life-changing dreams. Numbers 12:6 clearly indicates that God reveals himself through dreams: "I make-myself-known, in a dream I speak with him."[2] Some rabbis believed that everything that occurs is first revealed through dreams.

The Old Testament contains only twelve dreams, yet each one is of exceptional significance.[3] Some dreams speak for themselves and require no interpretation, such as Jacob's ladder dream. Other "royal dreams" are deeply disturbing and defy standard attempts at dream interpretation. Still other dreams are in a symbolic form, but their meanings are immediately clear to the dreamer and require no interpretation, as in the case of Joseph's own dreams of sheaves and stars all bowing down to him, which his entire family understands as his grandiose will to power. Dialogue between the dreamer and the divine is a key feature of many Biblical dreams.

Biblical dreams can be understood in terms of Jung's distinction between *personal* dreams and *big* dreams. Personal or little dreams deal with the dreamer's own psychological issues, whereas big dreams come from a deeper level and have a collective significance.[4] Joseph's dreams are a dramatic instance of how what seem at first to be purely personal dreams are understood only much later as big dreams, revealing how his fate is to save his family and nation.

The dreams of Pharaoh and Nebuchadnezzar[5] that defied the understanding of the court magicians are classic types of big dreams that affect not only the royal dreamer but also his (or her) entire kingdom. In contrast, the absence of dreams may be equally significant. When, on the eve of a decisive battle, King Saul[6] realizes that he has had no dream, he knows his cause is lost.

Biblical dreams, although few in number, reveal how profound the impact of a big dream can be and how important it is to find the correct interpretation. Not surprisingly, over the ages Jews became famous dream interpreters.

Dream Question Ritual—Hebrew: "She'elat Halom"

There is another traditional dream practice, mentioned in the Bible[7] and in the Talmud[8] and still practiced today, called the *dream question*.[9] It is a form of dream incubation whereby a person attains a wonderful prophetic-like state while dreaming and receives a divinely inspired answer to a question meditated on before falling sleep. In Jungian terms, we might say that the idea was to activate the Self, which would then provide a symbolic response to the concerns of the ego.

As in so much in Judaism, there is no standard accepted way of initiating a dream question. The early medieval master Hai Gaon notes one method for attaining a dream question state that involves fasting, purification, "mystical weeping," and meditation on a text such as Exodus 14:19-21, Ezekiel 1:1, or Deuteronomy 29:2, each verse of which contains 72 consonants—alluding to a mystical series of Hebrew letters said to represent the true name of God. Before falling asleep, one may also say the following:

> Master of Dreams, before I enter your world of healing and visions, I place myself in your hands. I need your guidance. Help me find my path. May this question in my dream be answered."[10]

The great Kabbalist, Haim Vital, proposed a visualization reminiscent of Jungian active imagination or even Jung's writings in *The Red Book:*

> Visualize that above the firmament, there is a very great white curtain, upon which the Tetragrammaton [four-letter divine name] is inscribed in [color] white as snow, in Assyrian writing in a certain color … and the great letters are inscribed there, each one large as a mountain or a hill. And you should imagine in your thought that you ask your question from those combinations of letters written there, and they will answer your question, or they will dwell their spirit in your mouth, or you will be drowsy and they will answer you, like in a dream.[11]

The dream question might be asked in the cemetery at the grave of a parent or spiritual teacher, or at home, after purifying one's home, especially of any smells. In some other cases, friends would promise to appear after death and give a full account of life after death. Rabbis would ask religious, legal, or mystical questions of long-dead scholars, and sometimes these dreams would resolve a difficult controversy. It is as if we could ask Jung or Marie-Louise von Franz to appear in a dream and help us understand some difficult psychological dilemma.

The Talmud

In the next section I discuss the most important rabbinic dream anthology, which contains by far the most concentrated narratives about dreaming that appear in the Talmud. Literally meaning "instruction" or "learning," the Talmud is the most important text in Judaism, after the Bible. It consists of rabbinic discussions on Jewish law, ethics, philosophy, customs, history, and much more. The rabbinic dream text is in the tractate dealing with "Blessings" and follows a section dealing with what to say upon seeing a place where a miracle has occurred, implicitly placing dreaming in that context of the miraculous. The rabbinic dream anthology follows a saying: "He gives wisdom to those who have wisdom."[12]

Rabbinic Dream Book: Babylonian Talmud, Berakhot 55a–57b

The first and most basic principle is stated at the outset: "R. Hisda also said: A dream that is not interpreted is like a letter that is not read (or like a decree not proclaimed)."[13] For Rabbi Hisda, dreams are coded messages that require interpretation. They speak in what Erich Fromm called "the forgotten language."[14] This symbolic view echoes the Jungian view that dreams are messages from the Self to the ego, from the unconscious to the conscious mind. Not trying to understand a dream can be compared to receiving an urgent telegram but not bothering to open it.

All cultures make a distinction between good dreams and bad dreams.[15] Good dreams must be carefully kept until they are fulfilled. Bad dreams must be told to allow their karma to be dispersed. Judaism has a formal ritual of "making a bad dream better," called *hatavat chalom*. Here is the Talmudic source:

> If one has a dream which makes him sad he should go and have it interpreted in the presence of three. He should have it interpreted! Has not R. Hisda said: A dream which is not interpreted is like a letter which is not read?— Say rather then, he should have it turned into good in the presence of three. Let him bring three and say to them: I have seen a good dream; and they should say to him, Good it is and good may it be. May the All-Merciful turn it to good....[16]

This ritual is still practiced today. A person with a bad dream will assemble three caring friends and recite prayers asking for the bad dream to be turned round for the good. For rabbis, a bad dream was understood as an evil decree from heaven. To overturn the decree, a person is urged to pray, to give charity, since "charity saves from death,"[17] and to fast. Particularly frightening dreams—for example, dreaming of one's teeth falling out, of one's house collapsing, or of the concluding prayer of the Day of Atonement—allowed the dreamer to fast even on the holy Sabbath.

Recovering Lost Dreams

Most of us as dreamers have the experience of waking from a dream only to have it slip through our mental fingertips. The more we try to recover the dream, the more it fades from view, back into the ocean of sleep. On the other hand, most people have had the experience of suddenly remembering a dream in the middle of the day. This experience suggests that dreams are registered somewhere in an inaccessible dream space until they become magically de-repressed. Is it possible to recover lost dreams? Some rabbis claimed that it was possible to recover lost dreams at the time of the priestly blessing. Here is the text:

> If one has seen a dream and does not remember what he saw, let him stand before the priests at the time when they spread out their hands, and say as follows: "Sovereign of the Universe, I am Thine and my dreams are Thine. I have dreamt a dream and I do not know what it is. Whether I have dreamt about myself or my companions have dreamt about me, or I have dreamt about others, if they are good dreams, confirm them and reinforce them like the dreams of Joseph, and if they require a remedy, heal them, as the waters of Marah were healed by Moses…[18]

The priestly blessing, "May the Lord bless you and keep you …" is the oldest part of the Hebrew prayer ritual. The priests (*cohen*) hold their prayer shawls (*talis*) aloft, with fingers separated like a cloven hoof so that they are covered, hidden by the prayer shawl. Each priest repeats the blessing, word by word, in an ancient chant led by the prayer leader. Since it is a moment of transmission of the divine blessings, traditionally, one is forbidden from looking directly at the priests while they are giving the blessing, when the divine channels are most open. The rabbis understood that at this special moment, dreams might resurface from the ocean of the unconscious.

The need to stay in touch with the unconscious and the Self is highlighted by another saying:

> R. Ze'ira said: "If a man goes seven days without a dream he is called evil, since it says, He shall abide satisfied, he shall not be visited by evil?— Read not *sabe'a* [satisfied] but *sheba* [seven]." What he means is this: He sees, but he does not remember what he has seen.[19]

This interpretation is based on word play so beloved by dream interpreters from ancient Egypt to Freud. In Hebrew, texts are usually written without vowels, only with consonants, and therefore *sabe'a* (satisfied) and *sheva* (seven) would be written in the same way. But in a more symbolic vein, losing touch with our dreams equals losing touch with ourselves. Once we are de-centered, we are prone to psychic possession—and that is, according to Jung, the root of evil.

The rabbis, significantly, were post-modern in the sense that they could happily hold diverse interpretations simultaneously, and this was especially true of dreams. Consider this delightful story:

> R. Bana'ah: There were twenty-four interpreters of dreams in Jerusalem. Once I dreamt a dream and I went round to all of them and they all gave different interpretations, and all were fulfilled, thus confirming that which is said: All dreams follow the mouth.[20]

This last line, "All dreams follow the mouth," is the most famous line in the entire dream book. The *mouth* refers to the spoken interpretation, which determines the significance of the dream, and not the dream itself. This view is relational in that the dream experience is situated within the context of a relationship in which the interpretation takes place.

In another story, we see how dangerous it is when the dream follows the mouth of a trainee interpreter: One famous dream interpreter was away and left his trainees in charge. A woman appeared and told her dream, and the fledgling interpreters said that her husband would die. When the dream master returned, he held his supervision session, and the trainees presented the "case" and their interpretation. When they finished, he cried out, "Oh no! You have killed a man! *For the dream follows the mouth*" (i.e., the mouth of the interpreter).

This story suggests that a dream and its interpretation interact in such a way that they cannot be separated. A good interpretation generates a good reality; a bad interpretation, a negative one. Just as when we are proud of our children, they do us proud, and when we are critically waiting for them to disappoint us, they are sure to start acting out.

The relational and countertransferential aspects of dream interpretation are poignantly revealed in the next narrative: "Bar Hedya was an interpreter of dreams. To one who paid him he used to give a favorable interpretation and to one who did not pay him he gave an unfavorable interpretation."[21]

In my clinical practice, I use a sliding fee scale. The well-to-do pay my full fee and others according to their means; it has happened that I have treated people for free, doing what a colleague called "God's work." I doubt whether the actual fee (or its absence) has a direct effect on my interpretation of dreams, but if we think of "payment" in more symbolic terms of transference and countertransference, then I suspect there is an effect. A delightful patient may receive delightful, even overly optimistic interpretations, whereas with a difficult, borderline patient, the analyst might unconsciously take revenge by giving harsh interpretations.[22] But, of course, it is true that the same dream may have different meanings to different people. Artemidorus,[23] the great Greek dream master, claimed that if a poor man dreams that he is eating whole wheat bread, it is a good sign since this is his usual fare, but for a rich man, it is a bad sign, indicating a lowering in the world.

Another rabbi, Johanan, provides guidelines for progressive dreams that deal with future possibilities and suggests that there are certain internal criteria that may help:

> R. Johanan also said: Three kinds of dream are fulfilled: an early morning dream, a dream which a friend has about one, and a dream which is interpreted in the midst of a dream. Some add also, a dream that is repeated, as it says, and for that the dream was doubled unto Pharaoh twice.[24]

Early morning dreams are linked with rapid eye movement (REM) sleep, which is typically associated with dreaming. The dream of a friend is presumably the creative unconscious intuition coming into play: Imagine meeting your dearest friend and hearing the most inspiring dream from him or her about you. Repeating dreams, however, would be understood very differently in modern Jungian terms from the way Rabbi Johanan understands them. Recurring dreams are typical of messages from the unconscious that have not been received and so are resent again and again until the message gets through. Repeating dreams are the urgent telegrams of the dream world.

Erotic Dreams

Another extraordinary series of commentaries concerns how the rabbis understood erotic dreams. Seemingly banal dreams of olives, pigeons, or eyes suggested illicit sexuality, whereas explicitly erotic, even incestuous, dreams were considered as indicative of the individuation process. Here are some examples: "A certain man said to R. Ishmael: I saw myself [in a dream] pouring oil on olives. He replied: [This man] has outraged his mother."[25]

To understand how Rabbi Ishmael concluded that incest had taken place, one must understand the symbolism in the dream. Olive oil is derived from olives, so olives can be said to be the "mother" of olive oil. Pouring olive oil on olives is a returning to the source and so reveals the hidden maternal incest. Another example: "He said to him: I dreamt that my eyes were kissing one another. He replied: [This man] has outraged his sister."[26] This dream uses a genealogical metaphor: the two eyes are on the same level in the human face and so can be compared to a brother and sister. The symbolism of the kiss, which is doing something impossible, further hints at the forbidden act of incest.

Few dreams for a man can be more frightening than that of actually having sex with his mother, with all its attendant psychotic Oedipal guilt and terrifying fears of engulfment by the Great Mother. But the rabbis, using their "mouths," found ways to turn incest into insight, as in the examples that follow:

> If one dreams that he has intercourse with his mother, he may expect to obtain understanding, since it says, Yea, thou wilt call understanding "mother." (Proverbs 2:3) ... If one dreams he has had intercourse with his sister, he may expect to obtain wisdom, since it says, Say to wisdom, thou art my sister. (Proverbs 7:4) If one dreams he has intercourse with a married woman, he can be confident that he is destined for the future world, provided, that is, that he does not know her and did not think of her in the evening.[27]

These dreams are surprisingly Jungian. Jung taught that sexuality in dreams may be symbolic of an inner marriage of the psyche with itself. Rabbis understood these erotic dreams with mother, sister, or married woman in similar fashion, turning incest to insight, using the principle that "the interpretation follows the mouth." Note how the Talmud distinguishes between an archetypal dream image of an unknown married woman as part of a spiritual inner marriage with an ideal anima, as opposed to a personal dream of lust and sexual arousal. In a similar context, the Talmud also states: "If one sees Ishmael in a dream, his prayer will be heard. And it must be Ishmael, the son of Abraham, but not an ordinary Arab."[28] In Hebrew *Ishmael* means "He will be heard by God" or "God will hear him."

We have reviewed some key features of rabbinic approaches to dreaming:

- Dreams are messages that must be interpreted.
- Interpretation follows the mouth.

- Lost dreams can be recovered.
- Association/amplification to Biblical passages provides the key.
- It is possible to turn bad or incestuous dreams into indicators of wisdom, as the soul connecting deeply with itself.

Now I want to turn to a modern Israeli dream pilgrimage tradition.

The Dream Pilgrimage of Rabbi Shimon Bar Yochai

Readers may be familiar with the incubational pilgrimage tradition of the temples of Asclepius,[29] of which Epidaurus was perhaps the most famous. Individuals would make a pilgrimage, speak to the priests, undergo a purification ritual, change their clothes, and then prepare to sleep in the *temenos* of the temple, in the hope that the god would appear. If the god appeared in traditional attire, then the dream was true; if not, then it was false. We have thousands of inscriptions testifying that, in many cases, healing would result from these dreams; the unhealed pilgrims might remain in the temple until they died, making it the world's earliest hospice.

What is less known is that comparable pilgrimage centers exist at Mount Meron, in Galilee, at the tomb of the *tzaddik* or holy man Rabbi Shimon Bar Yochai.

Lag BaOmer, on the thirty-third day following Passover, is the death anniversary of Rabbi Shimon Bar Yochai. It is a day of spiritual celebration. The death anniversary of a holy man is called a *hillulah* or mystical marriage of the soul of the *tzaddik* with the godhead. This *hillulah* has a special place in Jung's own life because, following his serious heart attack, Jung described an amazing series of visions or "near-death experiences":

> … an old Jewish woman … was preparing ritual kosher dishes for me. When I looked at her, she seemed to have a blue halo around her head. I myself was, so it seemed, in the Pardes Rimmonim, the garden of pomegranates, and the wedding of Tifereth with Malchuth was taking place. Or else I was Rabbi Simon ben Jochai, whose wedding in the afterlife was being celebrated. It was the mystic marriage as it appears in the Cabbalistic tradition…. It is impossible to convey the beauty and intensity of emotions during those visions. They were the most tremendous things I have ever experienced. And what a contrast the day was: I was tormented and on edge; everything irritated me; everything was too material, too crude and clumsy, terribly limited both

spatially and spiritually…. After the illness a fruitful period of work began for me. A good many of my principal works were written only then…. Something else, too, came to me from my illness … acceptance of my own nature, as I happen to be.[30]

Hillulah is celebrated throughout the Jewish world, but the main celebration is at Meron, the burial place of Rabbi Shimon and his son Elazar, where hundreds of thousands of Jews gather to light torches and sing and dance in honor of the *tzaddik*. In Hebrew the term *tzaddik* derives from the word for "justice," so that *tzaddik* can mean "a just man." But a *tzaddik* is able to act as a mediator or intercessor between heaven and earth, and in that sense he is a holy man with extraordinary powers beyond those of "a just man." In a different sense, a *tzaddik* is someone who is aligned on the ego-Self axis and is perhaps the prime symbol of the Self.

In the dream pilgrimage tradition, people come to sleep in the tomb or on the surrounding hillside with the hope that they will be favored by a dream. One memorable dream we collected was told by an elderly woman, living alone, often depressed and isolated, with no one on whom to rely.[31] She went to sleep and dreamed:

> I was in my bed when an elderly man in traditional Moroccan Jewish dress entered my room. He spoke to me and cried out, "Arise, Arise!" Suddenly, I felt energized. He gave me his hand and raised me up. I got up and he gave me mint leaves [a potent symbol of health and healing]. Then I turned to him and asked: "But who are you?" He said: "Don't you recognize me, my daughter?" "No, who are you?" "I am Rabbi Shimon Bar Yochai! You came to me, now I come to you."

The traditional dress lends authenticity to the dream and to the *tzaddik*, as it did in pilgrim dreams in the temples of Asclepius. There is also a literal physical raising up of the woman from the horizontal to the vertical and so out of her depression. Then there is the dramatic moment of unmasking or revelation, "Don't you recognize me?" The figure of the tzaddik may be identified with the Self, who radiates wholesome healing energy and power. Note that unlike R. Hisda's maxim, but similar to some Biblical dreams, this dream does not require interpretation. It speaks for itself. The dream itself is the healing, and so it reflects James Hillman's notion of staying with the image rather than the interpretation.[32]

This healing dream reveals the reciprocal nature of the relationship between *tzaddik* and devotee based on mutual responsibility and exchange. This mutuality is revealed in another rather amazing dream series. When most of the Moroccan Jewish community made *aliya* and came to Israel, they had to leave behind their many tombs of holy men. Migration, however successful in the host country, always involves cultural losses. One day, a simple forester in Safed had a dream in which one of these saints appeared to say that he was lonely in Morocco—no one visited his tomb, no one celebrated his *hillulah*. Later, in another dream, this *tzaddik* declared his intention of coming to Israel, and in a series of subsequent dreams makes the journey and declares to the surprised man and his wife that their bedroom will be his place in Israel. Under directions from the dream saint, the dreams were publicized among the community, and soon thousands of people were coming to the bedroom to commune with the *tzaddik*, pray, take water and oil, and receive blessings.

Another fascinating dream recalls the discussion concerning erotic dreams in the Talmud. A young woman told this dream, accompanied by her mother and young son near the tomb of the *tzaddik*. The woman began,

> I had great difficulty getting pregnant. Nothing seemed to work. Then one day, I had a dream. In the dream, my neighbor comes to my door and enters my apartment and stays.

There was the suggestion of a sexual encounter but nothing explicit. The woman continued,

> When I wake, I keep thinking about the dream and soon after, discover that I have fallen pregnant. Because you see, the neighbor, his name was Shimon. When the child was born, we called him Shimon, for the *tzaddik*, and here he is. Say hello, Shimon!

A religiously observant woman would never normally allow herself to be alone with a neighbor. Here, too, we can see how the interpretation follows the mouth by turning the dream of an illicit sexual encounter into a creative meeting with a holy man. In this "naming dream" we can see that the holy man has taken the guise of his namesake. In a symbolic way, he has allowed new animus energy to enter into the woman's house and something new to be created.

The beauty of this pilgrimage tradition is that the *tzaddik* is always available. He never goes on vacation. But he can be demanding. A woman thought not to come to the *hillulah* one year and then dreamed an ominous dream in which she was at the *hillulah*. She understood this dream not as wish fulfillment but as a warning dream from the *tzaddik* that something bad would happen to her if she did not attend, and the next morning she signed up to come.

Let me end on a more personal note of how a dream set me off on my own pilgrimage. When I applied to the Israel Association of Analytical Psychology to train as a Jungian analyst, I was searching to know if this was the right decision for me. Suddenly I had second thoughts. I wondered whether I really wanted to spend so much time, energy, and money in this enterprise. Then I had this dream: I am wondering through a medieval European city, through narrow alleyways and along high walls. I walk up some steps and come to a heavy wooden door. I go up to the door and knock. The door opens. Jung himself opens the door and invites me in. We are standing in the hallway that is also a little museum, with beautiful artifacts revealed behind sliding glass doors. Jung slides open one of the panels and gives me a beautiful object. When I awoke, I knew I had to do the training.[33]

Notes

1   There is no good introduction to Jewish dream interpretation, but probably the best available in English is Joel Covitz, *Visions of the Night: A Study of Jewish Dream Interpretation*.

2   Everett Fox, *The Five Books of Moses: A New Translation with Introductions, Commentary, and Notes*, is used as the source for all quotations from the five books of Moses.

3   For an excellent overview, see Erel Shalit, "Dreams in the Old Testament," in D. Leeming, K. Madden, & S. Marlan (Eds.), *Encyclopedia of Psychology and Religion*, Vol. 1, 251–253.

4   C. G. Jung, *CW 8,* par. 555 and par. 558.

5   Jung uses a drawing of the dream of Nebuchadnezzar as his frontispiece in Volume 8 of *The Collected Works of C. G. Jung* and discusses it in par. 559.

6   I Samuel 28:15.

7   I Samuel 28:6.

8   *Baba Metzia* 107b.

9   In Hebrew, *She'elat Halom*.

10   Based on V. L. Ochs & E. Ochs, *The Jewish Dream Book*.

11   Haim Vital, *Ketavim Hadashim l'Rabbenu Hayyim Vital*, 7.

12   Berakhot 55a. All quotations from the Talmud are from Maurice Simon, *Babylonian Talmud*, Tractate Berakhot ("Blessings"), 55a–57b. It can be accessed online at http://www.come-and-hear.com/berakoth/index.html or http://halakhah.com/berakoth/berakoth_55.html.

13   Berakhot 55a.

14   Erich Fromm, *The Forgotten Language: An Introduction to the Understanding of Dreams, Fairy Tales, and Myths*.

15   For more on this distinction, see Henry Abramovitch, "'Good Death' and 'Bad Death': Therapeutic Implications of Cultural Conceptions of Death and Bereavement" in *Traumatic and Nontraumatic Loss and Bereavement,* Ch. 10, 255–272.

16   Berakhot 55b.

17   Proverbs 10:2.

18   Berakhot 55b.

19   Berakhot 55b.

20   Berakhot 55b.

21   Berakhot 56a.

22   The best Jungian discussion of the impact of the fee on the therapist-patient relationship is by Mario Jacoby, *The Analytical Encounter: Transference and Human Relationship*.

23   Artemidoris, *Oneirocritica: Interpretation of Dreams*.

24   Berakhot 55b.

25   Berakhot 56b.

26   Berakhot 56b.

27   Berakhot 57a.

28   Berakhot 56b.

29   The classic Jungian treatment is C. A. Meier, *Healing Dream and Ritual*.

30   C. G. Jung, *Memories, Dreams, Reflections*, 294–297.

31   For more on the cultural context of these "visitational dreams," see Yoram Bilu and Henry Abramovitch, "In Search of the *Saddiq*: Visitational Dreams among Moroccan Jews in Israel," *Psychiatry 48*, 1985, 83–92; and "Visitational Dreams and Naming Practices among Moroccan Jews," *Jewish Journal of Sociology* 28(1), 1985, 13–21.

32   James Hillman, *The Dream and the Underworld*.

33   For a more detailed account of my pathway to becoming a Jungian analyst, see Henry Abramovitch "Into the Marginal Zone" in *Marked by Fire: Stories of the Jungian Way*.

References

Abramovitch, H., and Bilu, Y. "Visitational Dreams and Naming Practices among Moroccan Jews in Israel." *Jewish Journal of Sociology 28(1)*, 13-21, 1985.

Abramovitch, H. "'Good Death' and 'Bad Death': Therapeutic Implications of Cultural Conceptions of Death and Bereavement" in *Traumatic and Nontraumatic Loss and Bereavement*," eds. R. Malkinson, S. Rubin & E. Witztum. Madison, CT.: Psychosocial Press, 2000.

_____. "Into the Marginal Zone" in *Marked by Fire: Stories of the Jungian Way*, eds. Patricia Damery & Naomi Ruth Lowinsky. Carmel, CA: Fisher King Press, 2012.

Artemidoris. *Oneirocritica: Interpretation of Dreams*, transl. White, R. Torrance, CA: Original Books, 1990.

Bilu, Y. and Abramovitch, H. "In Search of the *Saddiq*: Visitational Dreams among Moroccan Jews in Israel." *Psychiatry 48*, 83-92, 1985.

Covitz, J. *Visions of the Night: A Study of Jewish Dream Interpretation*. Boston: Shambhala, 1990.

Fox, E. *The Five Books of Moses: A New Translation with Introductions, Commentary, and Notes*. New York: Schocken, 1995.

Fromm, E. *The Forgotten Language: An Introduction to the Understanding of Dreams, Fairy Tales, and Myths*. New York: Grove Press, 1951.

Hillman, J. *The Dream and the Underworld*. New York: Harper & Row, 1979.

Jacoby, M. *The Analytical Encounter: Transference and Human Relationship*. Toronto: Inner City Books, 1984.

Jung, C. *The Collected Works of C. G. Jung*. Vol. 8. Princeton: Princeton University Press, 1960.

———. *Memories, Dreams, Reflections*, Aniela Jaffe, ed. Transl. Winston, R. and Winston, C. New York: Vintage Books, 1989.

Meier, C. *Healing Dream and Ritual*. Einsiedeln, Switzerland: Daimon Verlag, 1991.

Ochs, V. and Ochs, E. *The Jewish Dream Book: The Key to Opening the Inner Meaning of Your Dreams*. Woodstock, VT: Jewish Lights, 2003.

Shalit, E. "Dreams in the Old Testament" in *Encyclopedia of Psychology and Religion*. Eds. D. Leeming, K. Madden, S. Marlan. New York: Springer, 2009.

Simon, M. *Babylonian Talmud*. London: Soncino Press, 1969.

Vital, H. *Ketavim Hadashim l'Rabbenu Hayyim* (Hebrew). Jerusalem: Ahavat Shalom, 1988.

Bi-Polarity, Compensation, and the Transcendent Function in Dreams and Visionary Experience

by Kathryn Madden

The raw material shaped by thesis and antithesis, and in the shaping of which the opposites are united, is the living symbol.[1]

—C. G. Jung

A strange drawing is reproduced in C. G. Jung's *The Archetypes and the Collective Unconscious.*[2] This image presents two back-to-back half-circles, one dark and the other light, each touching the other at a single point where also is found the drawing of a heart. A cross intersects the two half-circles, the vertical and horizontal lines of which pass through the centrally located heart image. Encompassing this display is a great circle. Numbers, letters, and words appear throughout, presumably as an interpretive guide to the significance of each component of the image. Labels such as Abyss, Eternity, Father, Son, Earthly Man, Soul, Craft, Devils, Tincture, and Fire seem to offer a roadmap to an understanding of what the image signifies. Atop the image is found the esoterically obtuse title: *The Figure of the Philosophik Globe, or Eye of the Wonders of Eternity, or Looking-Glass of Wisdom.*

This image (Fig. 12.1) is the work of the 17th-century German cobbler, philosopher, and mystic, Jacob Boehme (1575–1624). It appeared first in his volume of writings, *The Forty Questions of the Soul,*[3] originally published in 1620 and later in English in 1647 with a translation by John Sparrow. The title page of the English version reads, in part, as follows,

> In the first Question is contained, an *Explanation*, of the Philosophik Globe, or Wonder-Eye of Eternity, *or Looking-Glass* of Wisdom, being ONE half Light or Dark Globe or half Eye with a Rainbow about it, parted, with the Halves reversed, A Cross and Heart, appearing in the Centre, with the Abyss every where, within it, and without it, in Infinity, being all …. *Looking-Glass.*[4]

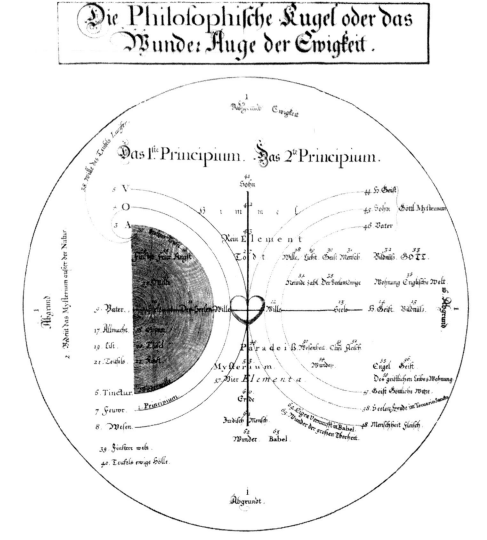

Figure 12.1 "The Philosophik Globe"

Was Boehme's unusual image a "dream image?" Was it the direct product of a night dream, a waking dream, a mystical vision—in other words, of the unconscious—or was it, rather, a consciously created graphical representation of a rational and theoretical understanding of the psyche and the cosmos? And the simple answer to this question is: it is not clear.

Boehme reported several mystical experiences that he said enabled him to see into the inner essence of things, specifically of nature and God. One of these experiences came, famously, as a result of his observing a beam of bright sunlight reflecting off a pewter dish. The vision was brief, lasting a mere fifteen minutes, and although it was profound, Boehme kept it to himself for some time, only writing about it some twelve years later in his first major opus entitled *Aurora*.[5] The experience is described in the following passage by Hans Martensen, one of Boehme's biographers:

> Sitting one day in his room, his eye fell upon a burnished pewter dish, which reflected the sunshine with such marvelous splendor that he fell into an inward ecstasy, and it seemed to him as if he could now look into the principles and deepest foundations of things. He believed that it was only a fancy, and in order to banish it from his mind he went out into the green fields. But here he noticed that he could gaze into the very heart of things, the very herbs and grass, and that actual nature harmonized with what he had inwardly seen.[6]

Boehme later said of the experience that "the gate was opened unto me, that in one-quarter of an hour I saw and knew more than if I had been many years together at a University; at which I did exceedingly admire, and I knew not how it happened to me; and thereupon I turned my heart to praise God for it."[7]

Now, it seems a long interval from Boehme's seeing a flash of sunlight reflecting off a pewter dish, a direct experience sparking an intuitive understanding of "the principles and deepest foundations of things," to the creation of a complicated and multi-faceted diagram of the inner workings of psycho-spiritual life and the cosmos as depicted in the "Looking Glass of Wisdom." So, what is going on here?

We know that prior to experiencing this vision Boehme had been devoutly reading scripture and participating in a study group organized by the pastor of his church—a Lutheran church—called the "Conventicle of God's Real Servants." The revelation was also "preceded by a period of deep melancholy, during which he had been in a profound quandary over the existence of evil and suffering in the world."[8] Writing in *Aurora*, Boehme describes his state of mind just prior to the experience. In this excerpt we are able to see something of the psychic and spiritual struggle that consumed him at the time:

[A]t last I fell into a very deep melancholy and heavy sadness, when I beheld and contemplated the great deep of this world, also the sun and stars, the clouds, rain and snow, and considered in my spirit the whole creation of this world...

...But finding that in all things there was evil and good, as well in the elements as in the other creatures, and that it went as well in this world with the wicked as with the virtuous, honest, and Godly; also that the barbarous people had the best countries in their possession, and that they had more prosperity in their ways than the virtuous, honest and Godly had.

I was thereupon very melancholy, perplexed and exceedingly troubled, no Scripture could comfort or satisfy me, though I was very well acquainted with it, and versed therein.[9]

In an attempt to liberate himself from this intense inner conflict, Boehme was finally able to penetrate through the clouds to another layer of being. He continues in *Aurora,*

But when in this affliction and trouble I elevated my spirit (for I then understood very little or not at all what it was), I earnestly raised it up into God, as with a great storm or onset, wrapping up my whole heart and mind, as also all my thoughts and whole will and resolution, incessantly to wrestle with the love and mercy of God, and not to give over, until he blessed me, that is, until he enlightened me with his holy spirit, whereby I might understand his will, and be rid of my sadness. And then the spirit did break through.[10]

In the above passage Boehme seems to be inviting us to stand beside him and observe as his dark mood is "enlightened" and his spirit illuminated. Did the flash of sunlight off the pewter dish happen exactly at the point he describes with the words "[a]nd then the spirit did break through?" From the immediacy and power of this writing, it certainly seems to me that what he is describing here is what has been called his primary vision or illumination. While he may not speak in *Aurora* in terms of sunlight and pewter dishes—the outer, visible moment—his language appears to refer to the inner experience which could easily have been propelled by the outer one.

Let us now attempt once more to answer the question: is Boehme's illustration (as shown in Fig. 12.1), the direct product of a dream or vision—i.e., from the unconscious? Or is it, rather, a schematic rendering of a rational system of thought? Though the evidence is slim, my own inclination is that Boehme was attempting, with this drawing, to better understand and to derive meaning from his mystical vision.

In other words, it seems to me that he turned to the medium of illustration to help him to externalize and then to further amplify what had been revealed to him in the illumination.

We have already described in some detail the various components of the illustration, and they can be clearly seen in Fig. 12.1. On the one hand, it is a complicated image with its somewhat bewildering display of labels. But, absent the numbers, letters, words, phrases, and decorative elements, it becomes a rather simple visual image. First of all, two semi-circles, one light, the other dark, are presented in co-equal opposition to one another. This primary, bi-polar image is then enclosed within a larger, encompassing circle. Two other non-verbal elements add a mystical dimension: 1) the thin, intersecting horizontal and vertical lines that divide the image into four equal parts, and 2) the drawing of the heart in the very center.

Now let us consider Jung's response to Boehme's mandala and explore the notion of compensation and the amplification of dream images (inclusive of those images in active imagination/visionary experience) with a focus on the "bi-polarity" inherent in the human psyche. After all, both men found in their dream or visionary life a prophetic quality of that which foreshadowed the culture: for Jung, the horrors of two world wars; for Boehme, the Reformation that squelched much of what had resonated of the symbolic life in the Christian tradition for the previous 1500 years and the Thirty Years War, which pitted Protestants against Catholics throughout Europe.

It is easy to imagine Boehme's mandala image emanating from the unconscious—whether from a waking dream or vision—with the addition of the words, letters, and numbers appearing later as Boehme attempted to further amplify the original illumination through an elaborate theological analysis. These elements are each extensively discussed in *The Forty Questions of the Soul*, the work first published in 1620 in which the image appeared.

It is not my purpose to conduct a critique of the analysis that accompanies the mandala, but rather to consider the mandala itself. According to Jung, mandalas universally represent the wholeness of the psychic ground, the archetype of the Self, or, in a mythico-religious sense, the God-image. In the chapter, "A Study in the Process of Individuation" from *The Archetypes and the Collective Unconscious*, Jung endeavors "to make the inner processes of the mandala more intelligible," saying that they are,

...self-delineations of dimly sensed changes going on in the background, which are perceived by the "reversed eye" and rendered visible with pencil and brush, just as they are, uncomprehended and unknown. The pictures represent a kind of ideogram of unconscious contents.... While painting them, the picture seems to develop out of itself and often in opposition to one's conscious intentions. It is interesting to observe how the execution of the picture frequently thwarts one's expectations in the most surprising way. The same thing can be observed, sometimes even more clearly, when writing down the products of active imagination.[11]

The wholeness represented by the mandala—that attains the likeness of the God-image—then, spontaneously arises from the unconscious. And, as Jung references above, the unconscious may even act in opposition (or in compensation) to preconceived notions from the conscious mind.

There are two distinct ways in which we can find Boehme's mandala to be compensatory. First of all, in a substantive sense, the mandala is in opposition to the prevailing theological and philosophical notions of the time that held, among other things, that evil is the absence of the good—also known as the concept of the *privatio boni*. Boehme had studied scripture which claims the victory of light over dark. And yet he had observed with his own eyes quite the opposite in nature—including human nature—a realization that caused him to fall into his aforementioned melancholy or depression. When he raised his spirit to God, however, he was given an illumination, beginning with observing a beam of sunlight reflecting off the pewter dish and culminating in a transformed understanding of the "nature of all things."

Jung references Boehme's mandala in the context of his discussion of the phenomenon and purpose of ritual mandalas:

Their object is the *self* in contradistinction to the *ego*, which is only the point of reference for consciousness, whereas the self comprises the totality of the psyche altogether, i.e., conscious *and* unconscious. It is therefore not unusual for individual mandalas to display a division into a light and a dark half, together with their typical symbols. An historical example of this kind is Jacob Boehme's mandala, in his treatise *XL Questions concerning the Soule*. It is at the same time an image of God and is designated as such. This is not a matter of chance, for Indian philosophy, which developed the idea of the self, Atman or Purusha, to the highest degree, makes no distinction in principle between the human essence and the divine. Correspondingly, in the Western mandala, the *scintilla* or soul-spark, the innermost divine essence of man, is characterized by symbols which can just as well express a God-image, namely the image of Deity unfolding in the world, in nature, and in man.[12]

In Boehme's worldview, then, dark and light are seen to be bi-polar co-inhabitants of the same ground. Light does not so much defeat the darkness—nor, for that matter, does the darkness defeat the light—but, rather, both are held in a coincidence of opposites to form a whole, in the world of nature as well as in the spirit. This is represented in the mandala by the opposing, co-equal, semi-circles, joined by the heart image. Significantly present, also, is the great circle encompassing both the opposing light and dark elements, giving the entire illustration an archetypal form as that of the Self which contains all opposites, or as a radically new God image, at least for Western Christianity.

Elsewhere Jung is critical of Boehme's attempt to "organize the Christian cosmos, as a total reality, into a mandala," saying he failed because he "was unable to unite the two halves in a circle."[13] Jung goes on to say that the two halves,

> …represent un-united opposites, which presumably should be bound together by the heart standing between them. This drawing is most unusual but aptly expresses the insoluble moral conflict underlying the Christian view of the world.[14]

On the other hand, Boehme did contain the opposing elements, not by completing a circle with the two half-circles, but rather joining them with the symbols of heart and cross, and with the entire display—dark/light, vertical/horizontal, with the heart at the very center—contained by the great circle. The archetype of the self is that which holds all opposites. Boehme's revelation was that so too does the Godhead, and his mandala—a new God-image—demonstrates that illumination.

Perhaps this image was also generated and utilized in unconscious compensation for what had been forcibly and violently suppressed by the Protestant Reformation that was already in full swing by the time Boehme was born in Eastern Germany in 1575. In other words, it was compensatory in this environment just because it was an image.

The symbology within Boehme's mandala image is powerful and seems to emanate from a vision in which he received knowledge that was otherwise inaccessible through conscious, rational thought alone. So, we might say that, at the very least, this mandala acted to compensate for the collective psyche's rejection of images during that particular time in the history of Western civilization—an attitude that was, itself, a compensation against what the Reformers took to be the idolatrous worship of statues, icons, paintings, and relics of the Catholic Church.

One cannot overestimate the extent to which the iconoclastic, puritan Protestant movement had taken over Europe. Images were highly suspect. Images, after all, arose from extra-rational, non-linear thinking. Dreams communicate in images. Prophets have visions and revelations and speak of them in imagistic terms. The radical Protestant theologians during the height of the Reformation condemned not only images, but also the visions and revelations that preceded them, saying that revelation happened once and only once, and that it was blasphemous to suggest otherwise. Many European cathedrals that survive today are a testament to this recklessness. Many lost the beautiful stained glass windows and statuary that communicated visually the stories of the Old and New Testament because the Reformers wanted the illiterate laity to receive the Word of God (the interpretation of which could be controlled through "orthodox" Protestant preaching) rather than images that were open to individual interpretation through direct experience. Boehme paid a price for his heterodox ideas, however, by being excoriated from the pulpit of the Lutheran church he dutifully attended despite his dogmatic and doctrinal differences with it, and, essentially, was run out of town as a heretic.

Some 300 years after Boehme, Jung became convinced that messages from dreams, or the unconscious in general, are worth listening to and attending to on their own terms. He felt that something was going on in dreams that could not be reduced to images simply signifying other objects, such as a cigar for a penis. The message of dreams, says Jung, may be veiled or hidden because "nature is often obscure and impenetrable, but she is not, like man, deceitful."[15]

The phrase that is often said in jest about Freud, "sometimes a cigar is just a cigar" is, nonetheless, a concept with which Jungians strongly identify. The images in a dream should rather be interpreted from the perspective of the dreamer with the assistance of a trained "guide," not from that of some third-party "expert" who has pre-codified all dream symbology and will tell you what your dreams "mean."

Jung believed that dreams specifically, and the unconscious generally, serve a compensatory function—in other words, that the images arising spontaneously in dreams somehow act to balance out the issues and attitudes of conscious life. "So far as our present experience goes," Jung says, "we can lay it down that the unconscious processes stand in a compensatory relation to the conscious mind."[16] Dreams and other unconscious process "contain all of those elements that are necessary for the self-regulation of the psyche as a whole"[17] in the event that it has gone too far down the road in one direction. For example, someone who has adopted a position of extreme introversion in her conscious life may experience a dream in which the dream ego is fully in charge of a social situation, in other words, who adopts an extroverted, take-charge persona with all of the power and exhilaration that comes from breaking out of the constrictive limitations of this introversion.

Psychiatrist and Jungian analyst James Hall delves into the compensatory nature of dreams by introducing Jung's use of the Heraclitian concept of *enantiodromia*, e.g. "the tendency of any extreme position to turn into its opposite."[18] So, by presenting an opposite position to the conscious one, the unconscious acts to "right the ship," as when the wind blows a sailboat too far in one direction and the sailor tacks back in the other direction to keep it moving forward.

The unusual mandala symbol sketched by Boehme might be seen to represent an example of Jung's notion of the compensatory function of the unconscious. Boehme's mystical visions and reflections revealed the dualistic, paradoxical nature of the creation and of the God-image. This notion, as has been shown above, was very much in opposition to the prevalent, Christian view of God as all-beneficent, all-good, with the source of evil in the world coming solely from humanity's act of turning away from God. Yet, the fact that his ideas were considered by many in the religious establishment to be heretical might lead one to conclude that Boehme may have been "onto something." The image of the presence of both light and darkness in nature, the psyche, and the godhead was later expanded by numerous theologians and philosophers. For example, Boehme's insights had a significant impact on Franz von Baader, Novalis, Tieck, Schelling, and Hegel, who were part of the intellectual elite of late 18th and early 19th-century German Romanticism. According to Mary Watkins and others, Jung was himself an intellectual descendant of this movement:

> Jung's notions of the purposive and creative aspects of the unconscious (not unlike those of the Romantics) as well as its objective status, required a different attitude toward and way of working with the unconscious than previously had been created by modern psychology.[19]

In addition to the numerous references to Jacob Boehme in the *Collected Works,* Jung addresses the previously mentioned concept of the *privatio boni* in his *Answer to*

Job,[20] an analysis that was directly influenced by Boehme's ideas of the presence of both good and evil in the Godhead.

Jung's theories of compensation, the coincidence of opposites, and the transcendent function combine to explain a natural process of the reconciliation of that clash of opposing forces in the psyche as well as in countless arenas of society and culture. The psyche is always working toward a synthesis of opposites, the solution often emerging from a complex mixture of factors. In the emergence of a symbol in dreams—"a coin split into two halves which fit together precisely"[21]—Jung found evidence of this synthesis in the circular symbols of unity—mandala symbols—archetypal images whose occurrence he attested to throughout the ages as representative of the wholeness of the self.

Jung describes this process in the following excerpt from *Psychological Types*:

> I have called this process in its totality the *transcendent function*, "function" being here understood not as a basic function but as a complex function made up of other functions, and "transcendent" not as denoting a metaphysical quality but merely the fact that this function facilitates a transition from one attitude to another. The raw material shaped by thesis and antithesis, and in the shaping of which the opposites are united, is the living symbol. Its profundity of meaning is inherent in the raw material itself, the very stuff of the psyche, transcending time and dissolution; and its configuration by the opposites ensures its sovereign power over all the psychic functions.[22]

Boehme's mandala, "Eye of the Wonders of Eternity," appears to be nothing less than the representation of an inner experience of what Jung calls the archetype of the self. This archetype embodies the holding in tension of the bi-polarities of light and dark, of good and evil, of the all and the nothing. This mandala also marked the appearance of a new God-image, born of a mystical vision, amplified through a simple yet profound drawing and further amplified by written text that expounds upon various elements of the image. The illumination and the mandala it produced led to a flurry of writings by an otherwise simple cobbler from Eastern Germany, writings that influenced theologians, philosophers, and psychologists for centuries to come.

In a letter to the Rev. David Cox, Jung discusses the need for Christ to be seen not only as an historical character who founded a new religion but also to become "an archetypal image or idea in the collective unconscious":

It seems to me of paramount importance that Protestantism should integrate psychological experience, as for instance, Jacob Boehme did. With him God does not only contain love, but, on the other side and in the same measure, the fire of wrath, in which Lucifer himself dwells. Christ is a revelation of his love, but he can manifest his wrath in an Old Testament way just as well, i.e. in the form of evil. Inasmuch as out of evil good may come, and out of good evil, we do not know whether creation is ultimately good or a regrettable mistake and God's suffering. It is an ineffable mystery. At any rate we are not doing justice either to nature in general or to our own human nature when we deny the immensity of evil and suffering and turn our eyes from the cruel aspect of creation. Evil should be recognized and one should not attribute the existence of evil to man's sinfulness. Yahweh is not offended by being feared.[23]

Jacob Boehme's hometown in Eastern Germany was the locus of much religious upheaval in the late 16th and early 17th centuries. Both Boehme and Jung lived and developed their ideas through periods of great social and political turmoil, and both were affected by horrible and protracted military conflict further adding to an immediate experience of evil and the clashing of opposites. In the case of Boehme, this was manifested as the great clash between Protestants and Catholics known as The Thirty Years War. For Jung it took the form of two awful world wars that left Europe and, indeed, the civilized world scorched and reeling from the realization that entire nations could be held in thrall by a powerful evil force that led to the disciplined murder of millions of civilians in addition to the killing of combatants on the battlefield.

In the first quarter of the 21st century we are confronted again with the politico-socio-religious conflict of peoples across the globe. Given these hard realities, the evolution of a new God-image is much more than an academic exercise or mystical speculation. A sober assessment of the current situation facing those alive today makes it hard to conclude that anything other than a great and desperate clash of opposing civilizations and worldviews is at work.

Boehme's revealing 17th-century illumination that co-existing in nature, the psyche, and the God-head are found the bi-polarities of dark and light, and evil and good, was never more germane than it is now.

Notes

1   C. G. Jung, *Psychological Types*, CW 6, par. 828.

2   C. G. Jung, *The Archetypes of the Collective Unconscious,* CW 9.i (Princeton: Princeton University Press, 1969), Fig. 1, 297.

3   Jacob Boehme, *The Forty Questions of the Soul*, 45.

4   Jacob Boehme, *The Forty Questions of the Soul*, viii.

5   Jacob Boehme, *Aurora*.

6   Hans Martensen, *Jacob Boehme: Studies in His Life and Teaching*, 5.

7   Robin Waterfield, *Jacob Boehme: Essential Readings*, 63–64.

8   Arthur Verslius, *Wisdom's Children*, 4.

9   Jacob Boehme, *Aurora*, 485–487.

10   Jacob Boehme, *Aurora*, 487.

11   C. G. Jung, *The Archetypes of the Collective Unconscious*, CW 9.i, par. 622.

12   C. G. Jung, *The Archetypes of the Collective Unconscious*, CW 9.i, par. 717.

13   C. G. Jung, *The Archetypes of the Collective Unconscious*, CW 9.i, par. 603.

14   C. G. Jung, *The Archetypes of the Collective Unconscious*, CW 9.i, par. 704.

15   C. G. Jung, *Two Essays on Analytical Psychology*, CW 7, par. 162.

16   C. G. Jung, *Two Essays on Analytical Psychology*, CW 7, par. 274 .

17   C. G. Jung, *Two Essays on Analytical Psychology*, CW 7, par. 275.

18   James Hall, *Patterns of Dreaming: Jungian Techniques in Theory and Practice*, 126.

19   Mary Watkins, *Waking Dreams*, 45.

20   C. G. Jung, "Answer to Job," *Psychology and Religion: West and East*, CW 11.

21   C. G. Jung, *Memories, Dreams, Reflections*, 335.

22   C. G. Jung, *Psychological Types*, CW 6, par. 828.

23   In Edward F. Edinger, *The New God-Image*, 184.

References

Boehme, J. *Aurora.* London: John M. Watkins, 1915.

_____. *The Forty Questions of the Soul.* London: John M. Watkins, 1911.

Edinger, E. *The New God-Image.* Wilmette, IL: Chiron Publications, 1996.

Hall, J. *Patterns of Dreaming: Jungian Techniques in Theory and Practice.* Boston: Shambhala, 1991.

Jung, C. *Memories, Dreams, Reflections.* New York: Vintage Books, 1962.

_____. *Psychological Types*, CW 6. Princeton: Princeton University Press, 1971.

_____. *Two Essays on Analytical Psychology*, CW 7. Princeton: Princeton University Press, 1966.

_____. *The Archetypes of the Collective Unconscious,* CW 9.i. Princeton: Princeton University Press, 1969.

_____. *Psychology and Religion: West and East*, CW 11. Princeton: Princeton University Press, 1975.

Martensen, H. *Jacob Boehme: Studies in His Life and Teaching.* New York: Harper, 1949.

Verslius, A. *Wisdom's Children.* Albany: State University of New York Press, 1999.

Waterfield, R. *Jacob Boehme: Essential Readings.* Wellingborough: Aquarian, 1989.

Watkins, M. *Waking Dreams.* Dallas: Spring Publications, 1984.

The Dream as Gnostic Myth

by Ronald Schenk

Dreams, as with all experience, are matters of interpretation and therefore present themselves as both the subject *and* object of many ways of being, depending upon the particular perspective used to engage them. We could say that as we read dreams, they also see us, read us, through a multitude of perspectives. One perspective, that of the mythic, seems particularly suited to dreams. Myth (*mythos*) means "story," but as etymologically associated with words of the unspoken—"mute," "mum," "mumble"— it also enhances our sensibility of the ultimately unknowable nature of dreams; they have us. Knowing the unknowable is the orientation of three great Middle Eastern religions—Judaism, Christianity, and Islam—all of which emerge from the underlying rhizome of mythic themes and images known in a general sense as gnosticism[*]—*gnosis* meaning "knowledge," or more specifically, "knowledge of God."

Gnosticism provides a complex set of themes and images interrelated through a storyline regarding the emergence and differentiation of the soul through the coming to knowledge of a previously unknowable aspect of its nature. In a religious context, this part would be considered an element of the "divine," whereas in a psychological sense, it would be considered the "unconscious," indications of which emerge through the dream. Like the dream, gnostic myth is a narrative, but one that is at once both linear and nonlinear, sequential and nonsequential, consisting of several stages that might be loosely differentiated as fallen world, descent, the call, the journey, the release, and the coming to knowledge. These stages are really psychological "worlds" with associated feeling tones, action patterns, imagery, and consciousness, all governed by an *archon* or tutelary power; in other words, they are archetypal.

From the standpoint of gnostic myth, dreams can be seen as signifiers of specific psychological spaces, which, taken together, form a pattern of transformation or change. Associations to dreams tell us what these imaginal places look like in the everyday world of the dreamer's life. Furthermore, the act of dreaming itself can be considered a manifestation of one or more of these realms. The intention of this chapter is to

---

[*] In this chapter the term *gnostic* refers to a general collection of themes and images and is not capitalized, as is the specific religion that incorporates some of these themes.

delineate these worlds and to show how the content of dreams, as well as the act of dreaming, give them expression.

Fallen World

The gnostic universe originates, divided and dualistic, without harmony, between two cosmic realms designated as the ideal and the mundane, knowledge and ignorance (*agnoia*), light and dark, heaven–earth, spirit–matter, above–below. The gnostic story takes place largely in the context of the "fallen world," the inferior aspect of any of these dyads, and moves toward an integration or "knowing" of the two worlds by each other. The "fallen" realm is any psychological space that is consciously or unconsciously experienced as flawed or mistaken, disenchanted or disillusioned, stuck or imprisoned—eliciting depression, despair, and the feeling of death. It is a form of alchemical *nigredo* or darkness, in which processes of rotting, decomposing, decompensating, and wasting away dominate. The atmosphere is bitter, putrid, seedy, staid, stale, petrified. Fallen situations are expressed metaphorically as those that are decrepit and decaying, structures that are falling apart, meetings never starting, dances not in step, parties that cannot get off the ground, planes delayed and grounded. There is a pervasive sense that nothing works, expressed in colloquial language as everything is "just fucked."

Life situations reflecting the fallen world include relationships, gatherings, organizations, and performances that cannot get going or have gone on too long, operating under corrupted value systems or foundations, or going past the point of diminishing returns. There is a sense of things "going sour" or working against themselves, expressed in images such as a sinking ship and conveying the "lost cause," where one is "mired in quicksand" or "running on a treadmill." The lower world is bodily as opposed to spiritual, existing in the mode of sleep or forgetfulness or just plain drunk. The gnostic phrase "the noise of the world" refers to what we might consider "low life" or anything undesirable. No direction is known; no goal appears. In gnostic terms, one finds oneself a "stranger" or a "stranger in a strange land," or held "captive" as an "alien." The pervading feeling is one of homesickness, melancholia, nostalgia, forlornness. The same old scenarios dominate, the "same old song and dance" prevails, and the "same ol', same ol'" remains the same.

"Rhonda," a writer/teacher married to a protective but emotionally distant and highly defended husband, reported a dream reflecting the fallen world. She was severely abused as a child by her mother and therefore developed a deeply masochistic identity, now modified but not given up. Her writing is focused on giving voice to the "abused girl" through fictional narrative. She is currently involved in an emotional affair with a geographically and psychologically distant man, T, who keeps her on a string through his seeming "understanding," which remains void of committed follow-through. She dreams the following:

> I am in T's house, exhausted after a long, arduous trip. I am in a small space. I hear arguing between T and his wife. I am too tired to deal with anything. T's wife comes in. She is a "suburban-Botticellian beauty." She coldly looks through me as if I'm not there.

Rhonda's association to the dream is that it took place after her last analytic session, that dealt with the felt "unspeakability" of the abused girl in her novel and the hopeless feeling her writing takes on as "more debris" is injected into the world. In the dream, we can see the fallen world as a tired, masochistic realm of self-abuse and devaluation, where the dreamer goes unseen as the "ruined woman." This is a world she enters every time she writes, comes into her analytic sessions, or contacts her "lover."

Here the act of dreaming itself can be seen as an experience of a fallen condition, a discomforting dwelling below the surface of consciousness, away from the world of habitual, secure survival with its rounds of custom, practiced by the dreamer in his or her everyday mode of accommodation.

The Descent

The lower, inferior world is attained through a fall, the purpose of which, in Jungian terms, is to achieve a more holistic being by incorporating something of the psyche that has been kept separate and apart. An aspect of the soul in the upper realm becomes attracted to the lower world and a descent occurs—a sinking, a focus downward, the higher pulled to the lower, the pure into muck, where its sparks are scattered, the original dispersed into the derived. The experience is often one of darkness, defeat, or trauma, yet there is a necessity about it. In everyday life, words coming out of the head and put down on paper, or ideas submitted to the practical test of the world, take a "fall" from ideality into a more material, tangible state of being. "Falling in love" takes one out of a "purer" singular existence into the more complex condition of relationship. This falling condition comes with literal falls in the form of accidents, disappointments, natural disasters, losses in competitive endeavors, and through larger life losses such as job, relationship, or literal death. In analysis, an intervention or simply the flow of associations may "tip" the patient into a cluster of repressed thoughts or feelings such that defenses slip reluctantly away. The fall occurs in dreams through any kind of downward movement—down the escalator or elevator, the ladder, or the stairs, falling down the rabbit hole or off the cliff, dropping to lower levels of geography or buildings.

"Mona" is a single, professional woman in her late thirties, hungry for a committed relationship with a man with whom she could create a family. With her fortieth birthday looming, she is carrying a history of relationships, sulfurous in their quick, flaming quality, with "beautiful addicts"—charming men void of capacity for commitment. These relationships have been somewhat in reaction to her earlier enmeshment with an invasive, controlling, self-involved mother, so that her desire for these unavailable men comes with a hidden resistance of her own and a burden of responsibility. As a result, a doubly determined defense comes into play along with her attraction to these men. In the midst of a budding new relationship, Mona had the following dream:

> I am walking. My foot comes down in a mass of snakes—copperheads—that wrap around my foot but don't bite.

Her association to the dream was that the snakes, although poisonous, were not rattlers, like her image of her mother. Gnostic myth might say that Mona is experiencing a fall into a complex of feelings (snakes) around (1) a developing relationship that seems to be of a different quality than those of the past; (2) an obsessional attitude that includes mixed feelings (entanglement), newly renewed, toward finding relationship; and (3) the mother-daughter configuration, now revisited in a mediated mode (i.e., as copperheads, not rattlers). (It could also be noted, as a sidebar, that copper, as a connector or conductor, is the metal of Aphrodite.) The fact that the original *pharmakon* or healing herb was both a poison and a healer would give evidence that the patient's fall also pertains to a growing intimacy within the analytic relationship. From a gnostic point of view, dreaming itself can be seen as an act of falling—that is, falling from a comfortable, rational mode of the "dayworld" into the relative discomfort of the irrational, inferior "nightworld" of images and feelings that comprise the dream experience.

The Call from Without

In gnostic myth the invisible counterpart of the lost soul embedded in the fallen world—that is, the spiritual "other"—at some point develops a yearning for its imprisoned or forgetful aspect and sends an emissary to correct the situation. This second descent is in service to a "retrieval" that involves a taking on of the "clothes of the world" by the messenger. The emissary appears to the lost soul and declares a revelation, a message of *re-minding* or *re-membering*, something like, "Greetings! ('*Ave, Maria!*') Awake, you drowsy sleeper! Become alive to your true being! The existence you are experiencing is inauthentic and temporary. Your condition is alien to the spiritual nature of your real self. You belong in a different place! Get back to where you once belonged! Return to your origins—come home! Realize your destiny!"

The "call" can be thought of as any indicator pointing to a need for change, usually accompanied by a feeling of discomfort. The change can be in identity, lifestyle, or stage in life. The call may evidence via a pull for regression, issued within an old way of being, now dysfunctional, and resulting in feelings of depression or yearning. The call can be an actual verbal communication, a physical or mental breakdown or dysfunction, or an unusual loss of control such as an emotional outburst. From the gnostic perspective, anything in psychotherapy regarded as a "symptom" could be seen as a call from the unconscious indicating that change is needed or is taking place according to the psyche's system of self-healing. Dreams of dark figures or of animals approaching or following the dreamer or trying to get into the dreamer's dwelling are manifestations of the call for change that is already underway.

"Bill" was sexually, physically, and emotionally abused by various family members, including his stepfather, R, as a child. Depressed and lonely, Bill wants a family of his own, yet relates to women in a style of emotional domination that compensates for his low self-esteem. He is working to separate himself from stringent family connections, literal and psychological, and dreams the following:

> I get a call from my mother and sister to meet them with R. I am waiting at the airport gate for them. Their flight is delayed until the next night. I go back to my hotel.

Next night, no arrival. It turns out they had arrived at the next gate, No. 28, two or three hours ago. I text my sister. They are staying with a friend of theirs. I drive there and ring the door bell. My sister answers in a matter-of-fact way. R walks over. He is a shell of a person, hunched and shaking, incoherent. I barely hear him mutter, "I love you," but the life force is gone from him. My sister gives me a look as if to make me feel guilty, but I don't.... She comments how treatments are killing him(!!!) ... and she is his caretaker.

Bill's association to the dream was that R was now lifeless, similar to the way he feels in his life. The call is bringing attention to a change that is occurring in Bill: His will to dominate is dying away through "treatment." The call also is from a guilt (sister) that resists the psychoanalysis ("treatment") that is working upon the domination–inferiority complex represented in R. Later Bill has another dream:

I am at my place, putting on a dinner party for three. Good time being had by all. Doorbell rings. I answer and it is M, my maternal grandmother.

Bill responded to this dream with the realization that in years of analytic work, he had forgotten about M and had left her out of his thinking related to his family. He said, "She died when I was seventeen, but was the only family member I was ever close to. She hated the other (abusive) members of the family, I could just tell. She read me stories and saw me as special." In the gnostic orientation, the emissary from beyond becomes a helper or guide to provide instruction. In the dream a self-affirming guide has appeared from within at a very dark time to influence Bill's identity in the world as a unique being whose presence is wanted. "Now *I* can show up!" he exclaimed, referring to his sense of self in relationship and work.

Within the gnostic framework, dreams act as the call, in and of themselves. Dreams *are* the animals and the unknown figures representing a new element to be included in the dreamer's personality, the harbingers of a more encompassing being.

The Journey

The theme of the return involves a journey of homecoming, not a return to a false condition, but to a *re-newed* or *re-membered* essential condition that has been left behind. For the gnostic, the present state is only a sojourn, and a journey of transformation is required. The journey is one of travail, involving a wandering through the unredeemed world, often imaged as following a meandering trail, gathering lost or forgotten "sparks" or aspects of the soul. The journey need not be one of space, but rather that of time, representing stages of transformation. These stages involve a process of assimilation or integration of that which is seen from a more limited, mundane perspective as "other." Psychologically speaking, dreams are journeys that include occasions for teaching through the appearances or epiphanies of characters or creatures representing different worlds or ways of being that are latent in the dreamer's unconscious.

Consider "Dolores," who is struggling with a conflict in identity between being a dependent, compliant daughter aligned with the values of a patriarchal culture and a cosmopolitan woman of the world. She dreams,

> I am at my house in this country. The house has a floor like that in my home country. A family member lets in a blind woman beggar from the backyard while I am in my room. I come out and see the woman finding her way around the house to beg. I am angry that she was let in. She is so intrusive! She finds me and begs. I say, "No," and kick her out. Then I feel guilty. My son may be harmed as a result of my action.

The patient's associations to the dream were that in her culture, the belief is that rejecting a beggar brings harm. The blind woman reminded Dolores of a certain woman in her community whom she was avoiding because this woman presumed to take a stance as "mother" to her. Applying agnostic sensibility, the patient is being confronted with a "poor, blind" neediness in herself that invites mothering and that she needs to integrate in order to attain her "destination" of authenticity as a woman.

Another example: "Kristin" brings in a poem as gift to her analyst, only to be traumatized by the analyst's spontaneous interpretive response. She dreams,

> I am with my grandson (age 8) in the backyard. There is a hole in the ground. A huge snake head appears. I am terrified.

From the gnostic perspective the snake would represent a primal force essential to her core being, evoked by a transference-countertransference enactment that took her to a place of the "child." Historically, the event corresponded to her own childhood experience of being "dissed" by her mother. The subsequent working through of her feelings and integration of the snake energy would allow Kristin to make a movement away from a dependent position with the analyst and in her life as a whole.

Dreams are the journey in that they take the dreamer on a "trip" into a different world with a different logic and a different set of underlying assumptions, inhabited by different subjects than the dayworld which forms his or her customary but limited identity—all of which can be "taken in" to form a new perspective, once perceived as foreign territory.

Release

During the gnostic journey of transformation a time comes when will and conscious intentionality give out. At this point of necessary surrender, a larger, autonomous force can take over and carry the process in conjunction with the exhausted will. This giving over of conscious intention allows for receptivity to the "otherness" of the soul that the weary traveler is destined to incorporate.

"Sonia" is struggling with the lifelong sense of always needing to organize herself around the values and expectations of others. This driving need stems historically from her unconscious need to be of "value" to her father. The struggle has often resulted in her resistance to others in a position of authority. At an annual business conference in which she had normally found herself skeptical and on-guard, she had a series of dreams:

> I dreamed of a young boy in my care. He had removed his own kidneys to present to CS, who I think was his mother. It was all very "clean," not bloody; they [the kidneys] looked a bit like living jewels.

Her association to kidneys was that their function is to screen out toxins, and that her father had had his kidneys removed as the first site of his cancer. "CS" is an old friend with whom she has been out of touch for years, a misfit who easily discounted others, who tried hard as if she had something to prove, who was self-deprecating, and who got by, slipping in "under the wire." These are all qualities to which Sonia had previously resonated.

Days earlier Sonia had dreamed of a plane being unable to successfully take off and being forced to come to a hard landing. A female passenger, who was associated with a woman who didn't get "pulled off her path by others," was catapulted into the row ahead of Sonia and straddled another seated passenger, face to face, as if a "descent" and "fall" had resulted in an encounter with something other than steadfast resilience. The giving up of kidneys could be seen as a giving over of the "filtering function" that represented her skepticism and defensiveness.

> There is a mother, a father, and a child in the dream (not me or my parents). The child is somehow connected to electricity from a wall socket, which keeps the child attached and unable to move away. Both the mother and the father try to "pull" the child away from the electricity. Neither of them is impacted by the electricity. This doesn't work. Finally, the father takes the child outside and "releases" the child, like you would release a balloon, and it disappears. I also sense the child being a duplex figure, like it is a child and a frog or toad, at the point where the father releases it.

Sonia's associations were that electricity was a form of energy and that a frog was a "caring" amphibious creature at home in two elements. A gnostic understanding of this dream would see a "release" from that which the boy had been heretofore "plugged into" as a central source of energy. The release was brought about by the inner character, representing father/authority/analyst, indicating a new relationship to this figure. (These dreams were the first in several years of analysis that were typed and given to the analyst.) The letting go also marks the place of a crucial connection to an amphibious or instinctual nature. In a larger sense, dreaming itself is a way of letting go of rational consciousness and will, "letting it all hang out," providing for the experience of release that leads to an ultimate integration of knowledge.

Knowledge

In gnostic mythology, the journey of transformation through the realization of knowledge via encounter with representatives of the "other" culminates in the ultimate meeting with the unknowable counterpart. Psychologically, the *apotheosis* consists in the soul redeeming itself by meeting its unknown aspect, now "knowing" itself as if for the first time. The redemption is one of knower and known in complete sympathy with each other through a unique, essential state signified by harmonious alignment. Sonia had the following dream, subsequent to those in the "release" realm:

> There are four groups of horses; each group is forming a circle. The horses remind me of Lipizzaners. They are moving into a precise position in each circle. There is one circle that I have an especially clear view of. I have a sense of the last horse in that circle

settling into position. At that moment I felt a shudder run through the middle of my body (horizontally) and I woke up.

A *shudder* is the bodily sensation that signals an encounter with an encompassing or "larger than" entity. In mythology, encounters with gods are often accompanied by a shudder on the part of the mortal. Sonia has come to feel that she is "of value" regardless of whether or not "father" ("other" as authority) knows she knows and whether or not she has sufficiently prepared to prove herself "ready." Her performative horse power has come into alignment; she now *is* the readiness itself.

"Don," a young man in the middle of a prolonged identity crisis, dreams the following as he is coming to realize what his lifework will be:

I am by a pool in the forest. It looks inviting, and I go in swimming. While in the pool I notice there is a snake in each of the four corners. I quickly get out. As I stand up on shore and look back into the water, the snakes converge at one end of the pool. They are joined by a fifth snake with four tails in the shape of a lute or some kind of musical instrument or notation. The snakes form a straight line and swim across the pool in formation.

Ironically, the analysis of this man is still a "long way from home," with the journey of self-discovery having just gotten underway, but the dream gives a premonition of getting there. The snakes represent primal energies that are finding their way into alignment. The dreamer can connect to this energy only when he gains a reflective perspective.

The function of apotheosis works through dreams as such, in that dreams act as a mirror image of the "other"—the unknowable sides of ourselves through which our unique sense of being may be experienced in its fullness.

The gnostic cycle is never completed, and dreams do not mark a lasting change. The psyche, as fundamentally hermetic, works in elliptical cycles, always coming round again to the point from which it started, but a little different each time around. In addition, dreams need to be considered within the context of the associations they elicit and the immediate everyday context that the psyche is taking into account through the dream. In the interplay of the dream with these various elements related to the dream, a web may be woven, decipherable through a gnostic orientation, giving an image of the sacred within the mundane of everyday life.

Four Hands in the Crossroads
Amplification in Times of Crisis

by Erel Shalit

In amplification, we reach out beyond the boundaries of our ego, beyond the realm of ego consciousness, which by definition is temporary and limited. We humbly admit that our ego-identity is not the one and only, the grand-all and be-all. By amplification we recognize that the images that arise from the unconscious have a life of their own, and that the world of matter and psyche exists in itself, even when out of the beholder's sight. The "I" of my awareness is not the grand creator of the image, but participates, sometimes actively, in that greater whole, in a reality of spirit and matter that exists and lives, even if I am absent. When in dialogue with the living image, I neither deny its existence, nor do I believe that I am its sole creator.

Thus, amplification does not only entail seeking parallels to one's personal experience in mythology and in the history of humankind, but it implies a shift of focus from ego-centeredness to a dialogue between personal consciousness and the objective psyche. Consequently, when amplifying, we consciously reach out and recognize the image's existence *in itself*, as well as allowing the image and its symbolic energy to enter consciousness.

Just as the Self seeks its realization in the ego, the objective psyche seeks to manifest itself in the world of consciousness. Amplification facilitates this process, whereby the Self of the objective psyche gains access to the ego of the individual psyche. By means of amplification, the Self, as archetype of meaning, anchors the personal ego in substance and significance.

ભ   ભ   ભ

If the images of the objective psyche are too compelling, and the ego and its defenses are too weak, the archetypal world will implode and crash into consciousness, destabilizing the psyche. In psychosis, the archetypal unconscious has unmediated access to the individual psyche. The complexes have sometimes not constellated well enough to carry out their teleological, purposeful process of personalization. In a psychotic condition, the complexes are unable to connect between the realms of archetype and ego, to mediate archetypal substance into the area of the ego and to regulate its assimilation in such a way that archetypal energies mold into personal manifestations. When the ego is too weak and does not have solid enough boundaries, it becomes inundated.[1]

Individuals react to crisis and turmoil in a variety of ways. On the one hand, some are paralyzed by anxiety, while in others Martian energy is triggered, leading to an increased capacity to act. In times of upheaval and disorder, the objective psyche, the archetypal unconscious, is activated and set in motion. Potentially traumatogenic archetypal matter is heated up and energized, boiling in the vessels more closely beneath the surface. Archetypal forces and images will more easily penetrate cracks in the ego's defenses, triggering collective fears and complexes, such as the fear that the Holocaust may be repeated.

Activated archetypal material will find its way and sometimes emerge in the psyche of the person whose doors to the unconscious are open, as happened to Jung prior to World War One (see below). In other instances, the archetypal forces that have been set in motion will penetrate into the psychologically unprepared or unsophisticated individual, as in the case of the young soldier below, and sometimes in the psychologically sensitive and conflicted person, as in the officer, whose dream is also described.

Dreams and Upheaval

Jung's World War One Premonition

In *Memories, Dreams, Reflections*, Jung vividly describes his dreams and visions prior to World War One. He writes,

> Toward the autumn of 1913 the pressure which I had felt was in *me* seemed to be moving outward, as though there were something in the air… It was as though the sense of oppression no longer sprang exclusively from a psychic situation, but from concrete reality…
>
> In October, while I was alone on a journey, I was suddenly seized by an overpowering vision: I saw a monstrous flood covering all the northern and low-lying lands

between the North Sea and the Alps. When it came up to Switzerland I saw that the mountains grew higher and higher to protect our country. I realized that a frightful catastrophe was in progress. I saw the mighty yellow waves, the floating rubble of civilization, and the drowned bodies of uncounted thousands. Then the whole sea turned to blood ... I was perplexed and nauseated, and ashamed of my weakness.[2]

Two weeks later, Jung had the same vision again, "even more vividly than before." He recalls how someone at the time asked what he thought about the future of the world, to which Jung replied that he "saw rivers of blood." Yet, at the time he still believed these visions were idiosyncratic, and he was concerned about his mental condition.

During the spring and summer of 1914, Jung had three frightening dreams in which "in the middle of summer an Arctic cold wave descended and froze the land to ice... the entire region totally deserted by human beings. All living green things were killed by frost." He then ends, saying,

> On August 1 the world war broke out. Now my task was clear: I had to try to understand what had happened and to what extent my own experience coincided with that of mankind in general.[3]

Jung was, of course, exceptional in his sensitive reception of unconscious material that erupted into consciousness; we know, for instance, that it was in a dream that his concept of the layers and structure of the unconscious was conceived, and it was he who formulated amplification as an approach to the archetypal significance of images. Jung's psyche may have been particularly open to the unconscious during the years of his mid-life crisis—the years during which he wrote his *Liber Novus*, which became the basis for all his future work.

The War Is On

In a social setting, I was once approached by a man who wanted to inquire of me about dreams. "I have heard that you interpret dreams," he said, contemptuously. Feeling somewhat uncomfortable, and respectful of the sincere labor of understanding the messages from the unconscious, I remained silent. He soon declared his conviction that he does not "believe in dreams. I never dream. Dreams are arbitrary responses to external stimuli, and have no value." Well aware that if you do not sense the gold in the garbage, it simply is not there, I saw no reason to challenge his views on the topic.

However, I cannot but observe how strikingly different that view is to a perspective that bears in mind the poetic essence of the dream. "Poetic experience," says the French philosopher Gaston Bachelard, "must remain dependent on oneiric [i.e., dream] experience."[4] James Hillman gives voice to this approach when he says, "Dreaming is the flickering activity of the mind participating in the world's imagination."[5]

The fellow soon left, only to return at the end of the evening, somewhat elated. Seemingly inspired by the liquid spirits, he said, "To tell you the truth, I did have one dream in my life. As a young soldier stationed in Sinai, in September 1973, I had an extremely vivid dream about a war-scene. Two weeks later, after the outbreak of war, exactly what I had dreamed took place in reality—explain that to me!" he said, sharing with me some of the details of his dream and the actual experience.

Explanations were superfluous. This man, who in such an overwhelming way had been inundated by shattering archetypal energies, did not need any more dreams in his entire life. The violent penetration from the unconscious by means of a photographically prospective dream required he implement strong and rigid defenses against further intrusions into his disconcerted consciousness.

Who Shall Live and Who Shall Die

"War is the father of all things," says Heraclitus.[6] Strife and conflict constitute an indispensable precondition of life, even within the realm of the life-giving Great Mother, who in death claims her children back into the chest of her earth. The conflict of opposites causes day to break the night, winter to turn into summer, and life to be created from what has died. The tension between Eros and Thanatos, the principles of life and death, is necessary for life itself.

While serving as commander of an army unit, a man, whom we shall call David, woke up from a dream in which either he or his second-in-command was shot in the forehead. Waking up in panic, he was not sure who had been killed, he or his friend. Several weeks later, after the outbreak of yet another war, when running through fortified trenches, his second-in-command was killed, hit by a bullet in his forehead. That very moment the dreamer David knew he would be safe and survive. However, still decades later, he remained trapped in the simultaneous feeling of relief of being alive and a killing pain and ontological guilt vis-à-vis his fellow officer. He understood the dream as telling him that his own survival depended upon the death of the other. Henceforth, he was unable to experience himself as a fully living person; his soul had frozen in the horror of an unresolvable dilemma.

While the dream preceded external reality, *who* was to be killed was left an open question, to be answered in the eternity of a few seconds, during the moment of battle and instant death, as the dream was concurrently *recalled, reenacted*, and *concluded*.

As psychic and physical reality merged, the dilemmas and conflicts of life and death came to light, who shall live and who shall die, who at his predestined time and who before his time.[7] The trauma, augmented by the dream and the awareness that when his friend was killed, he would survive, reminded him of the Nazi death camps and the selection between those gassed upon arrival and those whose extermination was, temporarily, postponed. The trauma of the dream and his friend being killed in battle would have required the dreamer to consciously ponder the existential dilemma and the awe of its enactment. However, unable to do this, he tried to suppress the dream and the battle, the death and the tragic conflict, and remained possessed by them, unable to live his life.

ᏋᏉ   ᏋᏉ   ᏋᏉ

These three examples illustrate unmediated eruptions of the unconscious. Jung believed the material that emerged was solely personal, fearing he was going crazy. When inundated by archetypal forces, we find ourselves, phenomenologically, in a psychotic condition, even if the ego remains relatively intact and conscious.

The young soldier who dreamed about a war scene, which then took place in actual reality, needed to protect his sanity, defending himself by dissociating from the archetypal psyche. He tried to discard psychic reality to the garbage bin of insignificance.

In the third case, the officer who had survived the dream and the ensuing battle remained trapped, possessed by an existentialist dilemma, similar to the ontological guilt of many survivors of the Shoah, the Nazi Holocaust of the Jews. He was unable to do the psychological work that possibly would have deepened the pain, but that might have helped him feel more alive.

Four Hands in the Crossroads

"Four hands in the crossroads" was dreamed by a man in his forties whom we shall call Jeremiah,[8] a couple of weeks after the onset of what soon would become known as the Intifada, the Palestinian uprising that began in December, 1987, against Israel's occupation of the West Bank and Gaza from the Six-Day War in 1967.

The Arabic term *Intifada* took root as quickly as the uprising spread and appears as the last word in the dream. At the time, the political and psychological impact of the Intifada was not yet apparent, including its influence on Israeli-Palestinian relations over the ensuing decades, which came to see dramatic turns of the tide.

Jeremiah was a social worker with a degree in law. He was married with four small children. He had been active in the Israeli peace movement, but since establishing himself as mediator, he had withdrawn from public activity. He dreamed,

> I see a small Arab boy crawling on his knees in the street, screaming in despair, "My hand is cut off." It is in the grass, some meters away from where he is crawling. At the crossroad of the streets are four cut-off hands, reaching up through the asphalt. The sight is too frightening for me to approach. I don't dare reach out a helping hand to bring his hand back to him, to the Arab boy. On the opposite side of the crossroad there is an overturned van. Underneath it, also on his knees, there is a Jewish man, dressed in blue overalls. His hands are tied together and bandaged. It is Intifada.[9]

The dream-ego, the "I" in the dream, is paralyzed by fear as the scene of horror unfolds in front of his eyes. He is called to see, to be exposed to and to witness a frightening sight. He is drawn into a situation of pain and horror, helplessness and bewilderment. The images impinge upon the dreamer's usually calm and confident, seemingly conflict-free ego.

The frame of this dream is defined by its beginning and its end. It begins from an entirely individual perspective, with the personal ego, "I," and ends by being defined in its social, collective, and geo-political context, the Intifada. Within this frame, the images distinctly reflect different attributes of the psyche, as confirmed by the dreamer's associations: while the Arab boy embodies an aspect of the shadow, the man in blue overalls represents the cultural persona of the Sabra, the Israeli-born Jew. The asphalt, as a solid, hardening layer of cultural norms, covers and suppresses the earth and prevents its growth. The asphalt stops Mother Earth from breathing, and her fruit dies in her womb before it is born. Furthermore, *hands* appear in different (in)capacities in the dream, and the image of the Self appears as the praying and suffering hands, stretching up from Mother Earth in the center of the crossroads. The anima as a possible fourth aspect in the directions of the crossroads is strikingly absent, especially considering that all the men are handicapped, whether in their capacity as ego (the dreamer's I), shadow (Arab boy), or persona (Sabra in blue overalls).

ဢ ဢ ဢ

While the dreamer's associations primarily referred to social and political circumstances, the dream carries, as well, a personal message for him. Jeremiah must relate to his own emotional upheaval, to the forces that arise from his shadow, making him aware of his inner, agonizing conflict. External events provide the garb for the dreamer's own, hitherto-repressed conflict.

But the collective soul is, likewise, reflected in the dreamer's private conflict. His psyche has picked up and responded to the emotional bearings that had yet to be fully sensed by the social collective. The despair, helplessness, and entanglement reflected aspects of the outer collective, as well as of the dreamer's personal shadow.

In the dream, it is the image of the Arab boy that calls upon the dreamer to see his projected shadow. Jews and Arabs, Israelis and Palestinians serve as each other's enemies. As such, they carry loads of shadow projections.

There is no ego without shadow, and we often initially encounter what lingers in the shadow by projection onto the awesome enemy. The enemy is an image of one layer of the shadow, and as such, he is a convenient target for projections, evoking fear, threat, and aggression. However, in the present dream, the Arab boy does not threaten the dreamer by his presumed murderous intentions, but his wound and despair evoke the dreamer's fear and awe. Rather than constellating aggression and a need to fight, compassion is called for. There is a need to embrace the wounded boy, but the sight and the pain are too frightening, in spite of the dreamer's worldview and his ability to feel empathy for the suffering other. The emotional impact is shattering, beyond his ability to feel compassion. The dream-ego is incapacitated, unable to stretch out a helping hand and incapable of restoring the power of the other.

When the hand of the Arab is cut off, the ego-ideal of the down-to-earth Sabra in blue overalls, the persona-manifestation of the Israeli-born Jew, is inevitably wounded,

197

as well. A disturbance in one faculty of the psyche resonates in other faculties. Thus, just as the hands of the dream-ego are unable to bring the cut-off hand back to the Arab boy, the hands of the earthly Sabra are tied and injured. Shadow and persona are intertwined, a pair of opposing twins holding (wounded) hands, pulling the ego in contrary directions.

ಀ ಀ ಀ

It is terrifying when the enemy-shadow gains strength, yet necessary for a fully functioning ego. The ego is vitalized by its encounter with the shadow. However frightening and agonizing, without encountering the shadow and relating to it—both in strife and in embrace, whether collective or individual—there can be no process of individuation, that is, no vital and meaningful relationship between ego and Self. However, the shadow needs to be contained, to be limited by the ego's boundary-formation. Neither the individual nor the collective ego may survive unrestrained aggression, such as the spread of war, terror, genocide, and weapons of mass destruction.[10]

As reflected in the dream, the petrification of the ego in conditions of war and terror often freezes the capacity to relate. The anima, "the archetype of life itself,"[11] the image of the feminine as carrier of soul and relatedness, is necessary as a mediator between ego and Self, but conspicuously absent in the dream. The dream itself may help constellate the soulfulness needed to break the stalemate, leaving the dreamer no option but to *relate;* that is, the anima manifests in the ego's reaction to the image of the hands that spring up from the earth.

ಀ ಀ ಀ

Dreams are often compensatory to the one-sidedness of the ego, and the Self may appear in particularly powerful ways with pertinent images in times of crisis. In "Flying Saucers: A Modern Myth," Jung writes,

> If the round shining objects that appear in the sky be regarded as visions, we can hardly avoid interpreting them as archetypal images. They would then be involuntary, automatic projections based on instinct, and as little as any other psychic manifestations or symptoms can they be dismissed as meaningless and merely fortuitous… They are impressive manifestations of totality whose simple, round form portrays the

archetype of the self, which as we know from experience plays the chief role in unit-ing apparently irreconcilable opposites and is therefore best suited to compensate the split-mindedness of our age.[12]

At the center of the present dream, the powerful and deeply disturbing image of the four cut-off hands in the middle of the crossroads, reaching up through the asphalt, evokes overwhelming dread and bewilderment in the dreamer, who had no person-al associations to this archetypal image. While frightening, the image calls upon the dreamer to approach its symbolic significance. The Self, as the meaning-generating and symbol-forming capacity of the psyche, has generated a gripping image through the terrifying aspect of the Self, a *complexio oppositorum*, an image of itself.

Jung refers to the crossroads as union as well as division, "Where the roads *cross* and enter into one another," he says, they symbolize the union of opposites, the search for wholeness. On the other hand, "[w]here the roads *divide*" we find parting and separa-tion.[13]

In Roman mythology, Trivia[14] is the deity of the crossroads. She requires the traveler to seriously contemplate his or her way, choose a direction and decide upon options, and to be part of determining one's destiny, rather than bowing in defeat to the triviality of one's predetermined fate. Thus, the crossroads is a central meeting place between wholeness and division, between conscious ego, direction, and decision, on the one hand, and archetypal fate and unconscious resources on the other. In the dream, the simultaneous union and conflict between the collective consciousness of cultural norms, represented by the earth-covering asphalt that impairs direct contact with inner and outer nature, and the hands that arise from the unconscious, is evident.

The four hands in the crossroads are, themselves, a union of opposites. Cut-off, castrated, they evoke fear and horror, awe and despair, reminiscent of Old and New Testament verses such as "If I forget you, O Jerusalem, let my right hand forget her cunning,"[15] and "if your right hand causes you to sin, cut it off and throw it away."[16]

These Biblical hands pertain to the human attitude in relation to cultural symbols, values, and morals. However, the hands in the crossroads are not human hands, unlike the other hands in the dream. They are the hands of the Great Mother, reaching up to-ward the realm of humans. They not only rise up as four wounded hands in the center, but are the fourth in a chain of increasingly wounded hands; from the dream-ego who is unable to stretch out and lend a helping hand, on to the Sabra's tied hands, to the Arab boy's cut-off hand, and then to the cut-off hands in the crossroads.

The alchemical dictum, ascribed to the alchemist Maria the Jewess,[17] spells out how the one reappears as the fourth, which Jung used as a metaphor for the individuation process. Not only do these hands constitute a wholeness in their foursome, but may in their very woundedness hold the potential of healing; healing can only come into being where there is pathology.

Figure 14.1
The Upstretched Hands of Tanit at Tel Hazor
Basalt Stela, Shrine of the Stelae, Hazor, Late Bronze period, 15th-13th cent. BCE
Collection of Israel Antiquities Authority, Photo © The Israel Museum, Jerusalem

These are the hands of Mother Earth that, in spite of their decimation and castration in the prevailing cultural climate, manage to penetrate the cultural layer of oppression and repression, to express the despair, the awe and the pain, but also the blessing and prayer of the earth. They reminded the dreamer of the Canaanite goddess Tanit at

200

Tel Hazor, her hands raised as in a ritual act of devotion. In the dream, Mother Earth provides her prayer and blessing by means of the hands that are not subdued by the asphalt, that are not silenced by the repressive collective consciousness. When, in times of severe distress, the multifaceted archetypal image can be related to by amplificatory reflection and understanding, then healing may materialize in place of suffering and despair.

The Healing Symbol

Amplification entails a search for the archetypal kernel of images, rather than remaining solely in the realm of the personal psyche. However, as Jung points out, amplification is not "a purely intellectual exercise," but brings "our total capacities into play."[18]

Thus, the method of active imagination, in which the individual carries out a [not necessarily verbal] dialogue with, for instance, dream images, is "a kind of spontaneous amplification of the archetypes."[19]

As has been mentioned, in times of crisis, upheaval, and sudden transformation, the Self and the archetypal psyche are activated close to the surface, often constellating powerful images that penetrate into the conscious psyche. Archetypal substances burst forth into the psyche, without the softening mediation of complexes.

The archetypal dramas played out leave little possibility for the individual ego to escape their impact. The objective psyche may intrude into the minds of individuals, for instance, by means of premonitions and predictive dreams. Jung was able to respond by sensing his vocation, to "understand what had happened and to what extent my own experience coincided with that of mankind in general." As has been seen, in others it may cause life-long conflict, or the engagement of rigid ego-defenses against the threats of the archetypal psyche. The unmediated manifestation of archetypal forces may be too powerful for the individual psyche.

Thus, in post-trauma we often observe how the archetypal images and the symbolic dimension have receded. They are noticeably absent. The symbolic dimension seems lost, dreams become concrete, photographic, and literal repetitions of the trauma, whereby no images remain to amplify. While in crisis the archetypal psyche is activated, in post-trauma the spirit is gone, and only the harsh matter of symbol-less factuality seems to prevail. Post-traumatic dreaming repeats the trauma, again and again. While it is important "that the traumatic content gradually loses its autonomy by frequent repetition and in this way takes its place again in the psychic hierarchy," says Jung, conscious assimilation of the post-traumatic dream, "which is essentially only a reproduction of the trauma, … [does not] put an end to the disturbance which determined the dream."[20] Without the symbolic imagery, the reality of the trauma loses its liquid, becomes dry matter, and can, therefore, not sink into the dream's drainage system, but bounces back, over and over again, requiring a therapeutic process of liquefaction, of reconnecting with soul and symbols.

With the intensity and heat of crisis, change, danger, and upheaval, compensatory Self-images, such as "four hands in the crossroads," may emerge, as Jung described in *Flying Saucers*. While usually we need to actively engage in the amplificatory search for the archetypal kernel of our images, in turbulent times the archetypal essence and meaning reach out toward us, sometimes bringing us the "numinous quality" and the "feeling-value"[21] of the archetype. The Self may then constellate and create a possibility for healing by bringing symbolic images into consciousness. A greater sense of meaning and vocation may then emerge from the soil of suffering, chaos, and confusion.

Notes

1. See Erel Shalit, *The Complex: Path of Transformation from Archetype to Ego*, 68f.

2. Carl Gustav Jung, *Memories, Dreams, Reflections*, 175.

3. *Memories, Dreams, Reflections*, 176.

4. Gaston Bachelard, *Water and Dreams: An Essay on the Imagination of Matter*, 22.

5. James Hillman, Foreword to Heraclitus, *Fragments*, translated by Brooks Haxton, xiv.

6. *Fragments*, fragment 44, 29.

7. From the composition "Un'taneh Tokef," which is part of the Yom Kippur liturgy. Cf. Lawrence A. Hoffman, *Who by Fire, Who by Water: Un'taneh Tokef.*

8. The Prophet Jeremiah wept, warned, and lamented the destruction of the land.

9. This dream appears in Erel Shalit, *The Hero and His Shadow*, 119.

10. For an elaboration of the shadow, its different layers and images, see my *Enemy, Cripple & Beggar: Shadows in the Hero's Path.*

11. Carl Gustav Jung, "Archetypes of the Collective Unconscious," CW 9i, par. 66.

12. "Flying Saucers: A Modern Myth," in Carl Gustav Jung, *Civilization in Transition,* CW 10, par. 622.

13. *Symbols of Transformation,* CW 5, par. 577.

14. Trivia is derived from the Latin *trivium*, which means "[the meeting of] the three roads." In medieval universities, the trivium comprised the three subjects grammar, logic, and rhetoric.

15. Psalms 137: 5.

16. Matthew 5:30.

17. "One becomes two, two becomes three, and out of the third comes the one as the fourth." Or, as Raphael Patai writes in *The Jewish Alchemists*, "Christianos… says that Maria uttered it in an ecstatic shriek…, 'One becomes two, two becomes three, and by means of the third and fourth achieves unity; thus two are but one,'" 66.

18. CW 10, par. 646.

19. CW 8, par. 403.

20. CW 8, par. 500.

21. CW 10, par. 646.

References

Bachelard, G. *Water and Dreams: An Essay on the Imagination of Matter*. Dallas: The Dallas Institute of Humanities and Culture, 1983.

Heraclitus. *Fragments: The Collected Wisdom of Heraclitus*. (Translated by Brooks Haxton, with a Foreword by James Hillman). New York: Viking, 2001.

Hoffman, L. *Who by Fire, Who by Water: Un'taneh Tokef*. Woodstock, VT: Jewish Lights, 2010.

Jung, C. *Memories, Dreams, Reflections*. New York: Vintage Books, 1962.

Jung, C. *The Collected Works*. (Bollingen Series XX). 20 Vols. Trans. R. F. C. Hull. Ed. H. Read, M. Fordham, G. Adler, W. McGuire. Princeton: Princeton University Press, 1953–1979.

Patai, R. *The Jewish Alchemists*. Princeton: Princeton University Press, 1994.

Shalit, E. *The Complex: Path of Transformation from Archetype to Ego*. Toronto: Inner City Books, 2002.

Shalit, E. *Enemy, Cripple & Beggar: Shadows in the Hero's Path*. Hanford, CA: Fisher King Press, 2008.

Shalit, E. *The Hero and His Shadow: Psychopolitical Aspects of Myth and Reality in Israel (Revised Ed.)*. Hanford, CA: Fisher King Press, 2012.

Dreams and Sudden Death

by Gilda Frantz

He looked at his own Soul
With a Telescope. What seemed
All irregular, he saw and
Shewed to be beautiful
Constellations; and he added
To the Consciousness hidden
Worlds within worlds.

—Samuel Taylor Coleridge, *Notebooks*[1]

It has been my unique experience to have witnessed the sudden death of several beloved family members. After my husband's totally unexpected death, when I was only in my late forties, I was eaten up by loneliness. For months I felt as though the house had a zipper that shut me out of life and kept life out of my home. I lived in the realm of the dead. It was then, in my sadness and pain, that I thought of my husband's dream journal. We were an inseparable couple, but both of us were extremely private people who had never looked at the other's dream journal or peeked into anything private. Now there I was, a bereft widow yearning for my husband, drawn toward taking a liberty I never would have imagined. Only after I spoke with his spirit and asked permission was I able to open his dream book. I turned to my own dreams at the same time and discovered a unique record in the dreams he'd dreamt not long before he died and in my dreams from about two months before that.

This paper is culled from my personal experience. Because it is personal, I took the advice of the ancient alchemists, who noted that there comes a time when one must throw away the books. This important statement has guided me to consider the dream and my own process rather than to pore over books to validate what I have written.

What now seems like a lifetime ago, the dream I had about two months before my husband's "sudden" death was a puzzle to me because I forgot the most important associations when I attempted to analyze it. The memory of two significant dreams that might have clarified the subject of this particular dream came later. It also appears that, unsurprisingly, I was very resistant to becoming conscious of the fact that my husband, Kieffer, was going to die soon. In *On Dreams and Death*, von Franz writes: "In cases where the dreamer has illusions about his approaching death or is unaware of its closeness, dreams may even indicate this fact quite brutally and mercilessly."⁷ I think the dream I had was fairly blunt, but I just didn't get it at the time.

This dream came at a very happy time in my life. I had been in the training program of the Jung Institute of Los Angeles for two years, and for the first time in decades I had time for myself and was enjoying the freedom as well as the studies. As our children were grown, my husband and I began having dinner dates after work, and life was good. Into my happy life came this dream:

> I am part of a very large group of people from my neighborhood who were running down the street as if to get away from a catastrophe. We are all terrorized. As I run, I look up the hill on my right and see my home. A huge bank of earth has fallen away, and I think, "This cleft in the earth has changed the landscape." I repeated this thought to a person who was running by my side: "Because of this catastrophe, the landscape will never be the same again. It has changed forever."

When I awoke, I had no idea what the catastrophe might be. The word *catastrophe* means a great and sudden calamity, a disaster. It was only much later that I recalled waking up on the morning of June 6, 1961, and finding out that Jung had died. My dream from that night:

> A huge bank of earth had broken away from behind the pool area and dropped down into the pool.

At my analytical appointment, I told my analyst the dream and wondered aloud what the Jungian world would be like with Jung gone. Her reply was interesting. She said that probably male analysts who didn't feel they'd had a chance to be seen or heard while Jung lived would now have that opportunity. It felt clear in the dream that Jung and his work had dropped down to an even deeper place.

In another dream, also dreamt in the early 1960s, I saw a huge owl land in our front yard. When I awoke from the dream in the middle of the night, I actually could hear an owl hooting. I then learned that my sister-in-law had died in a plane crash on her flight from New York. In my associations to this dream, I learned that the owl is a bird associated with death. After I remembered my associations, I thought that my dream

206

of a catastrophe might mean that someone had died, but there was no news of that, so my dream remained a puzzle. It just never occurred to me that my dream might be *pointing to a death to come*. I think it is clear that I didn't want to see what the dream was telling me.

About a month or two after I had this dream, my husband died suddenly at home, without illness or any warning. With all the shock and confusion sudden death brings, it took quite awhile for me to remember the dream. One day some time later, I was taking a walk early in the morning when the memory of the dream became conscious, and I realized that I was now living what the dream had referred to: My own earth had been changed by what now really was a catastrophic loss for me. When the memory of the dream came back to me, it also brought back what my husband was doing when he died. We were outside on a beautiful, sunny day, and he was repotting a small azalea plant that he felt needed to be in a larger-sized pot; its current pot was crowding the azalea's growth.

We in the Western world view death as a catastrophe or a tragedy. In the East there is more of a sense of destiny and fulfillment that comes with death. There is sadness, of course, but also acceptance of the continuation of one's journey. Holy men and women meditate for years to achieve within themselves what is a peaceful attitude toward that which is inevitable. We in the West say, for example, "He put up a *good fight*" or "She was ill for years and finally *succumbed after a long battle*." I think many in the East surrender to death when it feels right to do so and die with an understanding that they are continuing their journey. This is especially likely in cultures in which reincarnation is seen as a means of possibly improving one's karma in the next life. I think that most cultures see death as an end to suffering. One thing I never wanted to say about my husband's death was that it was tragic. It wasn't. I subscribed to the ancient Greek way of looking at tragedy. Death wasn't considered tragic unless there had been waste involved. My husband had lived a full life. He was a physician who was gifted in treating mental illness. He helped found the Society of Jungian Analysts and the Los Angeles Institute that bears Jung's name. He was director of the first low-fee adult clinic that offered Jungian analysis to those who could not afford private care. That clinic now is named after him, the Kieffer E. Frantz Clinic. And, he practiced meditation for over 30 years. He was a loving father to his two children. No waste here that I could see—although *I* felt cheated that he had died at what seemed to me to be so young an age.

My husband's dream journals now gave me great comfort; he had spent much time in this endeavor of writing down his dreams. I also read the active imaginations he did around his dreams. I looked to see what his dreams were saying before he died and found that he, too, was getting dreams about something foreboding. Kieffer's dream:

> Gilda and I are driving into a desert from which no one returns. There were eleven-legged wolves there.

I could see from his handwriting that this dream made a huge impression on him. He devoted a great deal of time writing about the dream and researching its symbols. He noted that often St. Paul was referred to as a wolf. His active imagination with his anima made it clear that he saw the dream as a warning about death and that he needed help from the archetypal figures in the unconscious to help him deal with this threat to his being. But with all this insight, he also made a note that he thought he would live another ten years.

It feels to me that the unconscious tries to shake us up and wake us up, but some of us have resistance to taking in information that we deem to be scary, unpleasant, or a threat to our status quo. That was true of my husband and true of myself. Neither of us could take in that our dreams were saying that life as we knew it was ending or was about to change dramatically.

In *Body and Soul* by Albert Kreinheder, I recall that he reported a dream in which he was digging his own grave. When he awoke, he felt that the dream was telling him to get his affairs in order.[3] This would be an example of a blunt dream in which the unconscious senses the dreamer's resistance to death. The dream makes it clear that it's not far off. The dream my late husband had may have been that kind of dream. His dream made him aware of his vulnerability. He took the dream about going to a desert from which no one returned seriously, talking with his anima about wolves and sheep. He "talked" with St. Paul, invoking him to do something about the wolves that were howling. So I know how much he took the idea of death seriously, but since he was well and only in his early sixties, he just couldn't believe that it was his time to die. But it was.

Many years later I was in Greece on a tour with the philosopher Betty Smith when I had another dream about a catastrophe. It happened that I was doing research on The

Fates, so being in Greece was the perfect environment in which to find out more about these goddesses. I traveled all over Greece and saw statuaries of the gods and goddesses in museums and temples. I totally fell in love with this magical place where Western civilization began. One night I had this dream:

> I am in Greece, swimming in the clear blue water of a small inlet dedicated to Demeter, and there are only a few people in the water, three or four. My back is to the ocean and I am facing the shore, which is near. I turn around and look out to sea and notice a huge wall of water at a great distance. It is a tsunami. I look away again and the next thing I know, the wall of water is above me and momentarily will crash down upon my head. I think, "No one can survive this catastrophe."

In thinking about this dream, I thought that "this catastrophe" might not be personal but instead be referring to a coming world catastrophe. When I looked up through the wall of water, I could see the sun through the blue-green fluorescent water. That might indicate spiritual light, not obliteration.

The next time I thought of the dream I was at a cemetery attending the funeral of my little granddaughter. When I recalled the dream, I grabbed a friend's arm and whispered that now I understood what the dream meant. While I was in Greece I could not stop thinking of my granddaughter and buying her little trinkets. She was always on my mind.

Demeter is the Great Mother. Her daughter Persephone was taken from her by Hades. He carried Persephone down to the Underworld, where she became queen. At the time of her rape by Hades she was a Kore, a very young child/woman. Demeter worshipped her daughter and went into mourning at her disappearance, refusing to allow anything to grow, as she was the goddess who ruled the growth of grains and plants and life itself. She dressed in black and became a nursemaid to a mortal child, attempting to make him immortal by holding him over a fire every evening. She was discovered and forced to leave. The child survived but never became immortal. Demeter pleaded with her brother Zeus to make Hades give her daughter back to her, which Zeus tried to do. They worked out an arrangement where Persephone stayed with her mother in spring and summer and returned to Hades and the Underworld in fall and winter. Thus, the myth goes, that is why the leaves die on the trees and nothing grows when Persephone remains in Hades during those months.

Seeing the setting in Greece and especially in a body of water sacred to Demeter, the dream seemed to place the catastrophe in the realm of the Great Mother. This dream seemed to tell me something huge was about to inundate my ego, and once more I used the word *catastrophe*, that sudden calamity from which no one can survive.

And when my grandchild was being buried, going down into the Underworld of Hades, I remembered the dream.

Our dreams of death or near-death signify that these deaths have meaning for us. They are not simply *sudden*—as in *unexpected*—but have much deeper roots in our souls, and their coming is already known in the unconscious and therefore expected.

I had an auditory, mystical experience in which a voice told me that people don't just die, they are *called*, and when they hear this *call*, they leave.

It feels to me that my late husband was called and that my granddaughter was called, and that is how I explain sudden death. I cannot even ask the question of why we are sent these dreams to help us become conscious of a mystical experience that is about to envelop us. When Jung was asked if he believed in God, his answer was, "I don't believe, I know." I feel that way about such dreams. I know that they are trying to help us prepare for this mystical and profound loss.

I think that it is important to look at a dream as a mystery—a mystery that uses symbolic language and that needs to be solved. Dreams can be extremely mysterious. One might even say they are veiled, elusive, and often hard to grasp.

We need to work to understand our dreams, although we all know of the experience of awaking from a dream and suddenly realizing what it is about. But that doesn't happen very often. More common is the experience of waking up with the mists of the unconscious still clinging to our nightclothes and our head feeling heavy and our eyes unable to fully open to the day. These are the times when the unconscious won't easily let go of us. Some dreamers awake this way daily and others of us occasionally, but it is an experience many of us have had.

But we have something besides our dreams to guide us here as well. A couple of months before my husband died, and around the time I had the dream of running from a catastrophe, my husband said goodbye to me as he departed for a one-week retreat to the mountains to study healing, a subject in which he was profoundly interested. I found myself alone in our home for the first time ever. My children were in college, and there I was in a huge home by myself. One evening I was sitting in front of the fire, my feet on the raised brick hearth. Our dog Pepper was at my feet and our big tomcat Eli in my lap.

My journal was open, as I had been writing in it. I closed my eyes and thought: "If I were to be widowed, this is how my life would be. I would be alone with my dog and cat as companions."

I had never thought about this possibility before in this way because I'd always had my children to care for when my husband went to conferences. Even though I had resisted the idea of my dream signifying something to do with death, my soul understood and tried, through a seemingly innocuous thought, to impart this information to me. The memory of this thought, much later on, helped me cope with being a widow. Something deep within me was directing my footsteps onto a new path during that week alone, and it saved my life. I did not become bitter when my husband died, leaving me alone in my late forties. I didn't know it, but I had been prepared. The unconscious understands that we can resist or fail to understand dream messages, so it sends us thoughts in our waking life to nudge us toward consciousness. Somehow I could accept the visual scene of sitting with my pets, alone in a big house, better than a dream about catastrophe. The two occasions worked together to bring me consciousness in however long it took for me to "get it."

The work of C. G. Jung and his colleague Marie-Louise von Franz has illuminated the world of dreams and the unconscious so that we know it is a part of us that is real, that we exist in both inner and outer worlds. That famous story of Jung describing a woman's dream of being on the moon to von Franz, when she first met Jung, comes to mind. He said that the dreamer was *on* the moon and von Franz interrupted, saying, you mean she *dreamt* she was on the moon, and Jung said, no, she *was on* the moon.

That is how real the unconscious is. I believe that these dreams and thoughts are gifts from the unconscious to bring me the understanding that the sudden deaths I witnessed in loved ones were not sudden after all, but were known in the unconscious, and that I was being informed that something momentous and life-changing was about to happen that would affect me profoundly.

When writing a long letter, many of us add a postscript to include a thought that has been left out. I often do, and I feel the need to do so today after rereading this article. I can see that my intuitive-feeling nature has not done a great job of explaining the leap I made from having a dream to concluding that it was a dream, a warning, about death.

What I neglected to explain is how I made that leap. Intuition often does that; it leaps and hurls itself across vast chasms, just because it "feels right." I have had a lifetime of dream interpretation in my practice with others and with myself. Sometimes a feeling simply tells me that what I am feeling is so. Others may not see it that way, but it satisfies me. In the event that you have a complex dream, you must have someone listen to it and help you understand what the dream is saying. It is better not to leap to conclusions unless that has been the way you access knowledge and have spent a lifetime doing it.

The most important thing to do with a dream is to write down all you can recall about it and then write down all of your associations to the elements in the dream. Remember at the early part of this article, I noted that I didn't recall an event when I was gathering associations, and that if I had, I would have better understood the dream? And sooner understood the dream? That is how important associations are. As an introverted intuitive with extraverted feeling (to use the parlance of Jung's typology), I am used to listening to my intuitions and feelings. That is how I drew the conclusions I did, through strong feelings and strong intuitions.

Notes

1 As cited in C. G. Jung, *Memories, Dreams, Reflections*, 1972.
2 Marie-Louise von Franz, *On Dreams and Death*, ix.
3 Albert Kreinheder, *Body and Soul*, 1991.

References

Jung, C. *Memories, Dreams, Reflections*, edited by A. Jaffe. New York: Vintage Books, 1972.
Kreinheder, A. *Body and Soul: The Other Side of Illness*. Toronto: Inner City Press, 1991.
von Franz, M. *On Dreams and Death*. Boston: Shambhala Publications, 1987.

Biographical Statements

Henry Abramovitch, psychologist and anthropologist, is Founding President and Senior Training Analyst in the Israel Institute of Jungian Psychology as well as a professor at Tel Aviv University Medical School, where he teaches the "human" side of medicine. He has served on Ethics and Program Committees of the International Association of Analytical Psychology (IAAP) as well as Chair of the Israel Anthropological Association and co-facilitator of the Interfaith Encounter Group. He has done fieldwork in the Malagasy Republic and Jerusalem on death rituals. He supervises "Routers" in the IAAP Developing Groups in Poland and Moscow. He is author of *The First Father* (2010) and the forthcoming *Brothers and Sisters: Myth and Reality*. His special joys are poetry, dream groups, and the holy city of Jerusalem, where he lives with his family.

Michael Conforti, Ph.D., is a Jungian analyst and the founder of The Assisi Institute. As a pioneer in the field of matter-psyche studies, he has presented his work at The C. G. Jung Institute, Zurich, and Jungian organizations in Venezuela, Denmark, Italy, and Canada. He is the author of *Threshold Experiences: The Archetype of Beginnings* and *Field, Form and Fate: Patterns in Mind, Nature and Psyche*. He is currently completing a new book, *When the Gods are Silent*. Michael Conforti has served as script consultant on a number of films, in addition to being selected by The Club of Budapest to be part of a twenty-member interdisciplinary team to examine the influence of informational fields. He is a recipient of the Vision Award presented by the National Association for the Advancement of Psychoanalysis and has recently been honored as a *Soci onorari* by the L'Istituto Mediterraneo di Psicologia Archetipica in Catania, Sicily.

Gilda Frantz, M.A., M.F.T., writer and Jungian analyst, served on the Board of Directors of The Philemon Foundation before and during the publication of *The Red Book* and is a Director Emerita of that foundation. Past President of the C. G. Jung Institute of Los Angeles, she has served on many of its boards and has taught advanced courses in Jung's theories. Mrs. Frantz is a noted speaker, having lectured in Japan and Switzerland, as well as many centers in the United States. Her most recent lecture was for a Jung on the Hudson conference on *The Red Book*. Currently she is co-editor in chief of *Psychological Perspectives* and is a founding member of the journal since its inception in 1969.

Christian Gaillard is a doctor of psychology (Sorbonne and EPHE), professor at the Ecole Nationale Supérieure des Beaux-arts (National Academy of Fine Arts) in Paris, training analyst and former president of the French Society of Analytical Psychology, and lecturer in several universities. He was president of the International Association for Analytical Psychology till 2007 and is a member of the international editorial teams of several Jungian journals. He has published essays on psychoanalysis and the arts in these journals and in many collective books, and, among other works, *Le Musée imaginaire de Carl Gustav Jung*, Paris, Stock, 1998; *Les Evidences du corps et la vie symbolique*, Paris, ENSBA, 2000; *Donne in mutazione. Saggi di psicoanalisi dell'arte*, Bergamo, Moretti e Vitali, 2000; "The Arts" in *The Handbook of Jungian Psychology*, R. Papadopoulos ed., London/New York, Routledge, 2006; *Jung* at the Presses Universitaires de France, 6th edition 2013.

Dr. Gotthilf Isler trained as a Jungian analyst at the C. G. Jung Institute in Zürich and worked for many years with Dr. Marie-Louise von Franz. He studied folklore, European folk-literature, and the history of religion at the University of Zürich. He is a founding member and past president, for 10 years, of the Research and Training Centre for Depth Psychology according to C. G. Jung and Marie-Louise von Franz.

Kenneth Kimmel is a Jungian psychoanalyst in private practice in Seattle, Washington, and author of *Eros and the Shattering Gaze: Transcending Narcissism* (Fisher King Press, 2011). Concurrent with his Guatemalan travels in 1974, excerpts of his research among the *Spiritist* healers in Brazil were published many years ago in *Realms of Healing*, by Stanley Krippner and Alberto Villoldo (Celestial Arts, 1976). These seminal studies gave rise to his work over two decades as the Director of the Pacific Northwest Center for Dream Studies. Over a thirty-year career he has taught widely on the subjects of dreams, patterns of initiation—both ancient and modern—and more recently, on love and narcissism. Today, his wide-ranging interests involve the interface of Analytical Psychology with contemporary schools of psychoanalysis, philosophy, and mystical traditions.

Naomi Ruth Lowinsky lives at the confluence of the River Psyche and the Deep River of poetry. She is the author of several Fisher King Press titles, including, *The Motherline: Every Woman's Journey to Find Her Female Roots* and *The Sister from Below:*

When the Muse Gets Her Way, which tells stories of her pushy muse. She is the co-editor, with Patricia Damery, of the new collection *Marked by Fire: Stories of the Jungian Way*. She is also the author of four books of poetry, including *Adagio & Lamentation* and *The Faust Woman Poems*. Her poetry has been widely published and she is the winner of the Obama Millennium Award. She is the Poetry Editor for *Psychological Perspectives* and a member of The C. G. Jung Institute of San Francisco. She has for years led a writing circle there, called Deep River.

Kathryn Madden, Ph.D., is a licensed psychoanalyst of Jungian/psychodynamic focus in private practice in New York City. She teaches at the Pacifica Graduate Institute and is a Lecturer at Union Theological Seminary of Columbia University. Kathryn is the Editor-in-Chief of *Quadrant*, author of *Dark Light of the Soul* (Lindisfarne) and co-editor of the *Encyclopedia of Psychology and Religion* (Springer). As President and CEO of the Blanton-Peale Graduate Institute, she offered a decade of executive leadership and administrative oversight to a psychotherapeutic training institute and state-licensed clinic. Her 15-year tenure with the *Journal of Religion & Health: Psychology, Spirituality & Medicine* was honored with The Distinguished Research & Writing Award presented by the American Association of Pastoral Counselors. Kathryn enjoys guest lecturing and leading workshops in the U.S. and internationally.

Nancy Qualls-Corbett, Ph.D., has been a practicing analyst in Birmingham, Alabama, since 1981. A diplomate of the C. G. Jung Institute, Zurich, she is the author of *The Sacred Prostitute: Eternal Aspect of the Feminine* and *Awakening Woman: Dreams and Individuation*. Nancy combines her love of mythology and travel in teaching seminars in Greece, Italy, Egypt, and Canada. She also serves as a board member for the Foundation of the International School of Analytical Psychology.

Ronald Schenk, Ph.D., is a Jungian analyst practicing and teaching in Dallas and Houston. His background is in theater, psychoanalytic training, work with Navajo, and phenomenological studies. He has served in various positions in the Inter-Regional Society of Jungian Analysts, most recently as President. He was recently elected to the Council of North American Societies of Jungian Analysis as President-elect. His interests are in culture as well as clinical work, and he has published four books: *The Soul of Beauty; Dark Light: the Appearance of Death in Everyday Life; The Sunken Quest,* the Wasted Fisher, *The Pregnant Fish: Postmodern Reflections on Depth Psychology;* and his most recent book, *American Soul: A Cultural Narrative,* as well as extensively in Jungian journals. He is currently working on a clinical work, *The Analytic Attitude: An Integrated Approach.*

Erel Shalit, Ph.D., is a Jungian psychoanalyst in Ra'anana, Israel. He is past President of the Israel Society of Analytical Psychology. He is Founding Director of the Jungian Analytical Psychotherapy Program at Bar Ilan University and past Director of the Shamai Davidson Community Mental Health Clinic at the Shalvata Psychiatric Centre in Israel. His books include *The Cycle of Life: Themes and Tales of the Journey; Requiem: A Tale of Exile and Return; Enemy, Cripple & Beggar: Shadows in the Hero's Path; The Hero and His Shadow (all Fisher King Press)*; and *The Complex (Inner City Books).* Entries, chapters, and articles of his appear in several books and journals. He wrote the chapter on Jerusalem in Thomas Singer (ed.), *Psyche and the City,* and "Silence is the Center of Feeling" appeared in Rob and Janet Henderson, *Living with Jung: "Enterviews" with Jungian Analysts.*

Thomas Singer, M.D., is a psychiatrist and psychoanalyst in the San Francisco Bay Area who writes about culture, psyche, and complex from a Jungian perspective. He is currently at work on a series of books that explore cultural complexes in different parts of the world. The first two volumes, *Placing Psyche: Exploring Cultural Complexes in Australia* and *Listening to Latin America,* have been published in the Spring Journal Books series of Analytical Psychology and Contemporary Culture, of which he is the series editor. Other recent Spring books that he has edited include *Psyche and the City: A Soul's Guide to the Modern World* and *Ancient Greece, Modern Psyche: Archetypes in the Making.* Dr. Singer also has a long-term interest in the Archive for Research in Archetypal Symbolism (ARAS) and serves on its National Board.

Nancy Swift Furlotti is a Jungian Analyst in California and Colorado. She is a past president of the C. G. Jung Institute of Los Angeles. As past president and founding director of the Philemon Foundation, she was instrumental in bringing Jung's *Red Book* to publication. An active member of the Inter-Regional Society of Jungian Analysts and the C. G. Jung Institute of Colorado, Nancy is also Chair of the Film Archive Committee at the C. G. Jung Institute of Los Angeles that oversees the "Remembering

Jung" Video Series and the films, *A Matter of Heart* and *The World Within*. She is a longstanding board member of the Archive for Research in Archetypal Symbolism (ARAS). Her publications include "The Archetypal Drama in Puccini's Opera *Madame Butterfly*," "Tracing a Red Thread: Synchronicity and Jung's Red Book" (*Psychological Perspectives*), and "Angels and Idols: Los Angeles, A City of Contrasts," in Thomas Singer (ed.) *Psyche and the City*. Her psychological amplification of the Maya *Popol Vuh* creation myth is forthcoming in 2014. Her interests include Mesoamerican mythology, initiation rites, and our relationship to nature.

Monika Wikman, Ph.D., is a Jungian analyst, an astrologer, and author of *Pregnant Darkness: Alchemy and the Renewal of Consciousness* (Nicolas Hays, 2005), along with various articles and poems in journals and periodicals. She coauthored an award-winning screenplay, *Rites of Passage* (Moondance Film Festival, 2010). She trained with the von Franz group of analysts in Switzerland after graduating from UC San Diego and the California School of Professional Psychology. She enjoys leading contemplative retreats on alchemy, dreams, healing, the *anima mundi*, active imagination, and the creative process, both in the United States and abroad.

Fisher King Press Jungian Psychology Titles

Advent and Psychic Birth
by Mariann Burke, Rev Ed., Trade Paperback, 164pp, 2013
— ISBN 978-1-926715-99-5

Re-Imagining Mary: A Journey Through Art to the Feminine Self
by Mariann Burke, 1st Ed., Trade Paperback, 180pp, Index, Biblio., 2009
— ISBN 978-0-9810344-1-6

Threshold Experiences: The Archetype of Beginnings
by Michael Conforti, 1st Ed., Trade Paperback, 168pp, Index, Biblio., 2008
— ISBN 978-0-944187-99-9

Marked By Fire: Stories of the Jungian Way
edited by Patricia Damery & Naomi Ruth Lowinsky,
1st Ed., Trade Paperback, 180pp, Index, Biblio., 2012
— ISBN 978-1-926715-68-1

Farming Soul: A Tale of Initiation
by Patricia Damery, 1st Ed., Trade Paperback, 166pp, Index, Biblio., 2010
— ISBN 978-1-926715-01-8

Transforming Body and Soul: Therapeutic Wisdom in the Gospel Healing Stories
by Steven Galipeau, Rev. Ed., Trade Paperback, 180pp, Index, Biblio., 2011
— ISBN 978-1-926715-62-9

Lifting the Veil: Revealing the Other Side
by Fred Gustafson & Jane Kamerling, 1st Ed, Paperback, 170pp, Biblio., 2012
— ISBN 978-1-926715-75-9

Resurrecting the Unicorn: Masculinity in the 21st Century
by Bud Harris, Rev. Ed., Trade Paperback, 300pp, Index, Biblio., 2009
— ISBN 978-0-9810344-0-9

The Father Quest: Rediscovering an Elemental Force
by Bud Harris, Reprint, Trade Paperback, 180pp, Index, Biblio., 2009
— ISBN 978-0-9810344-9-2

Like Gold Through Fire: The Transforming Power of Suffering
by Massimilla & Bud Harris, Reprint, Trade Paperback, 150pp, Index, Biblio., 2009
— ISBN 978-0-9810344-5-4

The Art of Love: The Craft of Relationship
by Massimilla and Bud Harris, 1st Ed. Trade Paperback, 150pp, 2010
— ISBN 978-1-926715-02-5

The Water of Life: Spiritual Renewal in the Fairy Tale
by David L. Hart, Rev. Ed., Trade Paperback, 158pp, Index, 2013
— ISBN 978-1-926715-98-8

Divine Madness: Archetypes of Romantic Love
by John R. Haule, Rev. Ed., Trade Paperback, 282pp, Index, Biblio., 2010
— ISBN 978-1-926715-04-9

Tantra and Erotic Trance: Volume One - Outer Work
by John R. Haule, 1st Ed., Trade Paperback, 215pp, Index, Biblio., 2012
— ISBN 978-0-9776076-8-6

Tantra and Erotic Trance: Volume Two - Inner Work
by John R. Haule, 1st Ed., Trade Paperback, 215pp, Index, Biblio., 2012
— ISBN 978-0-9776076-9-3

Eros and the Shattering Gaze: Transcending Narcissism
by Ken Kimmel, 1st Ed., Trade Paperback, 310 pp, Index, Biblio., 2011
— ISBN 978-1-926715-49-0

The Sister From Below: When the Muse Gets Her Way
by Naomi Ruth Lowinsky, 1st Ed., Trade Paperback, 248pp, Index, Biblio., 2009
— ISBN 978-0-9810344-2-3

The Motherline: Every Woman's Journey to Fnd her Female Roots
by Naomi Ruth Lowinsky, Reprint, Trade Paperback, 252pp, Index, Biblio., 2009
— ISBN 978-0-9810344-6-1

Jung and Ecopsychology: The Dairy Farmers Guide to the Universe Volume 1
by Dennis Merritt 1st Ed., Trade Paperback, 242pp, Index, Biblio., 2011
— ISBN 978-1-926715-42-1

The Cry of Merlin: Jung the Prototypical Ecopsychologist: DFG Volume 2
by Dennis Merritt 1st Ed., Trade Paperback, 204pp, Index, Biblio., 2012
— ISBN 978-1-926715-43-8

Hermes, Ecopsychology, and Complexity Theory: DFG Volume 3
by Dennis Merritt 1st Ed., Trade Paperback, 228pp, Index, Biblio., 2012
— ISBN 978-1-926715-44-5

Land, Weather, Seasons, Insects: An Archetypal View: DFG Volume 4
by Dennis Merritt 1ˢᵗ Ed., Trade Paperback, 134pp, Index, Biblio., 2012
— ISBN 978-1-926715-45-2

Becoming: An Introduction to Jung's Concept of Individuation
by Deldon Anne McNeely, 1ˢᵗ Ed., Trade Paperback, 230pp, Index, Biblio., 2010
— ISBN 978-1-926715-12-4

Animus Aeternus: Exploring the Inner Masculine
by Deldon Anne McNeely, Reprint, Trade Paperback, 196pp, Index, Biblio., 2011
— ISBN 978-1-926715-37-7

Mercury Rising: Women, Evil, and the Trickster Gods
by Deldon Anne McNeely, Rev. Ed, Trade Paperback, 200pp, Index, Biblio., 2011
— ISBN 978-1-926715-54-4

Four Eternal Women: Toni Wolff Revisited—A Study In Opposites
by Mary Dian Molton & Lucy Anne Sikes, 1ˢᵗ Ed, 320pp, Index, Biblio., 2011
— ISBN 978-1-926715-31-5

Gathering the Light: A Jungian View of Meditation
by V. Walter Odajnyk, Revised. Ed., Trade Paperback, 264pp, Index, Biblio., 2011
— ISBN 978-1-926715-55-1

The Promiscuity Papers
by Matjaz Regovec 1ˢᵗ Ed., Trade Paperback, 86pp, Index, Biblio., 2011
— ISBN 978-1-926715-38-4

Enemy, Cripple, Beggar: Shadows in the Hero's Path
by Erel Shalit, 1ˢᵗ Ed., Trade Paperback, 248pp, Index, Biblio., 2008
— ISBN 978-0-9776076-7-9

The Cycle of Life: Themes and Tales of the Journey
by Erel Shalit, 1ˢᵗ Ed., Trade Paperback, 210pp, Index, Biblio., 2011
— ISBN 978-1-926715-50-6

The Hero and His Shadow: Psychopolitical Aspects of Myth and Reality in Israel
by Erel Shalit, Revised Ed., Trade Paperback, 208pp, Index, Biblio., 2011
— ISBN 978-1-926715-69-8

The Guilt Cure by Nancy Carter Pennington & Lawrence H. Staples
1ˢᵗ Ed., Trade Paperback, 200pp, Index, Biblio., 2011
— ISBN 978-1-926715-53-7

Guilt with a Twist: The Promethean Way
by Lawrence H. Staples, 1st Ed., Trade Paperback, 256pp, Index, Biblio., 2008
— ISBN 978-0-9776076-4-8

The Creative Soul: Art and the Quest for Wholeness
by Lawrence H. Staples, 1st Ed., Trade Paperback, 100pp, Index, Biblio., 2009
— ISBN 978-0-9810344-4-7

Deep Blues: Human Soundscapes for the Archetypal Journey
by Mark Winborn, 1st Ed., Trade Paperback, 130pp, Index, Biblio., 2011
— ISBN 978-1-926715-52-0

Phone Orders Welcomed
Credit Cards Accepted
In Canada & the U.S. call 1-800-228-9316
International call +1-831-238-7799
www.fisherkingpress.com

Marked By Fire
Stories of the Jungian Way
ISBN 978-1-926715-68-1

A soulful collection of essays that illuminate the inner life.

edited by Patricia Damery & Naomi Ruth Lowinsky

When Soul appeared to C.G. Jung and demanded he change his life, he opened himself to the powerful forces of the unconscious. He recorded his inner journey, his conversations with figures that appeared to him in vision and in dream in *The Red Book*. Although it would be years before *The Red Book* was published, much of what we now know as Jungian psychology began in those pages, when Jung allowed the irrational to assault him. That was a century ago.

How do those of us who dedicate ourselves to Jung's psychology respond to Soul's demands in our own lives? If we believe, with Jung, in "the reality of the psyche," how does that shape us? The articles in *Marked By Fire* portray direct experiences of the unconscious; they tell life stories about the fiery process of becoming ourselves.

Contributors to *Marked by Fire: Stories of the Jungian Way* include: Jerome S. Bernstein, Claire Douglas, Gilda Frantz, Jacqueline Gerson, Jean Kirsch, Chie Lee, Karlyn M. Ward, Henry Abramovitch, Sharon Heath, Dennis Patrick Slattery, Robert D. Romanyshyn, Patricia Damery, and Naomi Ruth Lowinsky.

CPSIA information can be obtained at www.ICGtesting.com
Printed in the USA
LVOW11s1440130913

352041LV00004B/17/P